Brain Stimulation and Motivation

Research and Commentary

Contributing Authors:

S. P. GROSSMAN, *The University of Chicago*
NEAL E. MILLER, *The Rockefeller University*
JAMES OLDS, *The California Institute of Technology*
WARREN W. ROBERTS, *The University of Minnesota*
ELLIOT S. VALENSTEIN, *The University of Michigan*

Brain Stimulation and Motivation

Research and Commentary

Edited by ELLIOT S. VALENSTEIN

Professor of Psychology, The University of Michigan

Scott, Foresman and Company
Glenview, Illinois   Brighton, England

Library of Congress Catalog Card Number 72-90732
ISBN: 0-673-05443-8

Regional offices of Scott, Foresman and Company are located in Dallas, Texas;
Glenview, Illinois; Oakland, New Jersey; Palo Alto, California; Tucker, Georgia; and
Brighton, England.

Foreword

Electricity is an effective stimulus for the activation of neural tissue, because chemical-electrical activity is the basis for that initiation and propagation of membrane changes which is the neural impulse itself. The life of the brain is an electrochemical life, and so it is not surprising that the techniques of electrical stimulation of the brain are among those most frequently used in the study of the nervous system.

In his excellent introduction to the area of brain stiumulation, Dr. Valenstein points out that the surgical and electrical techniques required for brain stimulation studies were developed shortly after the middle of the nineteenth century. The advances that have been made in the preparation of electrodes since that time have been relatively few. The great increase in interest regarding electrical stimulation of the brain came about because of the development of more satisfactory behavioral techniques. Advances in behavioral analysis were derived from studies using operant conditioning techniques and ethology. Brain stimulation studies were given further impetus when it became clear to most investigators that the behavioristic approach of the 1930s and 1940s was inadequate for understanding the problems of man and the behavior of animals. When it became legitimate to talk about such things as pleasure and pain, as opposed to response frequencies and latencies, interest in the effects of brain stimulation increased. It may well be, in addition, that Olds' discovery of the pleasure regions of the brain helped overthrow a strictly behavioristic approach to the analysis of brain-behavior relationships. In any case, neurobehavioral science has become increasingly concerned with experience and verbal reports of experience, as well as with observing behaviors.

As revealed in this book, the tendency of brain stimulation research has been to look for more precise methods both for stimulating the brain and for analyzing behavioral changes. One area of research has been the use of chemical stimulation of the brain. Chemicals are introduced into the brain which are presumed to act on certain subsystems of the brain. A related recent approach has been to electrically stimulate the brains of animals treated with various types of drugs that alter the biochemical composition of the brain. In both cases, the aim is to get a better idea of the neural systems involved in the behaviors induced by the brain stimulation by identifying the chemical subsystems of the brain which are affected.

More precise behavioral analysis includes not only the use of more elaborate analysis of behavior by means of operant schedules, but also the more delicate evaluation of aggression in its many forms. It is no longer adequate to talk about electrical stimulation inducing "aggressive behavior." There are many types of aggressive behavior, and the type exhibited depends upon the conditions under which it is measured and other environmental factors. Science moves ahead not only by advances in technology, but also by the generation of new ideas, in this case about the effects of brain stimulation and, more globally, about how the brain works to govern behavior and experience. New ideas and concepts are the very backbone of scientific progress.

Brain Stimulation and Motivation is of value because the articles included represent significant contributions to the study of brain stimulation. The ideas they developed have helped shape the future of the field. The articles have been integrated and placed in historical context by Dr. Valenstein's introductory article, and the comments made by the various principal investigators responsible for this work make for enlightening and entertaining reading.

ROBERT L. ISAACSON
Gainesville, Florida

Preface

Science is a creative, almost artistic, process. The important discoveries are usually made by individuals who are able to perceive some aspect of nature in a new way. This is not an ability that can be taught by courses in scientific methodology.

The approach in the present volume is historical. The contributors have attempted to describe the thoughts and influences that generated their interest in pursuing a research problem. All of them clearly recognize that, like the three blind men and the elephant, they perceive only a part of the picture. Scientific "truth" is constantly evolving. What is important is the process—the asking of significant questions and the exploration of ways to make nature yield answers. The book also contains a number of illustrations of the importance of remaining open to unforeseen results.

The specialist may have some interest in the historical material and the new information presented, but the book was written with the student in mind. I would hope that the format of research papers and extensive commentaries may provide a "takeoff point" for a seminar on many topics in the biopsychology of motivation.

ELLIOT S. VALENSTEIN
Ann Arbor, Michigan

Contents

Brain Stimulation and Motivation

Research and Commentary

History of Brain Stimulation: Investigations into the Physiology of Motivation

ELLIOT S. VALENSTEIN

CHANGING VIEWS OF THE NERVOUS SYSTEM

Galen's "hydraulic theory" of the nervous system was so generally accepted prior to the eighteenth century that, had it occurred to anyone to stimulate the brain, he might have attempted to use a pump. Galen had perceived the nerves as hollow tubes containing fluids and gaseous substances that passed into muscles, causing them to balloon out and thereby shorten or contract.[1] This view had been postulated in the second century A.D. and, even though it had minimal explanatory power, it was never seriously tested or questioned for more than 1500 years. Leeuwenhoek (1632–1723) believed he could see hollow tubes in the nerves when looking through the microscope, but he claimed they were difficult to demonstrate to others because they dried and contracted too rapidly. About the same time, Thomas Willis, whose name is still associated with the arterial circle at the base of the brain, described the nerves in terms of "pores and passages" similar to those in sugarcane. Even in the middle of the eighteenth century, Alexander Monro found it necessary to provide experimental evidence against nerve fluid or "liquors," and he pointed out that it was not possible to detect any drops at the cut end of a nerve, nor did a nerve swell if it was tied firmly.

Anatomists had started to speculate about the possible role of electricity in nerve (and muscle) transmission about this time. "Animal electricity" had been identified in the electric eel by John Walsh in 1774 and a few of his contemporaries had attempted to stimulate muscles and nerves electrically, but it was Galvani who was first to work on this problem systematically. The controversy between the two great Italian scientists Galvani and Volta, in the 1790s, had a tremendous impact on the physiology of the nervous system and on electronic theory. Galvani had conducted a large number of experiments which demonstrated that electricity could produce muscular contractions in the frog. His dispute with Volta was over interpretation. Did the electricity reside in the animal or were the contractions all caused by an external source of

---

1. Several of the quotations from original sources cited in this section are from *The Human Brain and Spinal Cord: A Historical Study Illustrated by Writings from Antiquity to the Twentieth Century,* by Edward C. Clarke and C. D. O'Malley, originally published by the University of California Press, reprinted by permission of The Regents of the University of California. This excellent work was most helpful in preparing the early historical material.

electricity? In one series of experiments, the ability of atmospheric electricity to trigger contraction was demonstrated when a frog attached by a wire to a lightning rod twitched in synchrony with distant lightning flashes. A greater influence on Galvani's thinking, however, was his observation that a frog suspended from brass hooks would display muscle contractions every time its leg touched an iron railing. Galvani had almost favored the interpretation of external electricity and wrote:

> I was on the point of deciding that such contractions arose from atmospheric electricity . . . but when I brought an animal into a closed room, placed it on an iron plate, and began to press the hook fixed in the spinal cord against the plate, behold, the same contractions and the same movements. I performed the same experiment over and over, using different metals, at different places, and at different hours and days, with the same result except that the contractions differed according to the metals used; that is, more violent with some, weaker with others (Clarke & O'Malley, p. 181).

Clearly, Galvani did not appreciate that dissimilar metals could produce a "metallic electricity," but after Galvani's death Volta used this principle to develop a battery. It was not until the invention of the galvanometer by Schweigger in 1811 and its refinement by Oersted (1820) and Nobili (1825) that the evidence for the existence of "internal electricity" was well founded. In 1844, Matteucci reported his results of experiments in which frog muscles "prepared according to the method of Galvani" were stacked up in "frog piles." Matteucci wrote, "Thus I could obtain on my galvonometer 15°, 20°, 30°, 40°, 60°, etc., according to the number of half thighs . . . " (Clarke & O'Malley, p. 190).

ACCEPTANCE OF STIMULATION AS A RESEARCH TOOL

Galvani's demonstrations swept through the scientific community and a great number of physiologists began to stimulate animals in spite of the fact that questions about whether nerves actually accomplished their ends by electricity were still disputed. Johannes Müller had postulated the "law of specific energies," which in its essence proposed that no matter how sensory systems are activated they respond in their characteristic fashion:

> For the same cause, such as electricity, can simultaneously affect all sensory organs, since they are all sensitive to it; and yet, every sensory nerve reacts to it differently; one nerve perceives it as light, another hears its sound, another one smells it, another tastes the electricity, and another one feels it as pain and shock (Clarke & O'Malley, p. 205).

Although Müller took the position that electricity was an artificial stimulant that had no role in natural excitation, he had provided a practical justification for its use. Müller's students (duBois-Reymond, Virchow, Schwann, Helmholtz, and Koelliker) dominated German physiology during the second half of the nineteenth century and did not hesitate to use electricity to study the properties of the nervous system. Helmholtz used Galvani's preparation of a frog's gastrocnemius muscle and crural nerve, and calculated the speed of nerve transmission by noting the elapsed time between muscle contraction and electrical stimulation at different points on the nerve. Other techniques were available, but the popularity of electrical stimulation was on the increase. For example, duBois-Reymond wrote in his 1860 volume *Investigations of Animal Electricity:*[2]

> We can choose between the electric current, strychnine poisoning, and mechanical, thermal, and chemical stimulations applied directly to the nerve. . . . A great preponderance of certainty, convenience, strength, and duration of the stimulus are all in favor of the electric current (Clarke & O'Malley, p. 199).

It was not surprising, therefore, that Fritsch and Hitzig should have performed their classic study in 1870 on the elicitation of muscle contraction by electrical stimulation of the dog's cerebral cortex.[3] Apparently Fritsch and Hitzig were concerned with the problem of current spread, and they wrote, "When employing extremely weak currents, the possibility of isolated excitability of a narrowly delimited muscle group is, however, restricted to a very small foci, which we shall call centers for the sake of brevity" (Clarke & O'Malley, p. 509).

Several years earlier, Simonoff (1866), working in St. Petersburg, had used sewing-needle electrodes insulated with melted glass or "Firness" (a resin obtained from wood). Simonoff was interested in extending some of Sechenov's work on inhibitory regions of the brain and used puppies with chronically (permanently) implanted electrodes which were positioned by hand into deep regions of the brain. It took less than a minute to insert the electrodes through the skin and soft skull of the unanesthetized puppies. Simonoff compared faradic and constant current stimulation. He discovered that the latter produced lesions and he noted the relation between current intensity and duration and the extent of electrolysis. With faradic stimulation, using an inductorium adapted from duBois-Reymond, Simonoff was able to repeat experiments a number of times over several weeks on a single preparation. "On" and "off" effects of stimulation were observed and histology was routinely performed to confirm placements of electrodes in the brain. Simonoff even inserted fine cannulae in the lateral ventricles in order to study the effects of chemical solutions. The use of subcortical electrodes must have continued in Russia, as Bechterev (1887) reported stimulating the thalamus and Golsinger, who used insulated needles and an indifferent plate electrode attached to the abdomen, may have been the first to produce unipolar electrolytic lesions in deep-brain structures.

---

2. DuBois-Reymond had been experimenting with electrical stimulation for a considerable time before the appearance of this publication; his "Law of Stimulation" was formulated in 1848.

3. The time was certainly ripe. Fritsch had held a position in duBois-Reymond's institute in Berlin and Hitzig had previously observed eye movements following electrical stimulation of posterior regions of the cortex. Prior to collaborating with Fritsch, Hitzig had attempted some preliminary stimulation studies in the rabbit. According to an often-repeated account, Fritsch had originally noted that irritation of the brain caused twitching on the opposite side of the body while dressing the wounds of soldiers during the Prussian-Danish War in 1864.

The rapidity with which Fritsch and Hitzig's report was picked up by others also indicates the tenor of the time. In 1874, Dr. Roberts Bartholow of Cincinnati, Ohio, had a patient with extensive cranial damage. He was able to directly stimulate regions of the cortex and produce movements of different muscles on the opposite side of the body. After the patient died the doctor was forced to leave town by an irate citizenry, but he was able to perform an autopsy and publish some information on the cortical areas that produced specific muscle movements. Scientific communication was surprisingly adequate, as Bartholow was well aware of European investigations and wrote, "The needles being insulated to near the points, it was believed that diffusion of the current could be as restricted as in the experiments of Fritsch and Hitzig and Ferrier" (Clarke & O'Malley, p. 512).

Ferrier had just published his "Experimental Researches in Cerebral Psychology and Pathology" in the *West Riding Lunatic Asylum Medical Report* in 1873. He confirmed Fritsch and Hitzig's report on the dog and did extensive work on the monkey, the results of which were extended to a map of the human cerebral cortex. Two important trends can be detected in the electrical stimulation studies in many of the European laboratories.[4] One involved the emergence of a comparative approach, as could be seen in Grünbaum and Sherrington's (1902) study of the effects of stimulating the cortex in the orangutan, gorilla, and chimpanzee; the other involved exploration in lightly anesthetized animals and unanesthetized patients, as studied by such neurosurgeons as W. W. Keen of Philadelphia, V. Horsley of London, and F. Krause of Berlin (1911), who wrote, " . . . on the basis of my experience, the faradic investigation of the cerebral cortex in the operating room represents an indispensable method of investigation . . . " (Clarke & O'Malley, p. 526).

SUBCORTICAL ELECTRODES AND STIMULATION IN UNANESTHETIZED SUBJECTS

One of the most significant advances for those who were later to work in the area of brain stimulation and motivation was the development of techniques to stimulate fully awake, relatively unrestrained animals over a long period of time. Such "chronic" preparations would enable later investigators to observe the effects of stimulation on behavior under more natural conditions. Ewald's work around 1896 may have been the first to involve stimulation of relatively unrestrained animals. Ewald did not write up his results in any detail, but Talbert (1900), an American postdoctoral fellow studying in Germany, described the technique and his extension of Ewald's work. As ivory had been investigated for its usefulness in repairing skull damage, Ewald used this material to make a threaded cone that could be screwed into a hole drilled out of the skull. Platinum "button" electrodes within the cone were positioned on a dog's cortex and the attached wires were anchored to the cone before being led off to a battery in the experimenter's hand. The dog was led around on a leash and its brain stimulated while the animal was engaged in different

---

4. The reader interested in more details of this period may consult Brazier (1959), Clarke & O'Malley (1968), Haymaker (1953).

activities. Talbert was concerned with some of the problems which still are with us. He was aware, for example, of shifts in thresholds, only some of which seemed to be caused by scar tissue, of the fact that body position could influence the elicitation of responses, and of the dangers of producing generalized convulsions. Talbert also raised such questions as: How does the animal experience the stimulation (directly or only from muscle movements)? How can one interpret the results from nonresponsive sites? How should one estimate current spread? What is the relation of ablation and stimulation techniques?

Ewald's technique for stimulating awake animals was not overlooked by others. A few years later, Baer (1905) published an extensive account of his observations during stimulation of the cortex of unrestrained dogs. In his introduction, Baer asked why there was not more information available concerning the results of stimulating two cortical areas simultaneously. This gap in our information he attributed directly to the limitations of the Fritsch and Hitzig technique—it was very difficult to hold the electrodes in place with one hand while opening and closing switches with the other. Baer used Ewald's technique (as described by Talbert) with minor modifications for stimulating between electrode pairs selected from among four cortical electrodes positioned in the center of the pedestal. The metal pedestals were threaded and with the aid of a wrench they could be screwed into holes prepared in the skull. The electrode, which protruded slightly at the bottom of the pedestal, penetrated the exposed cortex. A battery was still used as the stimulation source and a switching device made it possible to pass current in either direction between two points. In common with Talbert, Baer noted that there was a lack of uniformity in responses obtained from the same stimulation site and wondered if this could be attributed to the use of awake and alert animals.

Up to the turn of the century, the portion of brain most extensively investigated was the cerebral cortex, primarily because of its accessibility. The development of an instrument by Horsley and Clarke (1908) made it possible "to direct a protected stimulating and electrolytic needle to any desired part of the brain with very fair accuracy" (p. 48).[5] The Horsley-Clarke stereotaxic device has become the model for a great number of instruments which permit the insertion of wires into the depths of the brains of animals and man. Essentially, a stereotaxic instrument positions the head in a fixed plane and, with the aid of three-dimensional anatomical maps (stereotaxic atlases), makes it possible to insert electrodes through small holes in the skull into almost any sector of the brain. This 1908 paper by Horsley and Clarke contains an almost overwhelming amount of basic information on electrode stimulation and coagulation techniques. For example, there are comparisons of faradic and direct current, anodal and cathodal stimulation (anodal, but not cathodal lesions were "generally spherical, circumscribed and precisely defined"), and descriptions of the size of lesions as a function of intensity and duration of current ("high milliamperage is wholly unnecessary; thus 1 ma. produces an adequate effect in a few seconds [fifteen] on a single group of cells, but 2 ma.

---

5. Horsley presented a preliminary description of the stereotaxic instrument at the meeting of the British Medical Association at Toronto, August 1906.

give a more constant result, and a hypermaximal effect is reached with 5 ma."). Horsley and Clarke also compared monopolar with bipolar electrodes, the latter of two types (double-barreled with tips 1–2 mm. apart, or concentric), and demonstrated experimentally the increasing spread of current with monopolar stimulation as the current intensity was raised. They used iridioplatinum electrodes, developed earplugs for accurate mounting of the animal's head in the instrument, made small lesions at the electrode tip after completing an experiment to more reliably locate an interesting stimulation point, and even placed "dummy" electrodes in brains at the termination of an experiment in order to guide the sectioning of the brain. Their histological techniques included "frozen sections" (head packed with frozen CO_2 softened with ether) and they described in great detail the histological changes (neuroglia infiltration and role of phagocytes) at different distances from the center of the lesion and at different times after its production.

Although some investigators continued to use their own techniques for inserting electrodes into the deeper regions of the brain, the development of stereotaxic devices provided a great impetus to the investigation of subcortical nuclei. About this time, Karplus and Kreidl (1909) began their classic series of studies on the hypothalamus. These collaborators, at the University of Vienna, electrically stimulated different regions of the hypothalamus of many animals (cats, apes, monkeys, dogs, rabbits, birds, reptiles, frogs, and fish) with bipolar, platinum electrodes. In earlier work, emphasis tended to be placed on the skeletal motor responses that could be elicited from the cerebral cortex, but hypothalamic stimulation initiated an interest in autonomic reactions such as smooth muscle and glandular responses that were activated from structures in the depths of the brain. Karplus and Kreidl observed that hypothalamic stimulation evoked such responses as pupillary constriction and dilation, urination, tearing, and salivation.

BRAIN STIMULATION AND MOTIVATION

The observation that hypothalamic stimulation could elicit "involuntary" (autonomic) responses led to speculation that electrical stimulation might also elicit emotional reactions and specific motivational states. Although it has been concluded that stimulation of the cerebral cortex is motivationally neutral, as the animal neither seeks nor avoids such stimulation (cf. review by Doty, 1969), gradually researchers realized that this was not necessarily true of some of the phylogenetically older, subcortical regions of the brain.

Around the beginning of the twentieth century, several investigators observed the changes in behavior that followed removal of the cerebral cortex. It was assumed that the hyperirritability seen after removal of the cortex and other higher centers was due to a reduction of inhibition and a consequent release of responses organized at lower centers. While rage could be induced easily in these animals by noxious stimulation, the aggressive responses were not well directed and they stopped much more abruptly at the end of stimulation than might be expected with a truly angry animal. For this reason it was popular to use such terms as "pseudoaffective" reflex (Goltz, 1892;

Woodworth & Sherrington, 1904). Cannon also used the term "pseudoaffective behavior," but then changed it to "sham rage." Bard (1928), who was Cannon's student, accepted this label for a while, but later he preferred to speak of "quasi-rage" in order to avoid the implication that there was anything fake about the behavior (Bard, 1934). The lower centers that appeared to be disinhibited following decortication seemed to be located in the hypothalamus. The evidence, primarily derived from transections of the brain at different levels, led to the conclusion that the hypothalamus (particularly the posterior portion) was critical for the *full expression of emotion* (Bard, 1928, 1934).

It was not clear whether the "hypothalamic animal" (the hypothalamus of which had been left intact, but which had been deprived of the influence of higher regions by transection of the brain) was capable of experiencing emotion or displaying motivated behavior. In the first place the observations were limited in scope, being restricted to the precipitation of rage reactions and, to a lesser extent, the induction of signs of sexual receptivity in female animals following the administration of appropriate hormones. More importantly, the question was in part philosophical or at least not easily answered by empirical data. Emotionality and motivation have never been adequately defined to the degree that would make it possible to apply an objective set of criteria to distinguish them from other behavior. Many still regard these concepts as the "phlogiston" of the behavioral sciences. Others are less frightened by the lack of precise definitions and refuse to concede that the terms are not pointing to processes that are important to an understanding of brain-behavior interactions. Emotionality is said to involve strong physiological responses associated with states that are not neutral—they may be positive or aversive. Motivation implies "goal direction" (toward or away from a goal), but the behavior cannot be completely reflexive, involving only inflexible responses to stimuli. Motivation is applicable only in instances where it is possible to demonstrate the animal's capacity to substitute responses to achieve the same end. Emotion and motivation probably represent different aspects of the same process. They are clearly interrelated, the difference being that motivation involves a more easily identifiable goal.

Although it was to be contested later, Masserman (1941) concluded that hypothalamic stimulation did not produce emotional experiences in cats even though it evoked retraction of ears, crouching, growling, arching of the back, and sympathetic reactions such as salivation, excessive pupillary dilation (mydriasis), hair standing on end (piloerection), biting, and striking movements with claws unsheathed. Lights or sounds that were repeatedly paired with such hypothalamic stimulation, for example, did not acquire the capacity to evoke any of the sympathetic or behavioral responses elicited by the stimulation. This certainly would have occurred if the unconditioned stimulus was foot shock. Masserman concluded:

Experiments on animals 'have indicated that the hypothalamus may integrate and possibly reinforce the effector neural impulses controlling some of the sympathetic and motor manifestations of fear and rage; however, there is little or no basis for the thesis that the hypothalamus governs or even mediates the emotional experiences themselves (p. 20).

Earlier Lashley had reached a similar conclusion. Originally the Cannon-Bard theory of emotion had placed more emphasis on the thalamic portion of the diencephalon. Lashley (1938) reviewed the evidence and concluded:

> The supposed evidence that the thalamus adds the affective or emotional character to sensations breaks down completely when subjected to critical analysis. The affective changes resulting from thalamic lesions are restricted to a small group of somasthetic sensations and cannot be interpreted as a general change of affectivity. . . . Thus the only part of the thalamic theory of emotion which has factual support is the localization of motor centers for emotional expression within the hypothalamus. It seems certain that these motor centers do not contribute directly to other aspects of emotion and there is no evidence for the existence of other affective or emotional centers (p. 58).

The work of W. R. Hess and S. W. Ranson and their respective colleagues serves as a bridge to the present era. Hess began his investigations in the 1920s and, because his work in Zurich was relatively uninterrupted by World War II, he was able to continue into the 1950s the studies that led to his being awarded the Nobel Prize. These investigations involved a mapping of the responses elicited by diencephalic stimulation (principally of the hypothalamus and thalamus) obtained from over 4500 points in about 480 cats. In most of his studies, Hess used fully awake animals which were restrained only by the connecting cables (cf. Gloor, 1954, for an English summary of the theories and experimental work of Hess). At approximately the same time, a group of distinguished anatomists working with S. W. Ranson at Northwestern University were using a modification of the stereotaxic device of Horsley and Clarke to explore the function of different regions of the hypothalamus and related neural structures (Ranson, 1937; Ranson & Magoun, 1939).

A large number of the reports from the laboratories of Ranson and Hess were initially concerned with hypothalamic regulation of isolated responses such as blood pressure, respiratory, and cardiac changes, as well as pupillary dilation and constriction. Later, an increasing amount of attention was devoted to more organismic or holistic functions such as responses characteristic of temperature regulation, defecation, vomiting, and sleep. Toward the end of their investigative careers, Ranson, and even more so Hess, described the stimulated animal in terms that implied affective states such as bulimia (insatiable hunger), flight, defensive reactions, and rage. In Hess's later writings, for example, he indicated that natural states could be induced by hypothalamic stimulation.

> Sherrington long ago showed how easily a decorticated cat may be brought into the state of rage, generally called sham-rage; however, when this state results from stimulation, there is no reason to consider it as different from natural rage (Hess, 1954, p. 20).

Up to this point, there was little of what would now be called objective behavioral tests used to evaluate these elicited states. The "Ranson School" primarily used restrained, lightly anesthetized animals. Hess was mainly interested in determining the range of responses that could be elicited from hypothalamic structures and did not vary the testing procedure to obtain a more complete qualitative and quantitative description of the animal's state when stimulated. Hess's experimentation stressed the elicitation of visceral and motor responses, as can be seen from his preface to his 1954 book:

> In April 1952 I accepted with pleasure the opportunity offered to me by the Harvard Medical School. . . . I wish especially to draw attention to an experimental technique, barely known in America, which meets important requirements for the investigation of the central nervous system, not only in regard to the central regulation of the function of autonomic (vegetative) organs, but also in regard to subcortical organization of motor functions (p. vii).

Actually, electrical stimulation of deep-brain structures in the fully awake subject was being adopted in America about this time but, interestingly, much of the work was with human patients. Spiegel and Wycis and their collaborators (1947, 1950) used stimulation techniques with patients suffering from disturbances in coordination of movement (basal ganglia dysfunction); Penfield stimulated the temporal lobes of epileptics (Penfield & Baldwin, 1952); Heath and his associates at Tulane began their stimulation work with chronic schizophrenics in 1951 (cf. Heath & Mickle, 1960); Sem-Jacobson and Torkildsen (1960) described stimulation studies with psychotics that had been initiated at the Mayo Clinic and the Rochester State Hospital in 1952; and Delgado, Hamlin, and Chapman (1952) speculated on the possible therapeutic value of their electrode-implantation technique (cf. Ramey and O'Doherty, 1960, for other references).

The introduction of more objective, behavioral tests to evaluate the elicited states had to wait for the adoption of techniques for stimulating unrestrained animals by investigators with training in the behavioral sciences. In the middle of the 1950s, physiologists (with the exception of those working in the Pavlovian tradition) tended to neglect behavioral methods. Psychologists, on the other hand, were generally trained within a different tradition and tended to rely exclusively on behavioral methods as the only way of analyzing what went on inside the organism. In the early 1950s, the great potential of these stimulation techniques was grasped by a number of researchers who were interested in the physiology of motivation either for its own sake or as it related to theories of learning. There was a period of fumbling and frustration while the techniques were being acquired (see, for example, the discussions by Neal Miller and James Olds in this volume), but by the middle of the 1950s a large number of technical articles had appeared which described different electrode assemblies and methods of attachment to the skull and the effects of various metals and stimulation wave forms on neural tissue (examples of this period can be found in the articles by Delgado; Spiegel & Wycis; Sheatz; Miller et al.; Lilly; Fisher et al.; Gengerelli and others in Sheer, 1961).[6]

---

6. Publication of this volume (Sheer, 1961) was delayed approximately five years. Most of the contents, therefore, reflect the state of the field in the middle 1950s. Delgado (1952) had described a technique for implanting multilead electrodes several years earlier. Sporadic reports of electrical stimulation techniques in awake animals, including remote stimulation by inducing a current in an implanted coil, were described between 1920 and 1950 by investigators in Europe and the United States (cf. Delgado, 1952, for specific references).

NEGATIVE AND POSITIVE REINFORCEMENT FROM BRAIN STIMULATION

Psychologists interested in learning theory developed explanatory models based on the rewarding or reinforcing properties of drive reduction. Indeed, for many strict adherents to the predominant learning theory in America, learning could not take place without such a reduction (Hull, 1943). As long as one studied drives in relation to states such as those produced by hunger or pain, it seemed obvious that any response that reduced the intensity of these states would be "reinforcing." In many situations where learning had obviously taken place, however, it required some fanciful *post hoc* hypothesizing to argue for drive reduction. Therefore, it could be claimed that drive reduction was really not necessary for reinforcement, but simply highly correlated with the conditions under which psychologists normally conducted their studies (primarily hungry rats rewarded with food and rats escaping from electric shock). The reports (mainly from Hess's laboratory) that stimulation could elicit eating and other adaptive behavior had obvious implications for those involved in understanding the mechanisms of learning, as it seemed possible now to measure and manipulate what up to this time could only be hypothesized. In his contribution to this book, Neal Miller is very specific about the initial impetus for his interest in brain stimulation studies:

> If I could find an area of the brain where electrical stimulation had the other properties of normal hunger, would the sudden termination of that stimulation function as a reward? If I could find such an area, perhaps recording from it would provide a way of measuring hunger which would allow me to see the effects of a small nibble of food that is large enough to serve as a reward but not large enough to produce complete satiation (pp. 54–55).

Fortunately, Miller had colleagues at Yale University at this time, such as Delgado, Stevenson, MacLean, Anand, and Bailey, who had experience in placing electrodes in animals' brains for either stimulation or ablation studies. The first of a series of interdisciplinary studies demonstrated that a conditioned fear response could be developed with brain stimulation serving as the unconditioned stimulus. Delgado had made some informal observations (later published) that cats stimulated in certain subcortical areas began to exhibit "anxiety-like responses prior to stimulation" (Delgado, 1955). In collaboration with Miller and Roberts (Delgado et al., 1954), he demonstrated that cats could learn a response to escape from such brain stimulation and that the stimulation could also serve as a punishment to make hungry animals avoid food.

Strictly speaking, these initial results did not contradict Masserman's conclusion, as the electrodes were located in the tectum, lateral thalamus, and part of the hippocampal gyrus, but not in the hypothalamus. The same may be said of Delgado, Rosvold, and Looney's (1956) report of conditioned fear responses obtained with stimulation of the medial nucleus of the amygdala in the monkey. Roberts (1958a), however, was successful in demonstrating that cats would learn an escape response to terminate stimulation of the posterior hypothalamus. Although this test was not comparable to Masserman's experiments, which employed classical conditioning procedures, the fact that the animal learned a new response to escape the stimulation indicated that there was more involved than an elicitation of unconditioned (built-in) motor patterns. Among other reports of emotion elicited from stimulation of nonhypothalamic sites, Roberts (1962) noted a "fear-like crouching or cowering response that could be elicited by stimulation of the dorsomedial thalamic nucleus of cats." Here too the emotion could be verified as the animals learned to avoid the stimulation that elicited this response. It soon became evident that Miller's hope that it would be possible to find neural areas that would provide a means to measure drives would not be simply realized. For example, Roberts and Carey (1963) observed that destruction of the dorsomedial nucleus did not reduce shock-induced fear and concluded that this area was not essential for the fear drive.

The demonstration of negative reinforcement with brain stimulation was most important. Although the question of what an animal experiences can never be adequately answered, the fact that animals would learn to escape and avoid brain stimulation of some areas provided a clue to what the animal *might* be experiencing. What made these observations particularly important was the possibility that brain stimulation might be revealing a neural system that played a basic role in the motivation underlying the acquisition of escape and avoidance behavior. Some investigators have concluded that the experimental evidence points to the existence of a negative reinforcing system in the brain, but this conclusion may be resting on a shaky foundation, as many of the sites stimulated seem to involve pathways mediating the sensation of pain (for example, parts of the reticular formation and the central gray and ventral portions of the tectum, which are known to receive input from the classical spinothalamic pain system). A number of experimental reports have described elicited behaviors that appeared to indicate "fear," "alarm," "flight," "defense," and "rage," but only in some of the cases would the animal escape the stimulation and, in fewer instances, avoid the stimulation that elicited these responses. The apparent aversive quality of brain stimulation could not always be demonstrated, despite the similarity to natural behaviors, such as "defense" and "flight" (Ursin & Kaada, 1960; Ursin, 1964).

The anatomical areas from which most of these aversive, or seemingly aversive, responses could be elicited by stimulation have included diencephalic structures (hypothalamus and thalamus) and some portions of the "limbic system" (e.g., medial amygdala nucleus). The "limbic system" has been called the "emotional brain" because destruction of areas within this region have produced such changes as transforming tame into wild rats (septal rage), wild into gentle, and normal into hypersexual animals (cf. reviews of behavioral changes following amygdalectomy and other limbic lesions by Brady, 1958; and Thomas et al., 1968). Broca's original anatomical definition of the limbic lobe consisted basically of the older cortical (paleocortical) structures forming the inner border of the cerebral hemispheres, but this was expanded to a functionally defined "limbic system" which now includes those regions of the hypothalamus and the midbrain ("limbic midbrain area") that seem critical to the expression of emotionality (Nauta, 1960). In general, aversive reinforcement was obtained from more medially placed electrodes, particularly within the diencephalon and midbrain, where structures close to the third ventrical and aqueduct of Sylvius (located in the midline) were judged to produce aversive reactions. For this reason this "system" has been referred to as a *periventricular punishment system* (e.g., Stein, 1969).

At about the same time as the initial demonstration of negative reinforcement produced by brain stimulation,[7] investigators at McGill University and the Montreal Neurological Institute were speculating about the significance of the *brainstem reticular activating system* (Moruzzi & Magoun, 1949; Magoun, 1952) for learning and motivation. This medially located area of mixed cells and fibers had been called the reticular formation by early anatomists because of its netlike appearance. A series of lesion and stimulation experiments had indicated that the reticular formation played a crucial role in maintaining arousal. Extensive destruction of this area produced coma, while electrical stimulation in sleeping animals produced the high-frequency, low-amplitude brain waves characteristic of an EEG from the cerebral cortex of an alert animal. Also influential at the time was Lindsley's (1951) postulation of an "activation theory of emotion," based on the assumption that marked changes in arousal level produced emotional expression by modifying the level of cortical inhibition normally exerted over diencephalic structures. Furthermore, the preliminary report by Yoshii that heightened EEG arousal accompanied an animal's approach to a goal suggested the possibility that this same system was involved in motivation and/or learning.

These germinal ideas formed the bases of much discussion about the role of arousal in learning and motivation, and encouraged Olds to attempt to stimulate the "arousal system" during learning tests. Miller's report that brain stimulation could be aversive and consequently might interfere with learning had apparently sensitized Olds to the desirability of testing for this possibility. The events surrounding the discovery of positive rewarding effects from stimulation with an electrode that accidentally ended up a great distance from the reticular formation are described in Olds's contribution to this volume. In terms of dramatic impact and amount of theoretical speculation and experimentation generated, no single discovery in the field of brain-behavior interactions can rival the finding that animals are highly motivated to stimulate certain areas of their own brains (Olds & Milner, 1954). Although many basic questions about "self-stimulation" remain unanswered, many people have speculated that this phenomenon may contain the key to understanding the physiological basis of motivation and reinforcement. The initial observations have been extended beyond the rat and self-stimulation has been demonstrated in a variety of animals including fish, chickens, rabbits, cats,[8] dogs, guinea pigs, monkeys, dolphins, and human beings (cf. Valenstein, 1964, or Olds, 1969, for specific references). The fact that self-stimulation has been obtained from approximately the same anatomical structures[9] in such a variety of species has served to increase confidence in the conclusion that a basic reinforcement mechanism of general evolutionary significance is involved.

---

7. The reciprocal influence of the studies leading to the discoveries of positive and negative reinforcement produced by brain stimulation are discussed in the separate contributions by Olds and Miller in this book.

8. The importance of a prepared mind cannot be overestimated. Much earlier, in the course of studying the convulsive properties of the cat's brain, Gibbs and Gibbs (1936) noted a "purring center" in the lateral hypothalamus. It is possible that their awake cats were indicating the existence of positive reinforcement.

9. In some of these species the anatomical information is too sparse to really say anything stronger than that no glaring discrepancies exist.

The importance of determining more precisely the neural structures that provided positive reinforcement seemed obvious. It was learned that self-stimulation (although not of equal strength) could be obtained from electrodes throughout the more lateral portions of the hypothalamus, from major portions of most limbic structures (septal area, amygdala, hippocampus, cingulate gyrus) and some sites in the reticular formation and brainstem (Routtenberg & Malsbury, 1969; Olds, 1956a; Olds & Peretz, 1960; Olds, Travis, & Schwing, 1960; Olds & Olds, 1963; Wurtz & Olds, 1963). Later studies searched for a critical area for self-stimulation. Most investigators had found it easiest to obtain self-stimulation from the medial forebrain bundle of the lateral hypothalamus, where the highest response rates and lowest intensity thresholds were obtained. It was only natural, therefore, to search for an essential region in this part of the brain. There is no general agreement about results of this work, as some investigators have claimed that the pathways are diffuse and no essential structure can be discerned in the lateral hypothalamus (Lorens, 1966; Valenstein & Campbell, 1966; Valenstein, 1966; Umemoto, 1968), while others have reported a critical focus in the lateral hypothalamus (Olds & Olds, 1969, and pp. 91–92 in this volume).

Several investigators have also attacked the problem of anatomical organization by utilizing histological stains (Nauta, 1957; Fink & Heimer, 1967) that make it possible to trace degenerating axons and axon terminals. After obtaining self-stimulation base lines, small lesions are produced with the stimulating electrode and the courses of the degenerating fibers are charted to their termination (Routtenberg & Malsbury, 1969; Scott, 1970). In another context, Chi and Flynn (1971) have used this technique to determine the pathways associated with elicitation of "quiet biting" and "affective" attack. It is still too early to discern if this technique will be useful in locating an essential pathway. One major obstacle is that, even if an effort were made to make the smallest lesions that would completely eliminate the elicited behavior, it might be difficult to prove that the ablated and stimulated fields were identical. There is always likely to be a combination of relevant and irrelevant cells (with respect to a specific elicited behavior) that are destroyed, and the task of determining the essential pathways may be overwhelmingly complicated.

Other experiments have attempted to clarify the behavioral side of self-stimulation. Originally most demonstrations of the reinforcement properties of brain stimulation utilized the somewhat stereotyped and repetitive responding involved in lever pressing. There were some people, therefore, who remained unconvinced that the brain stimulation acted as a reward. They argued that the stimulation forced the animals to repeat the response just made; the animals were really "trapped" rather than rewarded. Indeed, the frenetic way in which the animals often pressed the levers made this argument seem reasonable. Later, however, it was shown that animals could solve mazes (Olds, 1956b) and visual discrimination tasks (Keesey, 1964b; Kling & Matsumiya, 1962) when rewarded with brain stimulation. In these and numerous other testing situations, delays were interposed between successive responses and the results left little doubt that the animals were actively seeking out the stimulation. Animals that have not received any brain stimulation for several days may jump from the experimenter's hands in order to be able to make the responses rewarded by brain stimulation (cf. Olds, p. 85).

Of necessity, methodological questions had to be faced. Does the rate at which an animal self-stimulates provide a good measure of the reinforcement strength? If not, how can the reinforcement strength from different neural structures be compared? It had been shown that, when several electrodes were implanted, animals sometimes preferred stimulation at a neural site or at an intensity that produced lower response rates (Hodos & Valenstein, 1962). Apparently stimulation could have various influences on animals' ability to respond that did not necessarily affect the reward. For example, animals self-stimulating with electrodes in the septal area characteristically exhibit a very definite pause after each stimulation. This has been interpreted as reflecting the motor-inhibitory role of this area, which subsequent research has shown can be changed independently of the induced reward (cf. Valenstein, 1966, for a discussion of this question). Tests of reinforcement strength were designed which freed the animal from the task of pressing a pedal and thereby permitted it to engage in other behaviors while being stimulated. One such test used a two-compartment testing chamber, with the stimulation being presented in one of the two compartments on a random sequence. Animals could obtain stimulation for as long as they preferred (or they could escape from the stimulation) and the total time and the average duration the animal received stimulation provided a useful "profile" of other reactions to brain stimulation besides rate (Valenstein & Meyers, 1964). Methods that permitted the animal to self-adjust the intensity of the stimulus, by pressing one pedal to decrease and the other to increase the current strength, have provided a useful index of changes in the excitability of the reinforcement system, particularly following drug administration (Stein & Ray, 1959, 1960). For the reader who is considering doing research in this area it may be wise to become familiar with these methods, as well as with related problems of interpretation (cf. a review by Valenstein, 1964).

REINFORCING BRAIN STIMULATION AND THE ELICITATION OF BIOLOGICALLY SIGNIFICANT BEHAVIOR

It became apparent that most of the neural sites from which many biologically significant behaviors such as eating, drinking, hoarding, sex, and some types of aggression could be elicited were within the reinforcing brain areas. It was only natural, therefore, to ask whether the positive reinforcement system could be differentiated into regions primarily concerned with particular biological homeostatic mechanisms. As a first approach to this question, a number of investigators have sought to determine if the self-stimulation rate at particular brain regions is modified by changes in motivational state. The evidence has not been clear, in spite of many statements in textbooks which suggest simple relationships between self-stimulation rate, anatomical area, and motivational state.

Although there are reports that the self-stimulation rate at one electrode site may be modified by one drive (for example, hunger) and a different drive manipulation (for example, castration and hormonal replacement therapy) might be effective at another site in the same animal (Olds, 1958b), there is no convincing evidence that a *specific region* can be identified with a particular biological regulatory system by changes in the self-stimulation rate. The strongest evidence that self-stimulation performance may be used to identify the functional significance of a neural area has been derived from the data on hunger and satiety. There are, for example, several interesting reports of a parallel relationship between the effects of lateral and ventromedial hypothalamic manipulations on feeding and self-stimulation rate (Hoebel, 1969). It seems to be well established that animals will self-stimulate in the lateral "feeding" area, but not in the medial "satiety" area, and that self-stimulation at this site will be increased by variables producing hunger (e.g., food deprivation, insulin or distilled water injections) and decreased by variables that decrease eating (e.g., stomach distension, injection of glucagon). Furthermore, concurrent stimulation in the ventromedial area decreases eating and lateral hypothalamic self-stimulation rates. The difficulties of interpretation arise from the fact that most of these variables will have the same effect on many self-stimulation electrodes not located in the lateral hypothalamic feeding area (Hodos & Valenstein, 1960; Hoebel, 1969). Moreover, ventromedial hypothalamic stimulation appears to be aversive; therefore concurrent stimulation at this site is likely to disrupt any behavior, including those that have little relationship to eating or the lateral hypothalamus. It is possible that the positive correlation between lateral hypothalamic self-stimulation and feeding is spurious. Although Hoebel (1965) has shown that ventromedial hypothalamic lesions increase lateral hypothalamic self-stimulation rates as well as feeding, Ferguson and Keesey (1971) have reported that this relationship is very transitory and can be disassociated. Following ventromedial destruction, feeding is elevated for several weeks, while self-stimulation decreases following a brief initial increase. It is conceivable, nevertheless, that the neural circuits concerned with the regulation of different biological needs are widely distributed, although functionally discrete, throughout the reinforcement system. Gallistel (1971), for example, has demonstrated that an animal may prefer to self-stimulate with one electrode when thirsty and another when hungry, but the locations of these electrodes are not consistent nor are they predictable from what is known about the neural regulation of feeding (cf. Olds, pp. 88–89).

There has been a prevailing impression that the elicitation of eating and drinking by electrical stimulation has been obtained exclusively from the far lateral hypothalamic feeding area. Actually the anatomical information derived from stimulation techniques never corresponded very closely with the results obtained from ablation studies. Mogenson (1969) was correct in pointing out that the area from which he elicited drinking did not correspond to the lateral hypothalamic region that inhibited drinking (adipsia) following ablation (Montemurro & Stevenson, 1957; Teitelbaum & Epstein, 1962); however, he may have generalized from too small a sample when he concluded that drinking could only be elicited from a "critical focus, dorsolateral to the fornix" in the rat's hypothalamus. More recently Cox and Valenstein (1969) have reported that in the rat they were able to elicit drinking as well as eating (most often from the same electrode) from very disparate hypothalamic sites.

It is not necessary to view the ablation and stimulation results as contradictory, as they may reveal different aspects of the total process. For example, animals may be able to regulate food intake after recovery from the effects of lateral hypothalamic lesions, but they do not show the normal increase in eating during insulin-induced hypoglycemia (Epstein & Teitelbaum, 1967). Even in the case of drinking, where the deficits may continue to be profound, the animals are still capable of performing the act of drinking. The deficits produced by lesions seem to be confined to assessment of the internal milieu. Eating elicited by stimulation may primarily activate the outflow to the motor system. It may not be accidental that this latter function has a broader representation, as there may exist many "centers" responding to the different stimuli which are capable of triggering responses. Glickman and Schiff (1967) have marshaled evidence which suggests that stimulation may be activating built-in response systems located at sites distant from the electrodes. Similar arguments and additional evidence have been presented by Valenstein (1969a, 1970).

The difficulty of determining a precise localization for different functions with electrical stimulation has prompted some investigators to explore other techniques of exciting neural tissue that may be closer to physiological conditions. It was natural to think first of chemical stimulation as an alternative. This was not a new technique, as Simonoff (described earlier) had experimented with chemical cannulae in 1866 and Landois (1887) applied creatine to the frontal cortex to evoke responses. In more recent times, Demole (1927) and Cloëtta and Fisher (1930) applied sodium, potassium, calcium, and magnesium salts into the region around the infundibulum (pituitary stalk). Masserman (1937) introduced a variety of drugs into the hypothalamus in an attempt to compare chemical and electrical stimulation. Neurotransmitters were also used, as Kennard (1953) developed a microinjection technique to study the effects of acetylcholine on spinal-cord activity, and MacLean and Delgado (1953) introduced acetylcholine solutions into the limbic system of awake cats and monkeys. MacLean (1957) was concerned with the problem of rapid diffusion with solutions and experimented with crystals that would dissolve more slowly; acetylcholine and carbachol (a long-acting cholinergic mimetic) crystals were tapped into the inner barrel of a double-barreled cannula system which was implanted in the hippocampus of cats, rabbits, and monkeys.

Two new elements accounted for the rapid adoption of chemical stimulation techniques in the 1960s. First was the general acceptance of the notion of neurotransmitters as the major mechanisms of synaptic connections and the availability of a large arsenal of transmitter substances (or synthetic mimetics) and numerous blocking agents whose mode of action was, at least in part, understood. More significant, however, was the finding that either eating or drinking could be elicited in satiated rats through the same hypothalamic cannulae, depending on whether adrenergic or cholinergic crystals were used (Grossman, 1960). This evidence supporting a "pharmacological coding," capable of maintaining the functional independence of a physically interlaced neural substrate, has provided the impetus for a great number of studies during the past decade (cf. Grossman and Miller in this volume).

It should not be assumed that chemical stimulation presents an easy road to the truth. Although the likelihood of triggering a specific behavior in the rat with a given chemical substance may be high, the differences between species have been a source of major concern. Why should carbachol be so effective in triggering drinking in the rat, but elicit a variety of different responses such as "foot thumping," rage, or sleep, apparently from the same anatomical regions, in rabbits, cats, and other species? Moreover, the hope that chemical stimulation would improve localization because it would not affect fibers passing through an area (Miller, 1965) did not seem to be well founded. Although chemical stimulation more readily affects unmyelinated fibers, it is likely to affect all fibers as well as nerve cells. For many, the observation that chemical stimulation could elicit drinking from such widespread neural areas was disappointing (Fisher & Coury, 1962). It is often difficult to distinguish between pharmacological and nonpharmacological actions of drugs as the pH, osmolarity, and other physical properties of the injected substance may produce the observed results.[10] It has been shown, for example, that all compounds that chelate (bind) calcium activate neural tissue (Brink, 1954). Furthermore, many drugs have opposite effects at different dose levels. It may be necessary, therefore, to expend a great amount of effort obtaining dose-response curves. The pressure placed on investigators to provide explicit evidence of research progress often makes it difficult to introduce the necessary, but very time-consuming, controls.

In spite of all these difficulties, chemical stimulation is a very powerful tool that will certainly be used with increasing frequency and sophistication in the future. An increasing number of drugs with different physical properties but similar pharmacological action should make it possible to control for nonphysiological effects. The injection of drugs with similar action but different capacities to penetrate the blood-brain barrier makes it possible to parcel out brain and systemic effects. The concept of "pharmacological coding" is important and emphasizes a major weakness of electrical stimulation, which chemical stimulation has the potential to eliminate. Ultimately we will have to face the limits imposed by the fact that the application of even physiological substances through relative gross cannulae cannot duplicate the physiological events at a synapse. It is likely that by that time we will have learned much more about neural functioning and newer techniques will then be available.

There are important questions that have to be asked quite apart from those related to the neural sites from which it is possible to elicit eating, drinking, and other behaviors. Regardless of the kind of stimulation employed, we have to remind ourselves that the processes underlying the elicitation of behavior may be quite complex. Various investigators have emphasized different factors, some stressing the activation of drive states such as hunger or thirst, while others concentrate on the triggering of fixed motor pathways or the modification of the responsiveness to different stimuli. Those who have stressed the activation of such drive factors as hunger have pointed out that the stimulation usually does not appear to be eliciting motor patterns directly; the stimulated animal responds appropriately to the physical demands of the goal object (the stimulus-bound eater may bite or lap, depending on the form of the available food). Also relevant to this argument is the observation that stimulated animals, like naturally motivated animals, are capable of performing

---

10. See Grossman (1962), reprinted in this volume, for an example of the type of controls which must be a part of these experiments.

learned responses to obtain food, water, or even a suitable prey (cf. Valenstein, Cox, & Kakolewski, 1970, for a review of this literature).

The investigators who stress the elicitation, or at least sensitization, of motor pathways have pointed out that stimulation at some sites elicits only very specific, stereotyped response elements that are involved in such behaviors as mating, attacking, feeding, and drinking. The fact that some stimulation may activate only a few elements of a more complex pattern would seem to support the motor innervation interpretation (Roberts et al., 1967). Few people have noted, for example, that the first report of drinking elicited by hypothalamic stimulation contained the observation that the rat "would stand on its hind legs and run vigorously around the glass-enclosed circular cage, licking wildly at the glass wall" (Greer, 1955). Later the animal started drinking great quantities of water during stimulation, but if the water bottle was removed the cage-licking behavior returned. This observation and others of a similar nature strongly suggest that some stimulation may elicit motor responses.

In spite of the fact that responses may be elicited reliably by stimulation, the relation to the electrode site may be quite indirect. Some responses may represent a species-specific reaction to a more general affective state and the assumption of a direct elicitation by the stimulation may be misleading. Black and Vanderwolf (1969), for example, found that "foot thumping" could be elicited in the rabbit by stimulation of diverse sites in the septum, fornix-fimbria, midline thalamus, central gray, and reticular formation, as well as in the hypothalamus. Rather than describing a complex "foot thumping" circuit in the brain, these investigators noted that the sites also evoked aversive states and that thumping was a characteristic rabbit response to noxious stimulation including foot shock. Similarly, Ploog (1970) has studied the vocalization of monkeys in groups and has correlated various sounds with social interactions that suggest fear, threat, submissiveness, and other states. Stimulation could elicit some of these same vocalizations and there is a good correlation between specific calls and certain brain structures. However, the brain structures that mediate these cells (specifically, parts of the amygdala, hypothalamus, stria terminalis, and periventricular gray) all are associated with attack and defensive behavior. It seems unlikely in such cases that the motor control over these vocalizations is directly elicited by the stimulation.

Valenstein (1969) has reviewed data indicating that it may be difficult to predict the specific elicited response from knowledge of the electrode location. Individual animal and species characteristics seem to be major determinants of the elicited response. Often the same response is elicited from electrodes having very different placements in a given animal (Valenstein, Cox, & Kakolewski, 1970; Wise, 1971). The behavior produced by brain stimulation reflects innate (and perhaps learned) *prepotent responses* which tend to be dominant in a particular stimulated animal as a result of the interaction of environmental conditions, the presence of compelling stimuli, and an induced state of arousal. Unquestionably the states induced by stimulation may differ and these would be expected to set limits on the behavior exhibited, but Valenstein (1969) has argued that these induced states are seldom as specific as such terms as "hunger" and "thirst" would imply. The information obtained from human stimulation seems to be consistent with this interpretation.

Nevertheless, we should not expect the same explanations to prevail in all cases. For example, MacLean et al. (1963) have charted the cerebral areas from which they could elicit penile erection in the squirrel monkey. Although penile erection may serve as a signal in different nonprocreative social interactions (for the squirrel monkey), the fact that this response can be elicited even under anesthesia suggests some direct activation of an autonomic, vascular response.

Evidence has also been accumulating that hypothalamic stimulation may direct behavior by selectively changing responsiveness to stimuli. Most of the evidence for this position has been obtained with hypothalamic stimulation that elicits attack behavior in the cat. MacDonnell and Flynn (1966) have demonstrated that such stimulation potentiates the response to touch on the side of the face contralateral (opposite) to the side stimulated. If a broad region around the muzzle is stimulated with a blunt rubber probe, the cat moves its head to bring the object to its lips; if the lip is stimulated a mouth-opening response is elicited. More recently, Bandler and Flynn (1971) have observed that a mouse presented to the eye contralateral to the hypothalamic stimulation is more likely to elicit a lunging response than the same mouse presented to the ipsilateral eye. The argument that hypothalamic stimulation is specifically influencing sensory systems is strengthened considerably by the fact that the sensory fields on both sides of the midline are not changed equally. There is the possibility that the differences between the two sides may be produced by an ipsilateral disruption rather than a contralateral facilitation, but the fact that increases in the intensity of the hypothalamic stimulation produce a facilitation even on the ipsilateral side may rule out this interpretation (Flynn et al., 1971). Earlier, Chi and Flynn (1968) had noted that hypothalamic stimulation may reduce the size of the evoked potentials in the visual cortex, and more recent studies from their laboratory have demonstrated that the response of some individual cells in the visual cortex may be increased while other cells may exhibit a decreased responsiveness to various visual stimuli presented during hypothalamic stimulation. The conclusion drawn from such studies is that stimulation is triggering hypothalamic "patterning mechanisms" which "impose specific influences on the sensory system appropriate to attack behavior" (Flynn et al., 1970). It should be noted, however, that all tests of sensory changes in animals must involve responses. It may be difficult, therefore, to be certain that sensory rather than motor changes have been produced by the stimulation.

Of course it is possible that more than one mechanism is operating. Flynn and his collaborators have concluded that stimulation also exerts a patterning influence on the motor system. Cats stimulated in the central gray region tend to strike out at a prey with the contralateral limb and this is believed to result in part from facilitating the appropriate portion of the corticospinal motor system (Edwards, 1970). Flynn and his collaborators do not believe that stimulation activates a drive independent of sensory and motor involvement and they suggest that if drive is to be "operationally" defined, the meaning should be restricted to those measurable changes in responsiveness of the sensory and motor systems. It could be argued, however, that this definition may unnecessarily restrict the phenomena to be studied. There is little doubt, for example, that motivated animals may expend a great amount of energy performing learned responses to obtain goal objects which are not in the immediate environment. Under such conditions the learned responses have no inherent relation to the goal objects, and furthermore the goal objects are not present so they cannot be considered sensory stimuli.

Some discrepancies in the literature may have been caused by overlooking important behavior distinctions. Behavior that superficially appears similar may be significantly different. For example, what had been treated collectively as "rage" at one time is now seen as at least two different behaviors. Wasman and Flynn (1962) have distinguished between the elicitation of "affective" and "quiet biting" attack in the cat. The former consists of a pronounced sympathetic arousal with arched back, hair standing on end (piloerection), and claws unsheathed, often with growling, hissing, and profuse salivation. This response, which is elicited by medial hypothalamic structures and the so-called central gray region surrounding the aqueduct of Sylvius, may be the type of aggression that is elicited by painful stimuli. This interpretation is supported by the fact that animals escape from stimulation that produces this response (Adams & Flynn, 1966).

"Quiet biting" attack, on the other hand, seems to be related to predatory, stalking behavior and does not involve a great display of affective rage, but it can lead to very efficient and deadly hunting behavior even in cats that normally are not mouse and rat killers (Flynn et al., 1970). This behavior in general is elicited by stimulation in lateral hypothalamic areas. Roberts and Kiess (1964) have shown that normally nonaggressive cats can be motivated to run through a maze to reach a rat when stimulated at these sites (cf. Roberts' discussion in this volume). In more recent studies it has been shown that the stimulation which elicits "quiet biting" attack in the rat (Panksepp, 1969) and some types of aggression in the monkey (Robinson et al., 1969) may actually be positively reinforcing. "Quiet biting" and "affective" attack may not be the only types of aggression to be distinguished. Moyer (1971) considers seven classes of aggression (predatory, intermale, fear-induced, irritable, territorial defense, maternal, and instrumental) and suggests that the response patterns and underlying neural mechanisms may differ.

In addition to those instances in which hypothalamic stimulation seems to be tapping into adaptive patterns built into the nervous system, there is the possibility that some of the elicited behaviors observed are reflecting more plastic mechanisms. Judging by self-stimulation performance, most of the neural areas from which stimulus-bound behavior can be elicited are within the positive reinforcement system ("affective" attack behavior would have to be excluded from this generalization). Although part of the reinforcement system may be involved in facilitating inborn mechanisms, other parts may be less committed and therefore more responsive to the vicissitudes of the environment and to sources of rewards that nature could not anticipate. Valenstein (1971) has recently described many instances in which a stimulus-bound behavior emerged only after long periods of testing and was then gradually elicited with increasing regularity. In such cases there was no evidence of the existence of a fixed connection between the hypothalamic area stimulated (or the state induced by such stimulation) and the specific response pattern that was eventually elicited. The implications of this aspect of stimulus-bound behavior are discussed in Valenstein's contribution to this volume.

POSITIVE BRAIN STIMULATION: RESEARCH APPLICATIONS AND THEORIES

Brain stimulation: An immediate reward

One of the more interesting and potentially useful features of rewarding brain stimulation stems from the immediate nature of the reinforcement. By contrast, when an animal eats, much of the reinforcement must be delayed until digestion and absorption have started. Even recognizing that some reinforcement is derived from taste and that there exist techniques for delivering food directly into the mouth, food cannot compete with brain stimulation for rapidity of reward delivery. This feature of positive brain stimulation has made it possible to modify rapidly occurring responses that would be beyond the capacity of conventional rewards. In principle, any discrete response that can be measured can be reinforced. Taking advantage of the naturally occurring variability in the responses, one can reinforce some preselected segment of the total distribution. Electrical activity of single cells can be monitored and, using brain stimulation to "reward" those interresponse intervals that are above or below the criteria, their spontaneous firing rate may be modified (Olds, 1965). In a similar vein, Miller (1969) and DiCara (1970a) and their associates have been able to modify such glandular and visceral responses as heart rate, salivation, rate of urine formation in the kidney, and vascular constriction and dilation. In the electrocardiogram, the P and R waves are correlated with auricular and ventricular musculature, respectively. Fields (1970) has reported that specific components of the electrocardiogram, such as the P-P and P-R intervals, can be independently conditioned. DiCara (1970b) has described further consequences of these autonomic modifications, as experimental animals with elevated heart rates may display heightened emotionality that persists beyond the training, and this in turn may influence their ability to learn to avoid aversive stimuli.

These experiments have obvious clinical implications, for they suggest that many unhealthy visceral patterns, such as those that might produce ulcers, tachycardias (rapid heartbeat), high blood pressure, and even abnormal brain patterns, may be learned and may therefore also be unlearned. As the experimental animals studied have usually been immobilized with curare, the possibility that the rewards are primarily modifying skeletal muscles, which have concomitant visceral changes, appears to have been ruled out. What mechanisms are being rewarded or reinforced is not clear, as up to this point most of the effort has been expended on demonstrating the range of organs and responses that can be modified. Analysis can be quite complex when consecutive responses such as heartbeats (which in the rat may be separated by less than 150 milliseconds) are to be monitored and rewarded. It is generally assumed that the neural pattern determining the intervals between heartbeats is reinforced by the stimulation, but when the interval to be rewarded has been identified, the neural pattern for the next heartbeat has already been initiated. This might imply that some systemic factor associated with a series of rapid or slow heartbeats has been modified, rather than the specific mechanism controlling heart rate. However, the demonstration that vascular changes can be modified in one ear and not the other suggests that this type of "learning" may be quite specific (DiCara & Miller, 1968).

Interaction of positive and negative reinforcing systems

A theoretical issue which has received considerable attention concerns the nature of the interaction between the positive and negative reinforcing systems. As described earlier, Roberts (1958a) demonstrated that cats with posterior hypothalamic electrodes display a "flight" response when stimulated, but, interestingly, they could not learn to avoid the stimulation even though they rapidly learned to escape. Roberts hypothesized, and demonstrated in a second study, that animals failed to avoid stimulation because the onset was positive and only the continuation produced negative reinforcement (Roberts, 1958b). Roberts' cats actually sought out the stimulus although they escaped from it when it remained on. Similarly, Bower and Miller (1958) demonstrated that rats would press one lever to turn hypothalamic stimulation on and another lever to turn the same stimulation off. These results seemed to indicate that in some hypothalamic areas prolonged stimulation would start to activate an adjacent, aversive site after initially activating part of the positive reinforcement system. The implication that the positive and aversive systems were in close proximity in only certain areas was weakened by the observation that animals appeared to terminate most, if not all, positive stimulation regardless of the placement within the system (Valenstein & Valenstein, 1964). Apparently turning brain stimulation on and off is not characteristic of a particular neural area where positive and negative sites are in close proximity, as this behavior can be seen with electrodes in the septal area, amygdala, and hippocampus, as well as the hypothalamus. It is possible that the aversive and positive systems are always in close proximity, but there is evidence that, at least for the rat, turning brain stimulation off may not be a simple reflection of an aversive experience. It was shown, for example, that animals would self-stimulate even when the current was fixed at durations that were much longer than they had self-selected (Valenstein & Valenstein, 1964). Similarly, when stimulus durations longer than those self-selected were used, animals responded faster (Keesey, 1964a) and worked harder (Hodos, 1965) to obtain the stimulation.

Actually, an alternative explanation could be offered for why animals may repeatedly turn brain stimulation on and off besides the possibility that the prolongation of the stimulation changes the motivational effects from positive to negative. One of the other possibilities considered is that habituation to the stimulation may cause a rapid diminution of the reinforcement and animals may turn off the stimulation in order to turn it on again and receive the positive reinforcement associated mainly with the onset of the stimulation (cf. Olds, p. 87).

Scientists have always tended to be entrapped by puzzling phenomena, but that is not the only reason for pursuing the question of why animals turn the same stimulation on and off. It has been often observed that pain and pleasure have an intimate relationship, which may reach abnormal proportions in sadistic and masochistic behavior. There has been some speculation that the spontaneous activity of the lateral hypothalamic reward system may be inhibited whenever the punishment system is activated. Pain, for example, may activate the punishment system, which reflexly inhibits the lateral hypothalamic system. It has been suggested that when the source of activation of the punishment system is removed, there may be an automatic rebound activation of the positive system (Olds & Olds, 1964; Stein, 1964). This interaction is postulated to be the basis of the "it feels so good when it stops" experience. The relationship between the two systems may be mutually inhibitory, like antagonistic spinal reflexes. Pleasure may mask pain and pain interferes with pleasure; the termination of either may partially activate the other. Some experimental evidence supports this speculation, as reinforcing brain stimulation may mask the experience of pain in animals and man (Heath & Mickle, 1960; Cox & Valenstein, 1965; Valenstein, 1965).

Pharmacology of positive reinforcement

One way to obtain more information about underlying mechanisms and the function of the positive reinforcement system is to examine its pharmacological properties. It has been shown that systemic administration of drugs that modify adrenergic transmission in the brain has the largest effect on self-stimulation performance (Stein, 1960). For example, substances that release norepinephrine, such as amphetamine or α-methyl-tyrosine, increase self-stimulation rates or lower intensity thresholds. Similarly, drugs that increase norepinephrine supply by inhibiting the action of its antagonist, monoamine oxidase, also increase the excitability of the presumed neural substrate for reinforcement. In contrast, drugs such as reserpine (which depletes the brain of norepinephrine) or chlorpromazine (which blocks adrenergic transmission) tend to decrease self-stimulation rate and raise its threshold. These findings become more meaningful when considered together with the reports that the medial forebrain bundle (the region of the most reliable self-stimulation performance) is particularly rich in norepinephrine (Hillarp, Fuxe, & Dahlström, 1966; Heller, Seiden, & Moore, 1966) and that increased brain norepinephrine may be the principal factor in counteracting depression (Brodie, Spector, & Shore, 1959). Viewed as a whole, the data indicate that self-stimulation may depend primarily on the activation of a norepinephrine-based reinforcement system. It has also been suggested that when this system does not function normally psychopathology results. The elation and depression of moods as well as fluctuations in the ability to sustain purposive behavior may be reflecting the state of the reinforcement system.

In a very bold extension of their work, Stein and Wise (1971) have postulated a possible metabolic destruction of the adrenergic reward system as a basis of schizophrenia. The theory suggests that a pathological gene leads to a reduction of the activity of dopamine-B-hydroxylase, the enzyme responsible for the conversion of dopamine to norepinephrine. This deficiency results in the release of an excess of unconverted dopamine into the synapse where it may be converted to 6-hydroxydopamine (6-OH-DA). Ungerstedt (1968) has demonstrated that 6-OH-DA selectively destroys norepinephrine synapses and Stein and Wise (1971) have reported that injection of 6-OH-DA significantly reduces self-stimulation rate for "at least five days after dosing was discontinued." The latter observation may indicate that there has been irreversible damage to the reward mechanism.

This theory is bound to receive a great amount of attention and challenge during the next few years. Judging by the reactions of many people, a major part of the challenge to the theory has come from an unwillingness to accept Stein and Wise's implicit equating of self-stimulation performance and schizophrenic symptoms. Stein and Wise seem to take the position that there is indeed a connection between self-stimulation and schizophrenia in that both involve the positive reward system, a part of the nervous system vital for the maintenance of goal-directed behavior. It could be argued, though, that schizophrenia may take many forms, and while a loss of ability to maintain directed behavior may be characteristic of some schizophrenic patients, it does not appear to be true of all. Paranoid schizophrenics, for example, may exhibit extremely well-directed and purposeful behavior if one grants their initial premises. All of this may be "nit-picking" at this point, as even though Stein and Wise apparently believe that deterioration of synapses in the norepinephrine-based reward system is at the root of all types of schizophrenia, if their theory applies to only a percentage of psychiatric disorders the contribution could be enormous. If some psychoses are the result of a specific metabolic deficiency it is possible that a preventative treatment could be developed as it has with phenylpyruvic oligophrenia (a feeblemindedness produced by a metabolic disorder resulting in an accumulation of destructive amounts of phenylpyruvic acid).

It should be noted that self-stimulation performance may not be related in a simple way to norepinephrine pathways. Animals may self-stimulate when rewarded with small quantities of carbachol (a synthetic acetylcholine compound) injected into the hypothalamus in place of electrical stimulation (Olds et al., 1964) and patients report "pleasure reactions" following acetylcholine injections into the septal area of their brains (Heath, 1964). In addition, Roll (1970) has reported that following administration of disulphiram (an inhibitor of norepinephrine biosynthesis) self-stimulation performance continues at normal rates, providing the animal is prevented from falling asleep. Poschel and Ninteman (1966), however, had reported earlier 'hat lowering the brain concentrations of norepinephrine by interfering with its biosynthesis with DL-*alpha*-methyl-tyrosine produces a suppression of self-stimulation in the absence of any sedation. Poschel (1969) concluded, however, that the "reward system" was not exclusively dependent on norepinephrine synapses as some "excellent self-stimulation points" were not influenced by modification of norepinephrine levels. Recently, Poschel and Ninteman (1971) found that serotonin also plays a role in self-stimulation performance, as interference with the biosynthesis of this neurotransmitter produced a marked elevation in self-stimulation performance (cf. Olds, p. 90).

Satiation, drive, reinforcement: Some theoretical speculations

One characteristic of reinforcing brain stimulation which has resulted in some dramatic demonstrations and which may also have considerable theoretical speculation is its great resistance to satiation. In some hypothalamic areas, animals may self-stimulate for forty-eight hours in a row, almost to exhaustion, with little change in response rate over this period (Olds, 1958a). In one study, a rat with a hypothalamic electrode self-stimulated at an average lever-pressing rate of thirty responses per minute over a twenty-day period (Valenstein & Beer, 1964). It has been demonstrated, moreover, that self-stimulating animals may not bother to avoid shock or drink water even though thirsty (Valenstein & Beer, 1962) and rats that have just given birth to pups may neglect them in order to self-stimulate (Sonderegger, 1970). Under certain experimental conditions, self-stimulating animals may starve to death even though food is available (Routtenberg & Lindy, 1965).

Clearly it would be maladaptive for any reward to be able to completely "capture" an animal's behavior. Under natural circumstances, there is little danger that an animal could receive such direct stimulation of its positive reward system. According to one hypothesis, the capacity of stimuli to activate the positive reinforcement system changes as a function of drive state. Satiation is normally brought about as changes in the internal state comprising the physiological basis of the drive begin to block the ability of relevant stimuli to activate reinforcing neural areas. As hunger subsides, for example, food-related stimuli lose their effectiveness and may even activate an aversive system. In the case of reinforcing electrical stimulation this normal shut-off or "gating mechanism" may be bypassed and satiation is not possible.

Not unrelated to the above discussion is the challenge provided by the self-stimulation phenomenon to drive reduction theories. As the theory is often postulated, reinforcement is derived from a reduction in the intensity of an internal drive stimulus, in essence, a reduction in the activity of a neural system that is related to some specific motivational state. Hunger, pain, and other motivating states are assumed to be represented by increased activity in a neural system subserving that state. A response that reduced the hunger or pain would be considered reinforcing because it could produce an appropriate decrement of the relevant neural activity. *Reinforcing brain stimulation, however, would appear to heighten, not decrease, neural activity* (Olds, 1955).

Although there may be a high correlation between drive reduction and reinforcement, the relationship may be indirect. During a period of high-drive state, "relevant" stimuli may have the capacity to activate the neural system underlying reinforcement. From an evolutionary point of view, it is not difficult to understand why reinforcing stimuli are highly correlated with drive reduction, but there may be no direct causal connection—*the critical intervening process may involve the activation of the reinforcement system.*

There are other ways of conceiving of the relationship between drives and reinforcement besides a literal interpretation of drive reduction theory. Deutsch (1963) has hypothesized that drive has a different neural substrate from reinforcement. The drive pathway conveys the energy (motivational excitement) to a response system, Deutsch maintains, while the reinforcement pathway establishes the functional link between the source of this energy and a particular response system. Under the impact of the same "drive stimuli," therefore, previously successful responses are likely to be tried again. According to this view, drive and reinforcement involve separate neural systems, but electrical stimulation artificially activates both together. Under natural conditions, the drive system is activated by some imbalance in a homeostatic system and is not likely to be dissipated very rapidly. If the drive system is activated by electrical stimulation, there are no systemic factors that can maintain the motivation and the drive may rapidly decay if stimulation is interrupted. This would produce an abnormally fast extinction of unrewarded responses. Howarth and Deutsch (1962) have demonstrated, for example, that the number of unrewarded responses an animal displays decreases significantly if even relatively short rest periods are introduced after the last administration of brain stimulation. According to this view, the stimulation provides not only reinforcement, but also the drive for the next response.

The drive induced by reinforcing brain stimulation does not always dissipate rapidly. It has been shown that, following some training procedures, extinction is not always rapid and long series of unrewarded responses are possible (Pliskoff et al., 1955). In a different experiment, brief delays were interposed between responding and the delivery of reinforcing brain stimulation in order to make this situation more comparable to the delay of reinforcement when animals receive food. Under these conditions, the extinction performance with rewarding brain stimulation was equivalent to that obtained with food-rewarded responses (Gibson et al., 1965). Furthermore, Sonderegger and Rose (1970) have demonstrated that rats running in a straight alley for rewarding brain stimulation exert the greatest pull against a restraining device when closest to the goal box, even though most time has elapsed since the previous stimulation. This evidence of an "approach gradient" indicates that drive decay may not be a critical element in the motivation to obtain brain stimulation.

The rate of dissipation of the drive induced by brain stimulation may not be as critical an issue as the distinctiveness of the drive and reinforcement processes. Deutsch and some of his former students have designed tests to distinguish between the drive and the reinforcement components of rewarding brain stimulation. In general, running speed or rate of lever pressing are believed to reflect drive, while a discrimination task such as accuracy in choosing between alternative paths in a maze is thought to reflect reinforcement. The difference between drive and reinforcement can be demonstrated by selecting two different brain stimulation intensities and using them as the reward in the separate goal boxes of a T-maze. If the stimulation intensity values are selected appropriately, the animal will run to the goal box that offers the higher intensity; this has been interpreted as reflecting its greater reinforcement value. On the other hand, if the animal's running speed is measured in a straight runway and the same two intensities alternately serve as the reward on a series of closely spaced trials, the animal may run faster on the trials rewarded with the lower intensity. The explanation offered for these seemingly paradoxical results is that in the runway the drive generated by the previous stimulation is the major determinant of drive level on a given trial.

Deutsch has also attempted to measure neurophysiological differences in refractory periods which may be characteristic of the two systems. If a second stimulating pulse is presented only a small fraction of a millisecond after a first pulse, it may have no effect because of the absolute refractory period of the stimulated neurons. However, when the interval is gradually increased the summative effect of the second pulse becomes evident. If animals are tested in situations that presumably measure drive or reinforcement, the estimates of the absolute refractory period of the underlying neural systems differ (cf. Gallistel, 1972, for more details).

BRAIN STIMULATION IN HUMANS

It might seem that many of the mysteries surrounding the motivational states and reinforcement elicited by brain stimulation would have been resolved by reports from humans receiving such stimulation. Although the results with humans have contributed to our understanding of the phenomena, most of the mysteries persist. This is due in part to the limitations inherent in clinical research, such as the inability to incorporate adequate experimental controls and the relatively little anatomical confirmation of electrode placements. Furthermore, the verbal reports from a patient population that has, to a large extent, been made up of psychotics has not proven very useful. Even with nonpsychotic patients, however, the feelings evoked by stimulation have not often been easily expressed in particularly helpful words and it has been difficult to extract the essence from these very idiosyncratic reports. The verbal descriptions are often similar to those one would obtain by asking smokers to describe the pleasures they derive from cigarettes.

As any mention of electrodes in humans often conjures up images of "big brother" control over a population, as well as questions concerning the ethics of experimentation on humans, it may be important to briefly discuss these issues first. Even if such a discussion is not reassuring, it may be helpful in clearing up some misconceptions about the extent of control that can be achieved with brain stimulation. The fears that brain stimulation might be utilized for control over the population of a "1984 society" are not well grounded, but they have been expressed over and over in the popular press and even by professional psychologists. For example, London (1969) has written:

> All the ancient dreams of mastery over man and all the tales of zombies, golems, and Frankensteins involved some magic formula, or ritual, or incantation that would magically yield the key to dominion. . . . This has been changing gradually, as knowledge of the brain has grown and been compounded since the nineteenth century, until today a whole technology exists for physically penetrating and controlling the brain's own mechanisms of control. It is sometimes called "brain implantation," which means placing electrical or chemical stimulating devices in strategic brain tissues. . . . These methods have been used experimentally on myriad aspects of animal behavior, and clinically on a growing number of people. . . . The number of activities connected to specific places and processes in the brain and aroused, excited, augmented, inhibited, or suppressed at will by stimulation of the proper site is simply huge. Animals and men can be oriented toward each other with emotions ranging from stark terror or morbidity to passionate affection and sexual desire. . . . Eating, drinking, sleeping, moving of bowels or limbs or organs of sensation, gracefully or in spastic comedy, can all be managed on electrical demand by puppeteers whose flawless strings are pulled from miles away by the unseen call of radio and whose puppets, made of flesh and blood, look "like electronic toys," so little self-direction do they seem to have (pp. 136–137).

This "science fiction" conception of brain stimulation's being used to exploit human robots or puppets does not seem remotely possible. The activation of muscles by brain stimulation is too crude to produce the smooth, organized flow of movements necessary for accomplishing any but the simplest acts. The neural control of movement involves complex feedback mechanisms with exquisite integration of information and control at many levels. There is no reason to believe that it will be easier to duplicate useful movements by brain stimulation than it has proven possible to produce meaningful images by stimulation of the optic nerve or visual areas in the brain. Furthermore, the evidence indicates that when "spontaneous" or voluntary movements conflict with those elicited by the stimulation, the former often dominates (Delgado, 1969).

If brain stimulation does not seem to be a practical means of dominating humans by controlling movements, conceivably the administration of rewarding and punishing brain stimulation might be effective for this purpose. There is little doubt that some brain stimulation can produce very pleasant sensations and other stimulation can evoke very aversive or even painful experiences. There is no reason to believe, however, that this would be as efficient or practical a means of controlling humans as the great number of physical and psychological tortures and temptations that mankind, in its more malevolent moments, has contrived throughout the ages. Moreover, the belief that positive brain stimulation in man constitutes such a compelling and "addicting" stimulus that its consequences cannot be compared with any other reward are not justified by the available information on human self-stimulation performance (Bishop et al., 1964), nor is there evidence that stimulation can induce a euphoria comparable to that induced by some drugs (Heath, 1964).

Although the danger of brain stimulation's being used to control people does not seem to be a real issue when examined critically, the ethical problems related to experimentation on humans should certainly be a matter of concern. The ethical issues are not unique, however, as the same questions must be faced with any new clinical procedure. In all cases it is necessary to obtain meaningful consent and to ask (1) How serious is the illness? (2) What are the risks involved in the procedure? (3) What is the rationale for the procedure and the probability of its helping the patient? and (4) What other alternatives exist? These questions and the weight given to the answers are interrelated in ways almost too obvious to specify. Clearly, the risks that one could justifiably consider with a patient who is likely to die or be seriously debilitated are different from those applicable to a person whose illness does not have the same consequences. Any new clinical procedure can be used to gratify someone's ego or professional advancement. It is necessary, therefore, to establish safeguards to ensure that decisions are based on answers to the above questions. This is not to imply that the decision is always easy or that brain stimulation does not involve some special problems as, for example, the psychological impact on a patient whose moods may be remotely manipulated by his physician. Nevertheless, even these more subtle consequences of human brain stimulation can be considered when the risks are evaluated. As far as one can determine from the published records of experience with animal and human electrode implantation, at least the physical risks connected with the surgery are not great. The possibility that stimulation or electrode implantation may produce permanent neurological changes is more difficult to evaluate.

Brain stimulation has been used with patients suffering from the effects of epilepsy, Parkinson's disease, and other tremors, psychosis (primarily schizophrenia), narcolepsy ("sleeping sickness"), carcinoma with intractable pain, severe rheumatoid arthritis, and a special group of patients that have exhibited seemingly unprecipitated outbursts of violent assault (often resulting in the killing of someone). A representative cross section of the stimulation studies with humans can be obtained from the books and articles by Delgado (1969), Heath (1954, 1964), Mark & Ervin (1970), Penfield & Baldwin (1952), Sem-Jacobsen (1968), and Spiegel et al., (1960).

In cases of epilepsy and Parkinsonism, the ethical problems are relatively straightforward. When patients are scheduled for surgery[11] the rationale for using brain stimulation, either as a technique for locating the abnormal focus or as a means of anticipating the effects of surgery, is readily evident even if the prognostic accuracy cannot always be evaluated quantitatively from the literature. In some patients subject to violent outburst, the behavioral history and standard electroencephalographic recordings from the scalp have strongly suggested an epileptic foci, usually in the temporal lobe. Electrical recordings from deeply implanted electrodes may facilitate the locating of a very discrete focus. Sometimes further verification of the anatomical location of the difficulty can be obtained by presenting "significant environmental stimuli," which may trigger abnormal neuronal patterns that could only be recorded with "depth" electrodes. Additional confirmation may be obtained by the precipitation of violent outbursts by electrically stimulating these loci. Treatment may consist of destruction of small, bilateral areas; this has been reported to eliminate the episodes of rage in some cases (Mark & Ervin, 1970). As the area destroyed may be quite small, it is possible that there may be no other consequences of the surgery. It is difficult to evaluate the efficacy of this treatment at present as there is too little quantitative information available to estimate the probability of success. For the same reason, it is not possible to evaluate the claim of these authors that many outbursts of violence are the result of "trigger zones" in the brain, as there is no reliable estimate of the occurrence of such EEG indices in a population normally not subject to violent outbursts.

A more speculative treatment has been described by Delgado, which involves the use of a "transdermal dialytrode," consisting of a brain cannula attached to a dialysis bag, all implanted under the skin. The dialysis bag would permit a prescribed infusion rate of a drug to be delivered to a specific brain area, in order to modify some abnormal activities. The advantage of such a system would be the elimination of side effects that frequently result from the relatively large doses that have to be injected systemically in order to achieve adequate levels in the brain. There are many potential dangers of such a technique, such as leakage from the reservoir, and at present there are few, if any, neurological disorders that would even remotely qualify for this radical procedure.

The rationale behind the use of electrical stimulation with other illnesses is much less evident. In the few cases in which electrodes were implanted in patients suffering from severe arthritis or narcolepsy, the hope presumably was that activation of hypothalamic areas controlling the release of the hormone ACTH, or those areas thought to be critically involved in sleep and wakeful-

---

11. It is now possible to use the drug L-DOPA to suppress some Parkinsonian tremors.

ness, might in some unspecified way be helpful (Heath, 1964). The rationale for electrode implantation in psychotic patients is not explicitly stated. The implied goal is to produce a change in some properties of the positive reward system. Some of these implantations, however, were undertaken before this system was identified.[12] Some consequences of stimulation were unanticipated. There have been reports, for example, of stimulation increasing a patient's communicativeness, and the hope has been expressed that some of the mood changes induced by such stimulation might facilitate the psychiatric therapeutic process. Heath (1964) reports that "striking and immediate relief from intractable physical pain was consistently obtained with stimulation to the septal region in three patients with advanced carcinoma," as stimulation "immediately relieved the intense physical pain and anguish, and the patients relaxed in comfort and pleasure" (p. 225). It is difficult to determine if these or any other patients have been helped beyond the relatively brief effects of the stimulation, but fairness would require that any evaluation of the justification of these procedures must give sufficient weight to the fact that often the only future for some patients is a predictably steady and complete physical and mental deterioration.

In recent years, Japanese neurosurgeons have increased the application of stereotaxic technique to human emotional and behavioral problems (Narabayashi, 1964). Although these surgical interventions generally involve destruction of hypothalamic areas, the procedures have been strongly influenced by the past and current results of stimulation in the laboratory and the clinic. Many of the reports of improvement are reminiscent of earlier accounts of the beneficial effects of frontal lobotomy—a benefit which was often more meaningful to the hospital staff rather than to the patient. For example, Sano et al. (1966) report that, following posteromedial hypothalamotomy, aggressive patients "became markedly calm, passive and tractable, showing decreased spontaneity" (p. 167). Narabayashi et al. (1963) note that following bilateral amygdalectomy "the patient had become so obedient and cooperative that it was almost impossible to imagine that it was the same child who had been so wild and uncontrollable preoperatively" (p. 17). Most impartial observers are likely to conclude that there is not sufficient data to evaluate the "increasing enthusiasm" of these surgeons for their operative procedures.

What have we learned from manipulating the brains of humans? The literature is quite complex, with many anecdotal reports and a minimum of confirmation of electrode placements, but certain general conclusions seem justified. There is little convincing evidence that human brain stimulation reliably produces a specific goal-oriented response from the same anatomical structure. It is true that Delgado (1969) has described two female patients who, following temporal lobe stimulation, became increasingly "flirtatious" with the therapist, and Sem-Jacobsen (1968) has reported two cases in which stimulation of the "posterior part of the frontal lobe, 2 cm. from the midline" (p. 173) produced in one case a sensation "like a sexual pleasure" (p. 172), and

---

12. Heath (1954) indicates that he had reported at a meeting in 1952 that following stimulation of the septal area "one noticed a pleasurable reaction to stimulation," and one patient commented during stimulation, "I have a glowing feeling. I feel good."

in the other case ejaculation.[13] However, these effects were not explored extensively, and while the possibility cannot be excluded, there is little to support the view that a similar motivational orientation can be obtained from the same structure in different individuals. At least for the present, these results seem to be highly determined by personal reactions of the patients, but there may also be some consistency in the emotional state elicited by stimulation of certain neural areas.

The emotional states that have been evoked by human brain stimulation are usually described by such phrases as relaxation (even "hyperrelaxation"), feelings of well-being, increased alertness and communicativeness, euphoria or confusion, depression, anxiety, agitation, fear, anger, and rage. There seems to be reasonably good agreement that stimulation of some regions may produce a predictable change of emotion, such as mood elation or depression. For example, Mark and Ervin (1970) report that they are able to elicit positive feelings (usually some dimension of relaxation) from more lateral amygdala placements and unpleasant reactions, such as pain or loss of control, from the more medial areas within this same brain structure. These investigators also report that, at least in patients with temporal lobe disorders, they can initiate and stop violent behavior by stimulating different parts of the hippocampus and amygdala, but they also describe some "highly individualized" responses to limbic stimulation (Ervin, Mark, & Stevens, 1969).

PROJECTION INTO THE FUTURE

It is just a little over a hundred years since stimulation techniques were systematically applied to the study of brain function. Although a great amount of information has been acquired as a result of these techniques, it is very easy to exaggerate the extent of our knowledge and the degree of control that can be exercised. Over the past few years we have been subjected with increasing frequency to such statements as, "Though their methods are still crude and not always predictable, there can remain little doubt that the next few years will bring a frightening array of refined techniques for making human beings act according to the will of the psychotechnologist" (*New York Times,* September 12, 1971, section E, p. 9).

Several techniques, including behavioral manipulations, were referred to in this article, but emphasis was given to Delgado's dramatic demonstration that charging bulls could be stopped by remotely controlled brain stimulation. The interpretation, which is commonly accepted by many people, is that the stimulation had some specific effect on the bull's aggressive tendencies. Actually there seems to be no good reason to believe that the stimulation that stopped the bull had any direct effect on aggression. The behavior of the charging bull suggested that it was stopped by a combination of neuro-muscular interference (an imposed head turning, leg lifting, and circling), surprise, possibly confusion, and perhaps even some aversive stimulation. Under such circumstances it is not at all surprising that the bull stopped

---

13. Van Dis and Larsson (1971) have reported that, in animals, stimulation at very diverse sights may produce penile discharge with motile sperm.

charging. To conclude from this demonstration that we are close to being able to *selectively* reduce aggression in the normal brain with electrical stimulation seems very questionable.

There is little justification for such speculation as, "We might be on the threshold of that type of scientific biochemical intervention which could stabilize and make dominant the moral and ethical propensities of man and subordinate, if not eliminate, his negative and primitive behavioral tendencies" (K. B. Clark, Presidential Address at the American Psychological Association Convention, 1971).

The possibility of treating pathological brains, which may contain a specific irritative focus that triggers abnormal behavior, is quite far removed from possession of techniques for suppressing socially undesirable behavior by people with "normal" brains. *It has yet to be demonstrated that electrical or chemical stimulation of any region of the brain can modify one, and only one, specific behavior tendency.* We have no data that should make us optimistic about the possibilities of eliminating aggression with chemical mediation without interfering with a number of adaptive and positive capacities. Centrally acting drugs exert their influence by modifying chemical transmission at the synapse, but there are only a relatively few neurotransmitters that have been identified and these must be "spread over" all behaviors and many neural structures. Interfering with one transmitter system must necessarily affect very many behaviors. Drugs that reduce aggression always seem to produce a significant alteration of other functions and usually involve a considerable loss of effectiveness due to sedation. Drugs may very well be able to accomplish many useful ends such as facilitating learning and memory and counteracting some aspects of depression and anxiety. That is quite different, however, from using drugs to assure moral integrity and eliminate socially maladaptive behavior.

For the most part, stimulation techniques have to be considered research tools that have generated interesting, even if highly speculative, guesses about how the brain is organized. In this account, emphasis has been placed on the possibility that there exist reinforcement systems which play a significant role in encouraging or discouraging behavior. Various investigators have applied different names to the two postulated systems that might control behavior in this way. Lilly (1960), for example, has written about "start" and "stop" systems, while others have preferred such terms as "reward" and "punishment," "pleasure" and "pain," or simply "positive" and "negative." Recently, Milner (1970) has developed a model with "response hold" and "response switch" neural systems which would determine whether the animal would continue what it had been doing or switch to something else. Although the words may be different, there is a common recognition of the importance of some mechanism for assuring that animals approach what is beneficial and withdraw from what is harmful. It is not necessary, however, to postulate the equivalence of positive and negative reinforcement systems to accomplish this end. In some animal forms, where behavior is less plastic, there are a great variety of approach-avoidance reflexes that are based on relatively simple sensorimotor connections. Animals with little ability to modify their responses can be adapted to a particular environmental niche as long as enough of them can survive long enough to reproduce in sufficient numbers. When animals need to make many new responses to accomplish their goals, and when even the goals themselves may be acquired and quite variable, new types of mechanisms are needed. Modifiable behavior depends upon the retention of responses that were successful in the past so that increasingly complex sets of alternative ways of accomplishing goals can be accumulated.

It would be very inefficient if all experiences were retained. There are obvious advantages for an animal to be able to process important experiences preferentially. What seems to be emerging as a common denominator of many preliminary theoretical statements is that there are systems in the brain that quickly identify responses significant to the organism. There is a need for a mechanism that can identify responses with evaluative labels such as "important," "good," "bad," or "that may work." The responses so identified may be overt, but it is conceivable that neural and visceral patterns that are not expressed as overt behavior may also be evaluated.

There is little agreement on specific details, but many investigators are suggesting that the first step in the process of determining significance for an animal may involve the activation of circuits in the brain which are basic to a general reinforcement process. Most speculation started with a recognition of a connection between some form of arousal and the memory process. Previously, arousal had tended to be identified with the hypothalamic-pituitary-endocrine system (cf. E. Roberts, 1966), but more recently emphasis has been placed on the activation of a norepinephrine- (or other amine-) based system in the brain that is considered to play a basic role in consolidating the pathways underlying meaningful responses. Kety (1970), for example, has speculated that the release of "consolidating amines" associated with affective states would strengthen pathways that were active at that time. In one form or another, this is the germinal idea in much of the current speculation. The suggested mechanisms that may influence consolidation range from facilitating the rate of synthesis of those proteins containing the "coded memories" to increasing synaptic efficiency by prolonging the activity of pathways that have just been used. Basically, all these theories seem to imply that a substance is released throughout the brain when a reinforcement system is activated and this substance can selectively change those neurons and synapses most active at the time. None of these "simple" reinforcement theories can explain the great range of phenomena known to the learning theorist. The important point, though, is that data are being collected at a rapid rate and explanatory models are constantly being discussed and revised.

REFERENCES

Adams, D., & Flynn, J. P. Transfer of an escape response from tail shock to brain-stimulated attack behavior. *Journal of Experimental Analysis of Behavior,* 1966, 8, 401–408.

Anderson, B., & McCann, S. M. Drinking, antidiuresis, and milk ejection from electrical stimulation within the hypothalamus of the goat. *Acta Physiologica Scandinavica,* 1955, **35**, 191–201.

Baer, A. Über gleichzeitige elektrische Reizung zweier Grosshirnstellen am undgehemmten Hunde. *Archiv. für Physiologie, Pflüger,* 1905, **106**, 523–567.

Bandler, R., & Flynn, J. P. Visual-patterned reflex present during hypothalamically elicited attack. *Science,* 1971, **171,** 817–818.

Bard, P. A diencephalic mechanism for the expression of rage with specific reference to the sympathetic nervous system. *American Journal of Physiology,* 1928, **84,** 490–515.

Bard, P. On emotional expression after decortication, with some remarks on certain theoretical views. *Psychological Review,* 1934, **41,** 309–329.

Bard, P. Discussion in G. E. W. Wolstenholme & C. M. O'Connor (Eds.), *Ciba Foundation Symposium on the Neurological Basis of Behavior.* Boston: Little, Brown & Company, 1958. Pp. 72–73.

Bechterev, W. Die Bedeutung der Schügel auf Grund von Experimentellen und Pathologischen Daten. *Virchows Archiv.,* 1887, **110,** 322.

Bishop, M. P., Elder, T. S., & Heath, R. G. Attempted control of operant behavior in man with intracranial self-stimulation. In R. G. Heath (Ed.), *The Role of Pleasure in Behavior.* New York: Hoeber, 1964. Pp. 55–81.

Black, S. L., & Vanderwolf, C. H. Thumping behavior in the rabbit. *Physiology and Behavior,* 1969, **4,** 445–449.

Bower, G. H., & Miller, N. E. Rewarding and punishing effects from stimulating the same place in the rat's brain. *Journal of Comparative and Physiological Psychology,* 1958, **51,** 669–674.

Brady, J. V. The paleocortex and behavioral modification. In H. F. Harlow & C. N. Woolsey (Eds.), *Biological and Biochemical Bases of Behavior.* Madison: University of Wisconsin Press, 1968. Pp. 193–235.

Brazier, M. A. The historical development of neurophysiology. In J. Field, H. W. Magoun, & V. E. Hall (Eds.), *Handbook of Physiology. Neurophysiology, I.* Washington, D.C.: American Physiological Society, 1959. Pp. 1–58.

Brink, F. The role of calcium in neural process. *Pharmacological Reviews,* 1954, **6,** 243–298.

Brodie, B. B., Spector, S., & Shore, P. A. Interaction of drugs with norepinephrine in the brain. *Pharmacological Reviews,* 1959, **11,** 548–564.

Chi, C. C., & Flynn, J. P. Neural pathways associated with hypothalamically elicited attack behavior in cats. *Science,* 1970, **171,** 703–706.

Clark, E., & O'Malley, C. D. *The Human Brain and Spinal Cord.* Berkeley and Los Angeles: The University of California Press, 1968.

Cloëtta, M., & Fischer, H. Über die Wirkung der Kationen Ca, Mg, Sr, Ba, K und Na bei intrazerebraler injektion. *Archiv. für Experimentelle Pathologie und Pharmakologie,* 1930, **158,** 254–281.

Cox, V. C., & Valenstein, E. S. Attenuation of aversive properties of peripheral shock by hypothalamic stimulation. *Science,* 1965, **149,** 323–325.

Cox, V. C., & Valenstein, E. S. Distribution of hypothalamic sites yielding stimulus-bound behavior. *Brain, Behavior and Evolution,* 1969, **2,** 359–376.

Delgado, J. M. R. Permanent implantation of multilead electrodes in the brain. *Yale Journal of Biology and Medicine,* 1952, **24,** 351–358.

Delgado, J. M. R. Cerebral structures involved in transmission and elaboration of noxious stimulation. *Journal of Neurophysiology,* 1955, **18,** 261–275.

Delgado, J. M. R. *Physical Control of the Mind.* New York: Harper and Row, 1969.

Delgado, J. M. R., Hamlin, H., & Chapman, W. P. Technique of intercerebral electrode placement for recording and stimulation and its possible therapeutic value in psychotic patients. *Confinia Neurologica*, 1952, **12**, 315–319.

Delgado, J. M. R., Roberts, W. W., & Miller, N. Learning motivated by electrical stimulation of the brain. *American Journal of Physiology*, 1954, **179**, 587–593.

Delgado, J. M. R., Rosvold, H. E., & Looney, E. Conditioned fear by electrical stimulation of the monkey brain. *Journal of Comparative and Physiological Psychology*, 1956, **49**, 373–380.

Demole, V. Pharmakologisch-anatomische Untersuchungen zum Problem des Schlafes. *Archiv. für Experimentelle Pathologie und Pharmakologie*, 1927, **120**, 229–258.

Deutsch, J. A. Learning and self-stimulation of the brain. *Journal of Theoretical Biology*, 1963, **4**, 193–214.

DiCara, L. V. Plasticity in the autonomic nervous system: Instrumental learning of visceral and glandular responses. In F. O. Schmitt (Ed.), *The Neurosciences*. New York: Rockefeller University Press, 1970. Pp. 218–223.

DiCara, L. V. Learning in the autonomic nervous system. *Scientific American*, 1970a, **222**, 30–39.

DiCara, L. V., & Miller, N. E. Instrumental learning of vasomotor responses by rats: Learning to respond differentially in the two ears. *Science*, 1968, **159**, 1485–1486.

Dis, H. van, & Larsson, K. Seminal discharge following intracranial electrical stimulation. *Brain Research*, 1970, **23**, 381–386.

Doty, R. W. Electrocortical stimulation of the brain in behavioral context. *Annual Review of Psychology*, 1969, **20**, 289–320.

Edwards, S. B. The corticospinal control of striking in attack behavior elicited from the midbrain. Unpublished Ph.D. dissertation, Yale University, 1970 (University Microfilms, Ann Arbor, Michigan, No. 70-25, 259).

Epstein, A. N., & Teitelbaum, P. Specific loss of the hypoglycemic control of feeding in recovered lateral rats. *American Journal of Physiology*, 1967, **213**, 1159–1167.

Ervin, F. R., Mark, V. H., & Stevens, J. Behavioral and affective responses to brain stimulation in man. In J. Zubin & C. Shagass (Eds.), *Neurobiological Aspects of Psychopathology*. New York: Grune & Stratton, 1969. Pp. 54–65.

Ferguson, N. B. L., & Keesey, R. E. Comparisons of ventromedial hypothalamic lesion effects upon feeding and lateral hypothalamic self-stimulation in the female rat. *Journal of Comparative and Physiological Psychology*, 1971, **74**, 263–271.

Ferrier, D. Experimental research in cerebral physiology and pathology. In *West Riding Lunatic Asylum Medical Report*, 1873, **3**, 30–96.

Fields, C. Instrumental conditioning of the rat cardiac control systems. *Proceedings of the National Academy of Science*, 1970, **65**, 293–299.

Fink, R. P., & Heimer, L. Two methods for selective silver impregnation of degenerating axons and their synaptic endings in the central nervous system. *Brain Research*, 1967, **4**, 369–374.

Fisher, A. E., & Coury, J. N. Cholinergic tracing of a central neural circuit underlying a thirst drive. *Science*, 1962, **138**, 691–693.

Flynn, J. P., Edwards, S. B., & Bandler, R. J. Changes in sensory and motor systems during centrally elicited attack. *Behavioral Science,* 1971, **16,** 1–19.

Flynn, J. P., Vanegas, H., Foote, W., & Edwards, S. Neural mechanisms involved in a cat's attack on a rat. In R. E. Whalen, R. F. Thompson, M. Verzeano, & N. M. Weinberger (Eds.), *The Neural Control of Behavior.* New York: Academic Press, 1970. Pp. 135–173.

Gallistel, C. R., & Beagley, G. The specificity of brain stimulation reward. *Journal of Comparative and Physiological Psychology,* 1971, **76,** 199–205.

Gallistel, C. R. Self-stimulation: The neurophysiology of reward and motivation. In J. A. Deutsch (Ed.), *The Physiological Basis of Memory.* New York: Academic Press, 1972.

Gibbs, E. L., & Gibbs, F. A. A purring center in the cat's brain. *Journal of Comparative Neurology,* 1936, **64,** 209–211.

Gibson, W. E., Reid, L. D., Sakai, M., & Porter, P. B. Intracranial reinforcement compared with sugar-water reinforcement. *Science,* 1965, **148,** 1357–1359.

Glickman, S. E., & Schiff, B. B. A biological theory of reinforcement. *Psychological Review,* 1967, **74,** 81–109.

Gloor, P. Autonomic functions of the diencephalon: A summary of the experimental work of Professor W. R. Hess. *Archives of Neurology and Psychiatry,* 1954, **71,** 773–790.

Goltz, F. Der Hund ohne Grosshirn. Siebente Abhandlung über die Verrichtungen des Grosshirns. *Pflüeger's Archiv.,* 1892, **51,** 570–614.

Greer, M. A. Suggestive evidence of a primary "drinking center" in the hypothalamus of the rat. *Proceedings of the Society for Experimental Biology,* 1955, **89,** 59–62.

Grossman, S. P. Eating or drinking in satiated rats elicited by adrenergic or cholinergic stimulation, respectively, of the lateral hypothalamus. *Science,* 1960, **132,** 301–302.

Grünbaum, A. S. F., & Sherrington, C. S. Observations on the physiology of the cerebral cortex of some of the higher apes. *Proceedings of the Royal Society,* 1902, **69,** 206–209.

Haymaker, W. *The Founders of Neurology.* One hundred thirty-three biographical sketches prepared for the fourth International Neurological Congress in Paris by eighty-four authors. Springfield, Ill.: Thomas, 1953.

Heath, R. G. *Studies in Schizophrenia.* Cambridge: Harvard University Press, 1954.

Heath, R. G. Pleasure responses of human subjects to direct stimulation of the brain: Physiologic and psychodynamic considerations. In R. G. Heath (Ed.), *The Role of Pleasure in Behavior.* New York: Hoeber, 1964. Pp. 219–243.

Heath, R. G., & Mickle, W. A. Evaluation of seven years' experience with depth electrode studies in human patients. In E. R. Ramey & D. S. O'Doherty, *Electrical Studies of the Unanesthetized Brain.* New York: Hoeber, 1960. Pp. 214–242.

Heller, A., Seiden, L. S., & Moore, R. Y. Regional effects of lateral hypothalamic in brain norepinephrine in the cat. *International Journal of Neuropharmacology,* 1966, **5,** 91–101.

Hess, W. R. *Diencephalon, Autonomic, and Extrapyramidal Functions.* New York: Grune & Stratton, 1954.

Hillarp, N. A., Fuxe, K., & Dahlström, A. Demonstration and mapping of central neurons containing dopamine, noradrenaline, and 5-hydroxytryptamine and their reactions to psychopharmaca. *Pharmacological Reviews*, 1966, **18**, 727–741.

Hodos, W. Motivational properties of long durations of rewarding brain stimulation. *Journal of Comparative and Physiological Psychology*, 1965, **59**, 219–224.

Hodos, W., & Valenstein, E. S. Motivational variables affecting the rate of behavior maintained by intracranial stimulation. *Journal of Comparative and Physiological Psychology*, 1960, **53**, 502–508.

Hodos, W., & Valenstein, E. S. An evaluation of response rate as a measure of rewarding intracranial stimulation. *Journal of Comparative and Physiological Psychology*, 1962, **55**, 80–84.

Hoebel, B. G. Hypothalamic lesions by electrocauterization: Disinhibition of feeding and self-stimulation. *Science*, 1965, **149**, 452–453.

Hoebel, B. G. Feeding and self-stimulation. In P. J. Morgane (Ed.), *Neural Regulation of Food and Water Intake. Annals of New York Academy of Science*, 1969, **157**, 759–778.

Horsley, V., & Clarke, R. H. The structure and functions of the cerebellum examined by a new method. *Brain*, 1908, **31**, 45–124.

Howarth, C. I., & Deutsch, J. A. Drive decay: The cause of fast "extinction" of habits learned by brain stimulation. *Science*, 1962, **137**, 35–36.

Hull, C. L. *Principles of Behavior*. New York: Appleton-Century-Crofts, 1943.

Karplus, J. P., & Kreidl, A. Gehirn und Sympathicus. I. Mitteilung. *Archiv. Physiologie* (Bonn), 1909, **29**, 138–144.

Keesey, R. E. Duration of stimulation and the reward properties of hypothalamic stimulation. *Journal of Comparative and Physiological Psychology*, 1964a, **58**, 201–207.

Keesey, R. E. Intracranial reward delay and the acquisition of a brightness discrimination. *Science*, 1964b, **143**, 700–702.

Kennard, D. W. Local application of substances to the spinal cord. G. E. W. Wolstenholme (Ed.), *Spinal Cord (Ciba Foundation Symposium)*. Boston: Little, Brown & Company, 1953. Pp. 214–221.

Kety, S. S. The biogenic amines in the central nervous system: Their possible roles in arousal, emotion, and learning. In F. O. Schmitt, *The Neurosciences, Second Study Program*. New York: Rockefeller University Press, 1970. Pp. 324–336.

Kling, J. W., & Matsumiya, Y. Relative reinforcement values of food and intracranial stimulation. *Science*, 1962, **135**, 668–670.

Landois, L. Über typische recidivirende Krampfanfälle, erzeugt durch Behandlung der Grossirnrinde mittelst chemischer wirksamer Substanzen und über Cerebrale Chorea. *Deutsche Med. Wchnschr.*, 1887, **13**, 685–686.

Lashley, K. S. The thalamus and emotion. *Psychological Review*, 1938, **45**, 42–61.

Lilly, J. C. Learning motivated by subcortical stimulation: The "start" and the "stop" patterns of behavior. In E. R. Ramey & D. S. O'Doherty, *Electrical Studies on the Unanesthetized Brain*. New York: Hoeber, 1960. Pp. 78–105.

Lindsley, D. B. Emotion. In S. S. Stevens (Ed.), *Handbook of Experimental Psychology*. New York: John Wiley, 1951. Pp. 473–516.

London, P. *Behavior Control.* New York: Harper & Row, 1969.

Lorens, S. A. Effect of lesions in the central nervous system on lateral hypothalamic self-stimulation in the rat. *Journal of Comparative and Physiological Psychology,* 1966, **62**, 256–262.

MacDonnell, M. F., & Flynn, J. P. Control of sensory fields of stimulation of the hypothalamus. *Science,* 1966, **152**, 1406–1408.

MacLean, P. D. Chemical and electrical stimulation of the hippocampus in unrestrained animals. *Archives of Neurology and Psychiatry,* 1957, **78**, 128–142.

MacLean, P., & Delgado, J. M. R. Electrical and chemical stimulation of frontotemporal portion of limbic system in the waking animal. *Electroencephalography and Clinical Neurophysiology,* 1953, **5**, 91–100.

MacLean, P. D., Denniston, R. H., & Dua, S. Further studies on cerebral representation of penile erection: Caudal thalamus, midbrain, and pons. *Journal of Neurophysiology,* 1963, **26**, 273–293.

Magoun, H. W. The ascending reticular activating system. *Research Publications of the Association for Research in Nervous and Mental Diseases,* 1952, **30**, 480–492.

Mark, V. H., & Ervin, F. R. *Violence and the Brain.* New York: Harper & Row, 1970.

Masserman, J. H. Effects of sodium amytal and other drugs on the reactivity of the hypothalamus of the cat. *Archives of Neurology and Psychiatry,* 1937, **37**, 617–628.

Masserman, J. H. Is the hypothalamus a center of emotion? *Psychosomatic Medicine,* 1941, **3**, 3–25.

Matteucci, C. *Traité des phénomènes électro-physiologiques des animaux.* Paris: Frotin, Mason, 1844.

Miller, N. Chemical coding of behavior in the brain. *Science,* 1965, **148**, 328–338.

Miller, N. Learning of visceral and glandular responses. *Science,* 1969, **163**, 434–445.

Milner, P. *Physiological Psychology.* New York: Holt, Rinehart & Winston, 1970. Pp. 301–413.

Mogenson, G. J. General and specific reinforcement systems for drinking behavior. In P. J. Morgane (Ed.), *Neural Regulation of Food and Water Intake.* Annals of the New York Academy of Science, 1969, **157**, 779–795.

Montemurro, D. G., & Stevenson, J. A. F. Adipsia produced by hypothalamic lesions in the rat. *Canadian Journal of Biochemistry and Physiology,* 1957, **35**, 31–37.

Moruzzi, C., & Magoun, H. W. Brainstem reticular formation and activation of the EEG. *Electroencephalography and Clinical Neurophysiology,* 1949, **1**, 455–473.

Moyer, K. E. *The Physiology of Motivation.* Chicago: Markham, 1971.

Narabayashi, H. Stereoencephalotomy in Japan. *Confin. Neurol.,* 1964, **24**, 314–320.

Narabayashi, H., Nagao, T., Saito, Y., Yoshida, M., & Nagahata, M. Stereotaxic amygdalotomy for behavior disorders. *Archiv. Neurol.,* 1963, **9**, 1–26.

Nauta, W. J. H. Silver impregnation of degenerating axons. In W. F. Windle (Ed.), *New Research Techniques of Neuroanatomy.* Springfield, Ill.: Thomas, 1957. Pp. 17–26.

Nauta, W. J. H. Some neural pathways related to the limbic system. In E. R. Ramey, & D. S. O'Doherty (Eds.), *Electrical Studies on the Unanesthetized Brain.* New York: Hoeber, 1960. Pp. 1–14.

Nobili, L. Über einen neuen Galvanometer. *Journal für Chemie und Physik* (Nuremberg), 1825, **45**, 249–254.

Oersted, H. C. Galvanic magnetism. *Philosophical Magazine,* 1820, **56**, 394.

Olds, J. A physiological study of reward. In D. McClelland (Ed.), *Studies of Motivation.* New York: Appleton, 1955. Pp. 134–143.

Olds, J. A preliminary mapping of electric reinforcing effects in the rat brain. *Journal of Comparative and Physiological Psychology,* 1956a, **49**, 281–285.

Olds, J. Pleasure centers in the brain. *Scientific American,* 1956b, **195**, 105–116.

Olds, J. Satiation effects in self-stimulation of the brain. *Journal of Comparative and Physiological Psychology,* 1958a, **51**, 675–678.

Olds, J. Self-stimulation of the brain: Its use to study local effects of hunger, sex, and drugs. *Science,* 1958b, **127**, 315–324.

Olds, J. Operant conditioning of single-unit responses. *Proc. XXIII International Congress of Physiological Science. Excerpta Medica International Congress Series No. 87,* 1965, 372–380.

Olds, J. The central nervous system and the reinforcement of behavior. *American Psychologist,* 1969, **24**, 114–132.

Olds, J., & Milner, P. Positive reinforcement produced by electrical stimulation of septal area and other regions of rat brain. *Journal of Comparative and Physiological Psychology,* 1954, **47**, 419–427.

Olds, J., & Olds, M. E. The mechanism of voluntary behavior. In R. G. Heath (Ed.), *The Role of Pleasure in Behavior.* New York: Hoeber, 1964. Pp. 23–53.

Olds, J., & Peretz, B. A motivational analysis of the reticular activating system. *Electroencephalography and Clinical Neurophysiology,* 1960, **12**, 445–454.

Olds, J., Travis, R. P., & Schwing, R. C. Topographic organization of hypothalamic self-stimulation functions. *Journal of Comparative and Physiological Psychology,* 1960, **53**, 23–32.

Olds, J., Yuwiller, A., Olds, M. E., & Yun, C. Neurohumors in hypothalamic substrates of reward. *American Journal of Physiology,* 1964, **207**, 242–254.

Olds, M. E., & Olds, J. Approach-avoidance analysis of rat diencephalon. *Journal of Comparative and Physiological Psychology,* 1963, **120**, 259–294.

Olds, M. E., & Olds, J. Effects of lesions in medial forebrain bundle on self-stimulation behavior. *American Journal of Physiology,* 1969, **217**, 1253–1264.

Panksepp, J. The neural basis of aggression in the albino rat. Unpublished Ph.D. dissertation. University of Massachusetts, August, 1969 (University Microfilm Inc., Ann Arbor, Michigan, No. 70-4556).

Penfield, W., & Baldwin, M. Temporal lobe seizures and the technic of subtotal temporal lobectomy. *Annals of Surgery,* 1952, **136**, 625–634.

Pliskoff, S. S., Wright, J. E., & Hawkins, T. D. Brain stimulation as a reinforcer: Intermittent schedules. *Journal of Experimental Analysis of Behavior,* 1965, **8**, 75–88.

Ploog, D. Social communication among animals. In F. O. Schmitt (Ed.), *The Neurosciences Second Study Program.* New York: Rockefeller University Press, 1970. Pp. 349–360.

Poschel, B. P. H. Mapping of rat brain for self-stimulation under monoamine oxidase blockade. *Physiology and Behavior,* 1969, **4**, 325–331.

Poschel, B. P. H., & Ninteman, F. W. Hypothalamic self-stimulation: Its suppression by blockade of norepinephrine biosynthesis and reinstatement by methamphetamine. *Life Sciences,* 1966, **5**, 11–16.

Poschel, B. P. H., & Ninteman, F. W. Intracranial reward and the forebrain's serotonergic mechanism: Studies employing *para*-chlorophenylalanine and *para*-chloroamphetamine. *Physiology and Behavior,* 1971, 7, 39–46.

Ramey, E. R., & O'Doherty, D. S. *Electrical Studies of the Unanesthetized Brain.* New York: Hoeber, 1960.

Ranson, S. W., & Magoun, H. W. The hypothalamus. *Ergebnisse der Physiologie,* 1939, **41**, 56–163.

Ranson, S. W. Some functions of the hypothalamus. Harvey Lecture. *Bulletin of the New York Academy of Medicine,* 1937, **13**, 241–271.

Roberts, E. Models for correlative thinking about brain, behavior, and biochemistry. *Brain Research,* 1966, **2**, 109–144.

Roberts, W. W. Rapid escape learning without avoidance learning motivated by hypothalamic stimulation in cats. *Journal of Comparative and Physiological Psychology,* 1958a, **51**, 391–399.

Roberts, W. W. Both rewarding and punishing effects from stimulation of posterior hypothalamus of cat with same electrode at same intensity. *Journal of Comparative and Physiological Psychology,* 1958b, **51**, 400–407.

Roberts, W. W. Fear-like behavior elicited from dorsomedial thalamus of cat. *Journal of Comparative and Physiological Psychology,* 1962, **55**, 191–197.

Roberts, W. W., & Carey, R. J. Effect of dorsomedial thalamic lesions on fear in cats. *Journal of Comparative and Physiological Psychology,* 1963, **56**, 950–958.

Roberts, W. W., & Kiess, H. O. Motivational properties of hypothalamic aggression in cats. *Journal of Comparative and Physiological Psychology,* 1964, **58**, 187–193.

Roberts, W. W., Steinberg, M. L., & Means, L. W. Hypothalamic mechanisms for sexual, aggressive, and other motivational behaviors in the opossum, Didelphis virginiana. *Journal of Comparative and Physiological Psychology,* 1967, **64**, 1–15.

Robinson, B. W., Alexander, M., & Bowne, G. Dominance reversal resulting from aggressive responses evoked by brain telestimulation. *Physiology and Behavior,* 1969, **4**, 749–752.

Roll, S. K. Intracranial self-stimulation and wakefulness: Effect of manipulating ambient brain catecholamines. *Science,* 1970, **168**, 1370–1372.

Routtenberg, A., & Lindy, J. Effects of the availability of rewarding septal and hypothalamic stimulation on bar pressing for food under conditions of deprivation. *Journal of Comparative and Physiological Psychology,* 1965, **60**, 158–161.

Routtenberg, A., & Malsbury, C. Brainstem pathways of reward. *Journal of Comparative and Physiological Psychology,* 1969, **68**, 22–30.

Sano, M., Yoshioka, M., Ogashiwa, M., Ishijima, B., & Ohye, C. Postero-medial hypothalamotomy in the treatment of aggressive behaviors. *Confin. Neurol.,* 1966, **27**, 164–167.

Scott, J. W. Self-stimulation and diencephalic fiber pathways. *Proceedings of the 78th Annual APA Convention,* 1970, 243–244.

Sem-Jacobsen, C. W. *Depth-Electrographic Stimulation of the Human Brain and Behavior.* Springfield, Ill.: Thomas, 1968.

Sem-Jacobsen, C. W., & Torkildsen, A. Depth recording and electrical stimulation in the human brain. In E. R. Ramey & D. S. O'Doherty, *Electrical Studies of the Unanesthetized Brain.* New York: Hoeber, 1960. Pp. 275–287.

Sheer, D. E. (Ed.) *Electrical Stimulation of the Brain.* Austin: University of Texas Press, 1961.

Simonoff, L. N. Die Hemmungsmechanismen der Säugetiere experimentell bewiesen. *Archiv. für Anatomie und Physiologie,* Leipzig, 1866, **33**, 545–564.

Sonderegger, T. B. Intracranial stimulation and maternal behavior. *Proceedings of the 78th Annual APA Convention,* 1970, 245–246.

Sonderegger, T. B., & Rose, G. H. Approach gradients obtained through intracranial stimulation of the medial forebrain bundle in rats. *Journal of Comparative and Physiological Psychology,* 1970, **71**, 52–58.

Spiegel, E. A., Wycis, H. T., Baird, H. W., & Szekely, E. G. Physiopathologic observations on the basal ganglia. In E. Ramey & D. O'Doherty (Eds.), *Electrical Studies on the Unanesthetized Brain.* New York: Hoeber, 1960. Pp. 192–202.

Spiegel, E. A., Wycis, H. T., Marks, M., & Lee, A. J. Stereotaxic apparatus for operations on the human brain. *Science,* 1947, **106**, 349–350.

Spiegel, E. A., & Wycis, H. T. Pallidothalamotomy in chorea. *Archives of Neurology and Psychiatry,* 1950, **64**, 295–296.

Stein, L. Reciprocal action of reward and punishment mechanisms. In R. G. Heath (Ed.), *The Role of Pleasure in Behavior.* New York: Hoeber, 1964. Pp. 113–139.

Stein, L. Chemistry of purposive behavior. In J. Tapp (Ed.), *Reinforcement and Behavior.* New York: Academic Press, 1969. Pp. 328–355.

Stein, L., & Ray, O. S. Self-regulation of brain-stimulating current intensity in the rat. *Science,* 1959, **130**, 570–572.

Stein, L., & Ray, O. S. Brain stimulation reward "thresholds" self-determined in the rat. *Psychopharmacologia,* 1960, **1**, 251–256.

Stein, L., & Wise, D. C. Possible etiology of schizophrenia: Progressive damage to the noradrenergic reward system by endogenous 6-Hydroxydopamine. *Science,* 1971, **171**, 1032–1036.

Talbert, G. A. Über Rindenreizung am freilaufendeu Hunde nach. J. R. Ewald. *Archiv. für Anatomie und Physiologie* (Physiol. Abt.), 1900, **24**, 195–208.

Teitelbaum, P., & Epstein, A. N. The lateral hypothalamic syndrome: Recovery of feeding and drinking after lateral hypothalamic lesions. *Psychological Review,* 1962, **69**, 74–90.

Thomas, G. T., Hostetter, G., & Barker, D. J. Behavioral functions of the limbic system. In E. Stellar & J. M. Sprague (Eds.), *Progress in Physiological Psychology,* Vol. 2. New York: Academic Press, 1968. Pp. 229–311.

Umemoto, M. Self-stimulation of the lateral hypothalamus after electrolytic injury of the medial forebrain bundle in the cat. *Brain Research,* 1968, **11**, 325–335.

Ungerstedt, U. 6-Hydroxydopamine-induced degeneration of central monoamine neurons. *European J. Pharmacol.,* 1968, **5**, 107–110.

Ursin, H. Flight and defense behavior in cats. *Journal of Comparative and Physiological Psychology,* 1964, **58**, 180–186.

Ursin, H., & Kaada, B. R. Functional localization within the amygdaloid complex in the cat. *Electroencephalography and Clinical Neurophysiology,* 1960, **12**, 1–20.

Valenstein, E. S. Problems of measurement and interpretation with reinforcing brain stimulation. *Psychological Review,* 1964, **71**, 415–437.

Valenstein, E. S. Independence of approach and escape reactions to electrical stimulation of the brain. *Journal of Comparative and Physiological Psychology,* 1965, **60**, 230.

Valenstein, E. S. The anatomical locus of reinforcement. In E. Stellar & J. Sprague (Eds.), *Progress in Physiological Psychology,* Vol. I. New York: Academic Press, 1966. Pp. 149–190.

Valenstein, E. S. Behavior elicited by hypothalamic stimulation: A prepotency hypothesis. *Brain, Behavior, and Evolution,* 1969a, **2**, 295–316.

Valenstein, E. S. Preface. Motivation, emotion, and behavior elicited by activation of central nervous system sites. *Brain, Behavior, and Evolution,* 1969b, **2**, 292–294.

Valenstein, E. S. Stability and plasticity of motivational systems. In F. O. Schmitt (Ed.), *The Neurosciences: Second Study Program.* New York: Rockefeller University Press, 1970. Pp. 207–217.

Valenstein, E. S. Channeling of responses elicited by hypothalamic stimulation. *Journal of Psychiatric Research,* 1971, **8**, 335–344.

Valenstein, E. S., & Beer, B. Reinforcing brain stimulation in competition with water reward and shock avoidance. *Science,* 1962, **137**, 1052–1054.

Valenstein, E. S., & Beer, B. Continuous opportunity for reinforcing brain stimulation. *Journal of Experimental Analysis of Behavior,* 1964, **7**, 183–184.

Valenstein, E. S., & Campbell, J. F. Medial forebrain bundle, lateral hypothalamic area, and reinforcing brain stimulation. *American Journal of Physiology,* 1966, **210**, 270–274.

Valenstein E. S., Cox, V. C., & Kakolewski, J. K. Reexamination of the role of the hypothalamus in motivation. *Psychological Review,* 1970, **77**, 16–31.

Valenstein, E. S., & Meyers, W. J. A rate-independent test of reinforcing brain stimulation. *Journal of Comparative and Physiological Psychology,* 1964, **57**, 52–60.

Valenstein, E. S., & Valenstein, T. Interaction of positive and negative reinforcing systems. *Science,* 1964, **145**, 1456–1458.

Wasman, M., & Flynn, J. P. Directed attack elicited from hypothalamus. *Archives of Neurology,* 1962, **6**, 220–227.

Wise, R. A. Individual differences in effects of hypothalamic stimulation: The role of stimulation locus. *Physiology and Behavior,* 1971, **6**, 569–572.

Woodworth, R. S., & Sherrington, C. S. A pseudoaffective reflex and its spinal path. *Journal of Physiology,* 1904, **31**, 234–243.

Wurtz, R. H., & Olds, J. Amygdaloid stimulation and operant reinforcement in the rat. *Journal of Comparative and Physiological Psychology,* 1963, **56,** 941–949.

Learning Motivated by Electrical Stimulation of the Brain[1,2]

JOSE M. R. DELGADO, WARREN W. ROBERTS, and NEAL E. MILLER

Departments of Physiology and Psychiatry, and Department of Psychology, Yale University School of Medicine

It has long been known that responses resembling an emotional disturbance can be produced by electrical stimulation of certain points in the brain (Hess, 1949; Kabat, Magoun, & Ranson, 1935; Ranson & Magoun, 1939; Maclean & Delgado, 1953; Gastant, Naquet, Vigouroux, & Corriol, 1952). A true emotion can be conditioned easily to new cues and can be used to motivate the learning of new behavior (Miller, 1951a). But Masserman (1941), giving as many as 480 training trials, failed to secure any convincing evidence for the conditioning of violent emotional responses elicited by electrical stimulation of the hypothalamus. Therefore, he concluded that such responses are only peripheral motor components and do not have the motivational properties of a true emotion. Similarly, Loucks (1935) failed in 600 trials to condition a leg movement elicited by stimulation of the motor cortex. Brogden and Gantt (1937) report the simple conditioning of an ipsilateral foreleg extension elicited by stimulating a point in the lateral cerebellar lobe. We have not found, however, any experimental studies proving that the direct stimulation of the brain can produce emotional conditioning or can motivate the more complex trial and error learning of an instrumental response.

1. Reported by Dr. Miller as part of his address as President of the Experimental Division of the American Psychological Association, September 1953, and at the International Congress of Psychology, June 1954, Montreal (Miller, 1954). A sound motion picture, describing these experiments, was shown at both meetings.
2. This investigation was supported by a research grant from the Foundations' Fund for Research in Psychiatry and Grant M647 from the National Institute of Mental Health, National Institutes of Health, Public Health Service. It is part of Dr. Delgado's program of investigating the relation of brain structures to nociceptive sensory integrations (1952, 1954a, 1954b; Delgado & Rosvold, 1954) and Dr. Miller's program of using behavioral techniques to study motivation, e.g., hunger (Miller, Bailey, & Stevenson, 1950; Berkun, Kessen, & Miller, 1952; Miller & Kessen, 1952) and fear (Miller, 1948, 1951a, 1951b).

In contrast with these negative results, previous observations by Delgado (1952b, 1954a, 1954b) suggest that the emotional disturbance elicited by stimulating certain points in the brain may become conditioned to the apparatus in which the animals are stimulated. The present experiments were designed to demonstrate in carefully controlled situations whether or not this type of centrally elicited emotional disturbance can be conditioned, can be used to motivate trial and error learning, and can function as a punishment to make hungry animals avoid food. A variety of tests was used in order to be sure of the generality of the effects.

Subjects were 11 adult cats with electrodes chronically implanted in the brain so that the experimenter could stimulate them while they were moving about normally. The electrodes were in areas producing emotional responses for six experimental animals, motor responses for four control animals, and both areas for one animal.

Electrodes were constructed and implanted by a method which has been described elsewhere (Delgado, 1952a). Each electrode consisted of a tiny bundle of six insulated stainless steel wires cemented together with Plexiglass and ending at different depths so that each could be stimulated separately. Two needle electrodes, with a total of 12 leads, were implanted in each animal with a stereotaxic instrument. They were cemented into a small burr hole in the skull, tied to the bone, led under the skin to emerge from the back of the cat's head, and terminated in a miniature radio socket.

Electrical stimulation was delivered by a Grass model S4A stimulator, which was set to deliver biphasic stimuli with a duration of 0.5 msec. and a frequency of 100 cps. Monopolar stimulation (active electrode negative) was generally used, but bipolar stimulation was also tested.

Responses evoked by electrical stimulation of the brain were studied in animals which were free to move in a special stage, with a transparent front for observation. A variety of motor and autonomic responses were evoked, including stereotyped movements, such as turning the head, circling, pawing, licking, etc. Stimulation of some thalamic, mesencephalic, and rhinencephalic structures, to be described later, evoked a fear-like response, characterized by hissing, opening the mouth, showing the teeth, and flattening the ear, accompanied by well-oriented and coordinated movements aimed at escape. During this response some of the usually docile animals became aggressive, trying to bite and scratch any obstacle placed in the way of escape, including the gloved hands of the observers. Pupillary dilatation regularly occurred; other autonomic reactions, such as urination and defecation, were often observed as well as motor reactions. The evoked stereotyped movements in some cases interfered with the fear-like response. For example, if the animal turned its head to the right, this effect could disturb or make impossible the attempt to escape. The points which elicited the best fear-like responses were selected for the experiments which follow.

EXPERIMENT I. TRANSFER AND CONDITIONING OF WHEEL-TURNING

If the central stimulation can motivate the performance of a learned habit, it must involve more than mere motor reflexes. Will a habit learned to pain and fear transfer to the emotion-producing central stimulation?

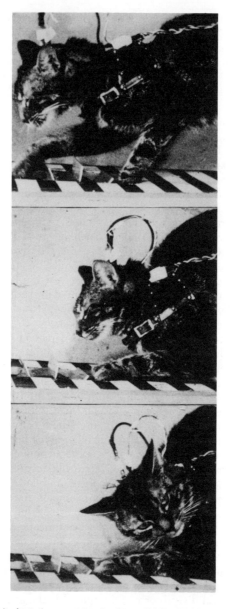

Figure 1. A learned habit of rotating a paddle wheel to avoid shock in the feet is elicited by electrical stimulation of specific cerebral structures. Stimulus turned on between first and second pictures. (Selected frames from motion pictures.)

Apparatus was a modification of the Mowrer-Miller (1942) avoidance-learning apparatus and is illustrated in Figure 1. It was a box 24 in. deep, 35 in. long, and 15 in. wide at the bottom and 21 in. at the top, with a glass front sloping outwards to facilitate observation and photography. Electric shocks

(100 to 400 volts AC through a series resistor of 50,000 ohms) could be administered via a grid floor and turned off by rotating a paddle wheel projecting through a hole at one end of the box. The latency of the response was timed automatically to $\frac{1}{100}$ second.

In order to secure a learned response to pain and fear which could easily be measured, five cats in the experimental group were trained to rotate the wheel to turn off the electric shock. Then they were given trials in which the buzzer anticipated the shock by 5 seconds. Rotating the wheel turned off both the frightening buzzer and the painful shock; if the cat turned the wheel within 5 seconds he avoided the shock. Training continued until all animals avoided the shock by responding promptly to the buzzer.

After this training, the electrodes were implanted and the cats allowed to recover from the operation. Then they were tested in the wheel-turning apparatus with electrical stimulation of the brain (ranging from 1–7 v. in different cats—averaging 4 v.) used instead of the fear of the buzzer and the pain of electric shock which had been used during the original training. Some experimental animals turned the wheel immediately at the first central stimulation, others seemed to be confused by the motor side effects, but learned rapidly during a very few trials in which turning the wheel was rewarded by escape from the central stimulation. The habit of turning the wheel seemed to transfer from the drives of pain (from shock) and fear (of buzzer) to the central stimulation; after retraining, it could be elicited consistently and immediately by central stimulation.

After this demonstration that the central stimulation could motivate the performance of a learned habit, four experimental cats were tested for conditioning. The conditioned stimulus was a flicker produced by the rotation of a toothed wheel in front of an overhead light for three cats, and a 2000-cycle tone for the fourth. Preliminary tests showed that these stimuli would not elicit wheel turning. The stimuli were then paired with the central stimulation in the same way that the buzzer had been paired with electric shock. After from 16–92 pairings, the new stimuli consistently elicited wheel turning. For each of these three cats the difference between the pre- and postconditioning tests could be expected by chance less than once in a thousand times; given a briefer test, the fourth was at the .02 level. It is clear that the response to the central stimulation was conditioned to the new stimuli.

The fourth cat referred to above also had a needle electrode in the motor area. Stimulation at one point on this electrode elicited vigorous licking but *not* wheel turning. Even with more extensive training than was given to any of the animals in which "fear-like" responses were evoked, no learning could be secured by stimulating this particular motor point.

In order to rule out the possibility that stimulation at the motor point produced some disturbance interfering with learning, stimulation of this point was used as a conditioned stimulus—i.e., followed by stimulation of the emotion-producing point. After such conditioning trials, stimulation of the motor point elicited licking followed by turning the wheel. The difference between pre- and postconditioning tests would be expected by chance less than twice in a hundred times. We conclude that the cat could learn to respond to stimulation of the motor point if motivation was supplied by stimulating the emotion-producing point.

EXPERIMENT II. CONDITIONED EMOTIONAL DISTURBANCE MOTIVATES NEW LEARNING

Miller (1948) has shown that, after fear has been conditioned to cues by administering painful electric shocks, the fear elicited by these cues can serve as a drive to motivate new learning on further trials without any electric shocks. Can the emotional disturbance conditioned to new cues by central stimulation serve as a drive to motivate new learning?

The apparatus consisted of two distinctive compartments, approximately 18 in. square and 25 in. high with hinged lids of coarse wire mesh and separated by a wooden barrier in the upper front corner of which was a 6 in. square hole through which the cat could climb. The barrier and floor of one compartment were painted white and the three sides were coarse wire mesh; the floor, barrier, and two wooden sides of the other compartment were painted black and the front was coarse mesh to facilitate observation and photography. Responses were timed automatically via weight-activated contacts on the floors.

All trials in the apparatus lasted 2 minutes. To test for initial preference, the hole in the barrier was open and each cat was placed for six trials in the black compartment, alternated with six in the white one. To condition the emotional disturbance to one of the two compartments, selected at random, experimental cats were given nine trials during which they received a brief central stimulation (averaging 7 v.) in that compartment, alternating with nine trials without any stimulation in the other compartment. The hole in the barrier was closed during these 18 trials. To test for learning motivated by a conditioned emotional disturbance, tests were given without central stimulation. The hole joining the two compartments was opened and each cat was started in the conditioned compartment on 12 trials alternated with 12 starts in the other compartment. During these trials, six of the seven experimental cats learned to jump promptly out of the compartment in which they had previously been stimulated; in each case the difference from the preliminary trials would be expected by chance less than one time in one thousand. The seventh cat, which did not learn, had been judged to give doubtful emotional responses.

Five cats with needle electrodes in sulci cruciatus and presylvius (sensorimotor area) were put through the same procedure with a slightly stronger stimulation (averaging 8 v.) judged to produce stronger motor responses.[3] Four of these showed no signs of learning. The fifth cat showed behavior suggestive of some transient learning. It climbed out of the conditioned compartment during the first six tests in it (different from the pretests at .07 level), but remained in it during the last six tests. One cat was included in both groups described above, being put through the entire procedure twice, first with motor stimulation in one compartment without learning to escape from it, and then with emotion-producing stimulation in the other one followed by reliable (.001) learning to escape.

We conclude that the emotional disturbance conditioned to the distinctive compartment by central stimulation can function as a learned drive to motivate

---

3. The electrodes in these cats had been implanted by Dr. Arnold Schulman.

the trial-and-error learning and performance of escape on later trials without central stimulation. Stimulation of the motor points tested seemed to produce much less, if any, learned drive.

EXPERIMENT III. CENTRAL STIMULATION CAN SERVE AS A PUNISHMENT

A painful electric shock can act as a punishment (presumably eliciting fear) to cause a hungry animal to avoid food (Miller, 1951b). Can the emotion-producing central stimulation function in the same way?

Hungry cats were trained to eat fish from a dish. On the first day they were given a succession of tests without any stimulation. On the next day they were tested after being momentarily stimulated immediately after touching the food. Stimulation of the sensorimotor area with an average voltage of 10.5 produced violent rearing back from the food, but three out of the four animals repeatedly returned as soon as the stimulation was turned off, showing no signs of learning to avoid. The fourth cat learned to avoid food (P for pre- vs. post-test = .001). (This cat had not learned in the two-compartment situation; the cat which had learned there did not learn to avoid food.) All five of the experimental animals learned to avoid the food in from one to four trials (P = .02, .001, .001, .001, and .001), when the specific thalamic, mesencephalic, or rhinencephalic structures were stimulated with an average of 6 v. (100 cps and 0.5 msec.). It is clear that the stimulation of the emotion-producing point acted as a punishment to motivate hungry animals to learn to avoid food, while the violent withdrawals elicited by stimulation of certain motor points produced considerably less learning of avoidance.

ANATOMICAL STUDY OF THE BRAINS

After the experiments were completed the animals were killed with overdoses of Nembutal, and then perfused through the heart with saline and neutral formalin, 10 percent. The top of the skull was removed, the dura opened, and the brain sectioned, with the head placed in a stereotaxic instrument in order to have slices oriented according to the Horsley-Clark coordinates. After 10–15 days' formalin fixation the brain was embedded in paraffin and serially sectioned (15 μ), and every 10 cuts stained alternately with Nissl and myelin stains; van Gieson stain was also occasionally used. Three areas proved to be responsible for the positive results in behavioral tests for motivation of learning: (a) the superior part of the tectal area in the neighborhood of the medial lemniscus and spinothalamic tract, (b) the lateral nuclear mass of the thalamus, and (c) the inferomedial part of the hippocampal gyrus.

Figure 2 shows a myelin-stained section of *cat P.S. 10,* showing the location of the different points of the needle electrodes. This slide is at about the same plane as that of Figure 18 of the paper of Ingram, Hannett, and Ranson (1932). As we see on the right side, point no. 1 (the most inferior) was in the cerebral peduncle; point 2 was in the neighborhood of the medial

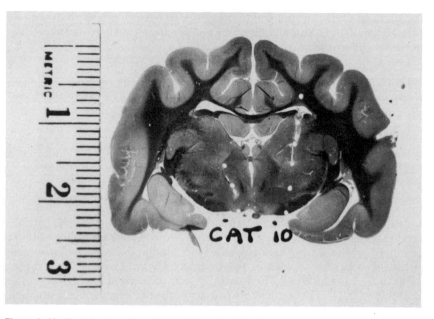

Figure 2. Myelin-stained section of *cat 10*. The six points of the right side, and the three inferior points of the left side have been marked with dots. 'Fear-like' responses were evoked by electrical stimulation of the superior part of the tectal area, and the lateral nuclear mass of the thalamus.
Figure 3. (Not reprinted.) Nissl-stained section of *cat 5*. 'Fear-like' responses were evoked by electrical stimulation of the hippocampus.

lemniscus or spinothalamic tract; point 3 was about at the limit between the medial geniculate body and the nucleus ventralis; point 4 was in the lateral mass of the thalamus; point 5 touched the fornix; and point 6 was in the white matter.

The left electrode was more medial. Point 1 was close to the mammillary peduncle; point 2 was close to the nucleus subparafascicularis; point 3 was in the nucleus ventralis (para arcuata); point 4 in the nucleus lateralis (pars posterior); point 5 touched the fornix; and point 6 was in the white matter. The superior part of the left tract is not visible in the figure, because it was a little more anterior than the right tract.

Emotional responses able to motivate learned behavior, as described previously, were evoked by electrical stimulation of points 2 and 4 of the right side (3 v.), and by points 2 (3 v.), 3 (1.5 v.), and 4 (6 v.) of the left side.

Violent motor responses were evoked by stimulation of points 1 (0.8 v.) and 3 (6 v.) of the right side, and point 1 (3 v.) of the left side. Strong motor effects and seizures were elicited by stimulation of points 5 and 6 of both sides (4–8 v.). The motor responses may have obscured any motivational effects which might possibly have been produced.

Electrical stimulation of the hippocampal gyrus also evoked emotional responses and motivation of learning, and in Figure 3 a picture of a Nissl-stained section of *cat P.S. 5* is shown [not reprinted], in which electrode 1, which gave positive results, was located at the tip of the tract, in the hippocampal gyrus.

DISCUSSION

The results of the three different types of experiments showed that centrally elicited emotional disturbance can be conditioned, can be used to motivate trial-and-error learning, and can function as a punishment to make hungry animals avoid food. These are positive answers to the questions which originated the present paper.

The negative results obtained in the control animals with electrodes implanted in the sensorimotor area, the negative results from some of the other points on the electrodes in the experimental animals, and observations on animals studied for other purposes demonstrate clearly that the emotional disturbance capable of motivating learning is not produced indiscriminately by electrical stimulation of any area of the brain, but is limited to the stimulation of specific areas. It is obvious that we cannot claim to have exhausted all the possibilities for such areas.

In the literature there is some indication that stimulation of the spinothalamic tract in cats at the mesencephalic level is able to elicit "pain-like" responses (Woodworth & Sherrington, 1904; Brown, 1915; Bazett & Penfield, 1922; Keller, 1932; Ingram, Ranson, Hannett, Zeiss, & Terwilliger, 1932; Magoun, Atlas, Ingersoll, & Ranson, 1936; Kelly, Beaton, & Magoun, 1946) but these investigations were done in animals under anesthesia. In the unanesthetized cat attack-defense reactions evoked by diencephalic stimulation have been reported by Hess (1949) and by Hunter and Jasper (1949). Very recently Delgado (1954a, 1954b) working with unanesthetized cats and monkeys showed that conditioned anxiety could be evoked by electrical stimulation of mesencephalon and hippocampus.

According to our present anatomical and physiological knowledge it is to be expected that stimulation of the spinothalamic tract would evoke painful sensations. In our experiments we have seen that the response originally learned to escape a painful electric shock on the feet transferred to the stimulation of the mesencephalon. Central stimulation of the mesencephalon seemed to have the same motivational properties as a painful peripheral electrical shock to the feet in a variety of learning situations, but stimulation of other brain structures, including the motor cortex, did not have these motivational effects.

Stimulation of the posterior hypothalamus and the middle line nuclei of the thalamus elicits a pattern of attack-defense, according to Hess (1949), and stimulation of the anteroventral and anterodorsal nuclei of the thalamus sometimes produces a fear reaction, according to Hunter and Jasper (1949). In our experiments in cats the pain-fear reaction was evoked by stimulation of the lateral nuclear mass of the thalamus, but we have no tests involving the other nuclei in these animals. In other experiments by Delgado and Rosvold (unpublished) on unanesthetized monkeys, habits learned in "fear" situations were elicited by stimulation of the nucleus ventralis posteromedialis of the thalamus, but not by stimulation of the nucleus medialis dorsalis.

In cats, fear responses evoked by hippocampal stimulation have been reported by several experimenters (Maclean & Delgado, 1953; Gastant, Naquet, Vigouroux, & Corriol, 1952). In our experiments we have shown that conditioning and trial-and-error learning can be motivated by stimulation of this area. It seems clear that the electrical stimulation of the described diencephalic and rhinencephalic structures evoked an emotion which could serve as a drive, but we cannot yet tell whether this emotion is produced by cerebrally stimulated pain or by the activation of some special central mechanism connected, for example, with fear. We are designing further experiments to differentiate pain from fear.

Another problem to be solved in the future is whether we are dealing with two independent systems, spinothalamic and hippocampal, or whether both regions are functionally connected to form different stations of one system of sensory perception, integrated with defensive-offensive mechanisms. . . .

REFERENCES

Bazett, H. C., and W. G. Penfield. *Brain,* **45**: 185, 1922.

Berkun, M. M., M. L. Kessen, and N. E. Miller, *J. Comp. & Physiol. Psychol.,* **45**: 550,1952.

Brogden, W. J., and W. J. Gantt. *Am. J. Psychol.,* **119**: 227, 1937.

Brown, T. G. *J. Physiol.,* **49**: 195, 1915.

Delgado, J. M. R. *Yale J. Biol. Med.,* **24**: 351, 1952(a).

Delgado, J. M. R. *Am. J. Physiol.,* **171**: 436, 1952(b).

Delgado, J. M. R. *Federation Proc.,* **13**: 34, 1954(a).

Delgado, J. M. R. *J. Neurophysiol.,* 1954(b).

Delgado, J. M. R., and H. E. Rosvold. *J. Comp. & Physiol. Psychol.,* 1954.

Gastaut, H., R. Naquet, R. Vigouroux, and J. Corriol. *Rev. neurol.,* **86**: 319, 1952.

Hess, W. R. *Das Zwischenhirn.* Basel: Schwabe, 1949.

Hunter, J., and H. H. Jasper. *Electroencephalog. & Clin. Neurophysiol.,* **1**: 305, 1949.

Ingram, W. K., F. I. Hannett, and S. W. Ranson. *J. Comp. Neurol.,* **55**: 335, 1932.

Ingram, W. R., S. W. Ranson, F. I. Hannett, F. R. Zeiss, and E. H. Terwilliger. *Arch. Neurol. & Psychiat.,* **28**: 513, 1932.

Kabat, H., H. W. Magoun, and S. W. Ranson. *Arch. Neurol. & Psychiat.,* **34**: 931, 1935.

Keller, A. D. *Am. J. Physiol.,* **100**: 576, 1932.

Kelly, A. H., L. E. Beaton, and H. W. Magoun. *J. Neurophysiol.,* **9**: 181, 1946.

Loucks, R. B. *J. Psychol.,* **1**: 5, 1935.

Maclean, P. D., and J. M. R. Delgado. *Electroencephalog. & Clin. Neurophysiol.,* **5**: 91, 1953.

Magoun, H. W., D. Atlas, E. H. Ingersoll, and S. W. Ranson. *J. Neurol. Psychopath.,* **17**: 241, 1936.

Masserman, J. H. *Psychosom. Med.,* **3**: 3, 1941.

Miller, N. E. *J. Exper. Psychol.,* **38**: 89, 1948.

Miller, N. E. In *Handbook of experimental psychology,* ed. S. S. Stevens. New York: Wiley, 1951(a).

Miller, N. E. *J. Person.,* **20**: 82, 1951(b).

Miller, N. E. Proceedings of the Fourteenth International Congress of Psychology, Montreal, June 1954, *Acta Psychologica,* 1954.

Miller, N. E., C. J. Bailey, and J. A. F. Stevenson. *Science,* **112**: 256, 1950.

Miller, N. E., and M. L. Kessen. *J. Comp. & Physiol. Psychol.,* **45**: 555, 1952.
Mowrer, O. H., and Miller, N. E. *J. Exper. Psychol.,* **31**: 163, 1942.
Ranson, S. W., and H. W. Magoun. *Ergebn. Physiol.,* **41**: 56, 1939.
Woodworth, R. S., and C. S. Sherrington. *J. Physiol.,* **31**: 234, 1904.

Commentary

NEAL E. MILLER

HOW THE PROJECT STARTED

My early work on conflict emphasized the importance of drives.[1] A hungry rat learns to run down a short alley to eat food at the goal. Then he suddenly gets an electric shock at that goal. Whether he will start again on the next trial and how far he will run toward that dangerous goal is strikingly dependent on how long he has been deprived of food and how strong the electric shock was. Similarly, naturalistic observations of people under extreme conditions of deprivation (Miller & Dollard, 1941), in combat, or in psychotherapy for abnormal behavior emphasize the importance of motivation (Freud, 1920; Dollard & Miller, 1950).

My interest in the drive-reduction hypothesis of reinforcement (Miller, 1963) also led me inevitably to investigations of the mechanism of motivation. Drives are not effective in producing efficient learning and sustained performance of behavior in the absence of reinforcement. One type of reinforcement is the escape from pain or fear. In this case, the sudden reduction of a strong, noxious stimulus serves as the reinforcement. But when the appetitive drives of hunger or thirst are used as motivation, the food or water that serves as the reinforcement also eventually reduces the drive. Thus there seems to be a close relationship between the operations that produce reinforcement and those that produce satiation. This is the basis for the drive-reduction hypothesis of reinforcement.

But is the relationship of satiation to reinforcement the essential mechanism of reinforcement, as the drive-reduction hypothesis assumes, or is it a spurious correlation which is the product of evolutionary pressure for the selection of animals which, when hungry, get pleasure from the food that satiates their hunger? In order to answer this question, my students and I conducted a series of experiments that involved manipulating drives in

---

1. This work has been described in part of the Langfeld Lectures "From Behavior to the Brain," given at Princeton University, which are now being written up as a book. There will be considerable overlapping in the two accounts. The work described was supported by Grants MH647, MH2949, and MH13189 from the National Institute of Mental Health of the U.S. Public Health Service.

unusual ways. One of the rationales of such experiments was that, if the correlation between drive reduction and reinforcement were indeed a spurious one, it might fall apart when drives were manipulated in unusual ways that had not been encountered in the natural selection involved in evolution. Another rationale was that the unusual manipulations would lead to a better understanding of the mechanism, which would be significant in its own right.

At this time, my interest in working on the brain mechanisms of motivation was greatly increased by conversations with my friend Dr. Robert Livingston, who was at that time in Professor Fulton's excellent department of physiology at Yale. Dr. Livingston called to my attention the fact that bilateral lesions in the ventromedial nucleus of the hypothalamus caused rats and a variety of other animals to overeat so that they became obese. He introduced me to Dr. J. A. F. Stevenson, who was skilled in making such lesions. My thought was that, if we could demonstrate that eliminating this area by lesions had all the functional properties of a genuine increase in hunger, then perhaps we could go on to demonstrate that stimulation in this area by an electrode would have all the functional effects of normal satiation, in which case, according to the drive-reduction hypothesis, such stimulation should serve also as a reward to reinforce learning. Since electrical stimulation would be a very abnormal way of producing satiation, positive results would be rather convincing evidence for the drive-reduction hypothesis of reinforcement.

With the help of a talented graduate-student assistant, C. J. Bailey, Dr. Stevenson and I set out to investigate in more detail the behavioral effects of such lesions. To our surprise we found that, although the lesions caused the rats to overeat palatable food, these rats would not work as hard as equally deprived, normal ones in order to get food—they were stopped more readily by weights on the lids of the food dishes or by having to work for food by pressing a bar on a variable-interval schedule. That this was not due merely to physical weakness was shown by the fact that, when the food was made bitter by adulteration with quinine, they were stopped at much lower concentrations than were normal rats, and that they also could be stopped more easily by electric shocks. Furthermore, after a period of fasting, such animals did not increase their food intake nearly as much as did normal rats. These findings (Miller, Bailey, & Stevenson, 1950), which have subsequently been confirmed in elegant detail and extended by Teitelbaum (1957), showed that the phenomenon was more complex than the simple release of hunger and led us to the hypothesis that the lesions interfered somewhat with the mechanism of hunger, but even more so with the mechanism of complete satiation. They also illustrated the value of using a variety of behavioral techniques to measure the effects of a physiological intervention in the brain. I was excited by the possibilities of using a combination of physiological and behavioral techniques to investigate the mechanisms of certain basic drives.

Although the effects of the lesions were not as simple as I had hoped, I was considerably encouraged to push ahead to the next step, that of devising a means of stimulating this area in unanesthetized, free-moving rats. At this time I was not yet aware of the earlier, beautiful work of Hess (1949) on using chronic electrodes to stimulate the brains of cats. But once I started to think about the idea of direct electrical intervention in the brain, a number of additional exciting prospects arose. If I could find an area of the brain where electrical stimulation had the other properties of normal hunger, would the sudden termination of that stimulation function as a reward? If I could find such an area, perhaps recording from it would provide a way of measuring hunger which would allow me to see the effects of a small nibble of food that is large enough to serve as a reward but not large enough to produce complete satiation. Would such a nibble produce a prompt, appreciable reduction in hunger, as demanded by the drive-reduction hypothesis? This reduction might, of course, be only temporary or might even be followed by a rebound of somewhat stronger hunger to account for the fact that a nibble may not produce complete satiation and may even whet one's appetite. How would the recording be affected by a cue that had acquired secondary-reward value by being associated with feeding? These and other problems could be investigated conclusively if I had a moment-to-moment measure of the strength of the hunger.

Similarly, a direct measurement of the neural activity involved in fear would help me test some of the predictions, such as the negative therapeutic effect, flowing from my analysis of approach-avoidance conflict behavior (Miller, 1944). It would allow me to determine more exactly the role of reduction of fear in avoidance learning and to check on my inference, based on observing the overt behavior of the animals, that the initiation of a coping response could elicit an anticipatory reduction in the strength of fear (Miller, 1951, pp. 451–452).

Finally, a series of experiments had failed to find a learned drive based on hunger or thirst analogous to the fear that I had demonstrated functions as a learned drive based on pain (Miller, 1948). Was this difficulty based on the fact that, whereas fear can be elicited quickly by pain, hunger or thirst build up gradually; or was it based on a fundamental difference in the existence of a learnable physiological drive-inducing mechanism? If hunger could be elicited quickly by direct electrical stimulation of the brain, I would have a means of answering the question.

With these various ideas in mind, I learned that William B. Knowles (1951), one of Don Lindsley's students at Northwestern, had been implanting recording electrodes in the brains of cats. I asked Bailey to visit Knowles and learn what he was doing. After Bailey returned we tried to put electrodes in the brains of rats, but we ran into many difficulties. Bailey had a far better idea than I at that time how many intricate functions were tightly packed in the small hypothalamus of the rat, and he was afraid that any wire stiff enough to be guided accurately was merely mashing up that part of the brain. Furthermore, Knowles had told him that he had tried to put electrodes in the brains of rats and had given up. There were certainly many difficulties. For example, the skull of the rat was so thin and moisture from bleeding interfered so much with the dental cement that the electrodes were always pulling out.

Scarcely any rats lasted long enough to be tested, but one did show signs of a pain-like distress to electrical stimulation of the brain. We decided to see if by any chance this was fear. The rat was given avoidance training to turn a wheel in order to turn off a buzzer that signalled shock. After he had learned this we stimulated his brain, but he did not turn the wheel. Shortly thereafter he pulled out his electrode. We probably started out with too sophisticated a test. If we had tried to see whether he would learn a response, such as turning a wheel or making a correct choice in a T-maze, to turn off the brain stimulation, we might have succeeded and been a couple of crucial years ahead.

RELATED DEVELOPMENTS

Meanwhile, work along a different line was progressing. Martin Kohn and I were trying to find ways of manipulating hunger by constructing a portal directly into the rat's stomach that we could open or close at will. We tried many different things, encouraged by the rat's enormous resistance to peritoneal infection, but amazed by his ability to get rid of the metal and plastic objects we sewed into him. At times it almost seemed as if the rat must have used the fourth dimension to circumvent the retaining flanges we had designed. For one thing, our devices were too heavy.

Finally we learned of a fistula technique that had been developed at the National Institute of Health by Dr. Evelyn K. Anderson, and embarked on a series of experiments (Kohn, 1951; Berkun, Kessen, & Miller, 1952; Miller & Kessen, 1952). We found that food injected directly into the stomach produced a prompt reduction in the strength of hunger, while food taken normally by mouth produced an even greater reduction. Furthermore, as the drive-reduction hypothesis predicts from the foregoing observations, food injected directly into the stomach functioned as a reward, but food taken normally by mouth functioned as a stronger reward. Bailey spent a good part of his time happily constructing for these experiments operant conditioning equipment, including the feeders, bars, and other components that are all available commercially today. Our device to train and test a number of rats simultaneously became affectionately known as "The Green Monster."

At the same time I was encouraging Bailey to continue to work on implanted electrodes. Because of the difficulty of anchoring them to the thin skull of the rats, Bailey decided to work with cats and use the multipolar electrode bundles that Dr. José Delgado had been developing to aim at one of the areas in the cat's brain from which eating could be elicited. By now Martin Kohn had translated for us from the unusually difficult, Swiss-type German the relevant parts of Hess's (1949) key book. I wanted Bailey to search in areas where Hess had found points that would arouse stimulus-bound eating, but he thought it safer to start by aiming at an area where Delgado and Anand (1953) had found that chronic stimulation produced a long aftereffect of increased food intake. After implanting a considerable number of cats and failing to elicit eating from any of them, it seemed undesirable for him to work for a dissertation on such a chancy project, so we agreed that he should turn to something else (Bailey, 1955).

Shortly after this decision, Dr. Delgado called to my attention a pain-fear-like response he was getting from certain areas of the brains of cats. Naturalistic observation of the cats' general behavior suggested that this response became conditioned to the apparatus in which the cats were stimulated, in marked contrast with the emotional responses that Masserman (1941) had described as not subject to conditioning. Therefore it seemed especially promising to test for the motivational properties of stimulating these areas that Delgado had discovered.

At this time I was very fortunate in having an unusually enterprising and capable young student, Warren Roberts, as a graduate assistant. Delgado implanted the electrodes, I was primarily responsible for designing the behavioral tests, and Roberts did most of the training. I reported the results as part of my address as President of the Experimental Division of the APA in

September 1953, and again to the International Congress of Psychology at Montreal in June 1954, in both cases showing a film of the experiments. These results, presented in the preceding article, furnished the first proof that trial-and-error learning could be motivated by direct electrical stimulation of the brain.

In these studies, all the tests for genuine motivational properties came out so well that Roberts and other students in my laboratory believed we were entering a new area of research with many exciting potentialities. This belief was encouraged by the fact that Olds and Milner (1954) soon thereafter discovered the fact that electrical stimulation of certain areas of the rat's brain could function as a reward. In fact, I came back from the International Congress in Montreal with the exciting news of their initial observations, the subsequent development of which is described later in this volume.

ADDITIONAL BEHAVIOR FROM BRAIN STIMULATION IN CATS

One of the things that Roberts, Delgado, and I tried to do was to devise tests to see whether we were stimulating pain or fear. We trained cats to run down a straight alley, first to escape an electric shock, and then to turn off the buzzer that signaled the electric shock and hence to avoid it. When they showed a high level of avoidance, we assumed that they had learned to fear the buzzer. Then we trained them to turn in one direction in a simple T-maze to escape pain from electric shocks to the feet and in the opposite direction to escape fear by turning off the buzzer. They did learn this discrimination, but were they discriminating between pain and fear or only between shocks to the feet and the sound of a buzzer? In order to test for this, we first retrained them in the alley using a different painful stimulation, shocks to the flanks, and a different cue, a 1000-cycle tone, that initially did not elicit avoidance. After they had learned the avoidance we tested them in the T-maze. Some gave the correct response, but others did not and had to be retrained.

But a shock to the feet and a shock via electrodes implanted in the flanks are relatively similar, so we tried yet other sources of pain and fear. We rigged up a long, flexible cable like that used to operate the shutter on a camera, but much larger, to create a Rube Goldberg device for pinching the cat's tail. And we repeated the procedure with a flashing light as the new fear-eliciting stimulus. In the tests in the T-maze, some of them seemed to generalize but others required retraining. After this retraining, we tested the stimulation of various areas in the brain. Here the results were even more ambiguous. We wanted to use a variety of other sources of pain in an attempt to teach the cats a more reliable generalized response (i.e., concept of pain), but were running out of ideas for new, distinctive sources. Furthermore, Roberts was getting interesting results in other exploratory work, so we allowed this difficult project to lapse.

As Hess (1945) had discovered, there are a number of places in the cat's hypothalamus where electrical stimulation will elicit a spectacular display of rage. This is not a mere blind reflex response; the cat will strike quite accurately at a moving stick or a gloved hand. We tried various ways of conditioning this response, and finally succeeded with one cat. Subsequent histology, however, showed that the particular electrode point eliciting the conditionable response was outside the brain, so we must have been eliciting the attack via painful stimulation of the meninges (Miller, 1957). Thus this cat became a control to confirm Masserman's early observation (1941) that aggression elicited by stimulating these areas of the brain is, at the very least, vastly harder to condition than is fear.

Electrical stimulation at other points caused cats to flee instead of fight. Using a behavioral test, Roberts discovered that the electrodes in these cats could be divided into categories. At some points electrical stimulation could be used to reinforce the learning of both avoidance and escape responses, exactly as reported in the preceding article. But to our great surprise, Roberts found that stimulation at other points could be used to reinforce the learning of escape but never of avoidance. For his dissertation, Roberts (1958a) designed a convincing series of elegant experiments to prove that he had indeed discovered a true functional difference. In his dissertation he expressed an idea which seemed to me exceedingly improbable, namely, that the puzzling failure to learn to avoid might be caused by an initial rewarding effect of the stimulation. Later, in 1956, he proved that his idea was correct; he discovered that stimulation of exactly the same point in the brain can have, paradoxically, first rewarding and then punishing properties (Roberts, 1958b).

OSMOSTIMULATION

During this time, Bailey and I were greatly interested by Bengtt Andersson's (1953) report that a minute injection of hypertonic saline in the region of the third ventricle of a goat will induce extensive drinking.

Bailey developed a cannula made of a hypodermic needle with its hub turned down so that a plastic cup could be fitted over it. With the cap removed, this cannula served as a guide through which a second needle could be inserted. By now the students in my laboratory were much more skilled at operations, so that, compared with his frustrating early experiences with trying to implant electrodes in the brains of rats, implanting these cannulas in the thick skulls of cats was easy for Bailey. Nevertheless there were some difficulties. The cannula tended to get clogged quickly so that injections became impossible. This problem was solved by Melissa Richter, who used a small hypodermic needle fitted snugly into a larger one. The hubs were turned down and threaded so that the smaller one could be screwed into the larger. Then both needles were cut off at the same length. When this assembly was implated in the brain of the cat, the smaller needle could be withdrawn, leaving a clear opening in the larger one.

Using the foregoing procedures, we were able to confirm Andersson's finding of the thirst-inducing effects of a hypertonic injection and, even more significantly, to show that a minute injection of pure water would reduce the amount drunk (Miller et al., 1955; Miller, 1957, 1961). The results of this study, as well as much of the previously mentioned work by Roberts, are included in my first progress report to the National Institute of Mental Health, dated December 1954.

This work on brain stimulation was handicapped by chronic difficulties with buying healthy cats. The typical acute experiment in the Medical School could use practically any cat, but we had a much bigger investment in each animal and wanted to keep it for a much longer time. Sometimes it was difficult to buy any cats at all. It was a happy day when two little old ladies living in a huge, castle-like house on the outskirts of town phoned in to say that they had a number of cats to sell, all of which turned out to be tame and in splendid condition. But this bonanza, alas, was the exception.

SEARCH FOR MOTIVATIONAL EFFECTS IN RATS

Difficulties such as these with cats, plus our much greater experience in training and testing rats, which also required much less cage space, kept us at work trying to develop chronic electrodes for rats. Coons, Lewis, Jensen, Bailey, and our technician, Mrs. Levine, had many lively discussions on how to improve the technique. We were encouraged by Olds' success, but wanted a method that would allow us to use the accuracy of the stereotaxic instrument. There were many problems: keeping the skull absolutely dry so that the dental cement would stick, making a small but rigid and straight electrode, insulating it effectively, connecting it to the stimulator. After much trial and error for over a year, these petty but crucial problems were at last finally solved one by one (Miller, Coons, Lewis, & Jensen, 1961).

Having at last evolved a workable technique, we set out in the summer of 1955 to make a systematic three-dimensional grid of the hypothalamus of the rat and to test the stimulation at each point for the elicitation of motivated behavior such as eating, drinking, aggression, fear, or sex. Setting up an assembly-line system, my laboratory workers implanted and tested that summer two electrodes in each of approximately one hundred rats. We observed a wide variety of motor side-effects, but none of the motivated behavior we were seeking. Orville Smith's (1956) subsequent report of eating elicited by stimulation in the lateral hypothalamus held out some hope, but our own search for such effects continued to be discouraging for some time thereafter.

In order to make some use of the implanted rats, we tested for rewarding and aversive effects and did find an area where both effects could be secured from the same electrode, replicating the phenomenon that Roberts had observed on cats. Thinking that this reward-aversion effect might be a useful test for the action of drugs, we prepared a number of additional rats with electrodes aimed at this point. And indeed, we did find that methamphetamine had the interesting effect of causing rats to speed up at pressing a bar that turned the stimulation on and to slow down at pressing a second bar that turned it off. Apparently this methamphetamine tipped the balance in the direction of the rewarding effect, a result congruent with its clinical euphoric effect. Interestingly enough, chlorpromazine appeared to have the opposite effect of slightly slowing down the time required to turn the stimulation off, but greatly slowing down the time to turn it on, a result congruent with its clinically opposite effect of tending to produce a depression (Miller, 1957, 1958).

Among other things, we were concerned with the amount of damage to the brain that might be caused by the electrical stimulation. We used some of the rats with motor side-effects to compare the amount of damage, as indicated by an increase in threshold, produced by two hours of stimulation (spread out over a period of eight hours) by either the extremely brief reversed pulse pairs described by Lilly (1961) or an ordinary 60-cycle sine wave AC. Since the increase in threshold was relatively small and equal for the two measures, we used thereafter the vastly simpler 60-cycle AC (Miller, Jensen, & Myers, 1961).

Unexpectedly, the two preceding studies had one highly gratifying by-product. Using rats discarded from the drug experiments because they had relatively weak aversive effects, and the more sensitive control on the AC stimulator developed for testing damage, E. E. Coons was studying the effects of hunger and thirst on the thresholds for motor movements elicited by electrical stimulation of the brain. Incidentally, the drives did lower the thresholds. But at 11:30 on the night of June 28, 1957, he was giving a test under conditions of satiation to rat No. 253 when he noticed that the brain stimulation caused this animal to nibble at some of the feces in the test cage. With admirable ability to capitalize on an unexpected observation, he threw in some pellets of food and found that the stimulation caused the rat to eat them. Then he spent the rest of the night carefully testing the other ten rats. By 6:30 A.M. he had found that stimulation would cause three more of them to eat also. He restrained himself enough to wait until 8:00 A.M. before calling me, and I rushed to the lab to see his results. It was a happy day. We had been looking for something like this for almost two years without any success; now it turned up as a chance observation!

We were greatly excited and proceeded to aim more electrodes at this point, which was in the lateral hypothalamus. At first our success was only approximately one in twenty rats—in fact, Jim Olds failed to replicate our results and refused for some time to believe that we really could elicit eating. However, by a number of progressive refinements in placing the electrodes, our success is now approximately one in three, and Olds and many others have replicated our results.

TESTS FOR MOTIVATIONAL PROPERTIES OF HUNGER

We did not wait for additional rats. That very morning we started to design a series of experiments to investigate whether the electrical stimulation of the lateral hypothalamus (ESLH) that induced eating did indeed have the other motivational properties of hunger (Miller, 1957, 1960; Coons, 1964).[2] In some of these first rats ESLH would not only elicit eating but also, especially at higher levels, elicit gnawing at an inedible object such as a stick. This posed the question of whether we were eliciting normal hunger or merely a reflex gnawing response. How could we be sure?

Normal hunger will elicit not only eating but also learned food-seeking responses. Therefore we trained rats when normally hungry to press a bar that would deliver food at infrequent, unpredictable times. When satiated, they did not press the bar. If ESLH elicited merely reflex gnawing, it should cause them to gnaw the apparatus, but if it elicited hunger, it should cause them to press the bar. To our delight, it caused them to press the bar.

---

2. Some of these experiments are presented as a part of an unusually good educational film which also includes Olds's work, distributed by McGraw-Hill Book Company and entitled "New Frontiers of the Brain."

But perhaps the stimulation was not specific to hunger-motivated behavior; conceivably it might only wake the animal up and produce a general activation. Since bar pressing was the dominant habit in this situation, that was what the rat did when activated. How could we test for this?

In quite a number of the rats ESLH elicited both eating and drinking, but Coons and I were able to find some rats for whom stimulation elicited only eating. We trained these rats when thirsty to drink at a water spout and when hungry to go to a specific place and push back a panel to get food hidden behind it. Then, when they were completely satiated on food but just thirsty enough to drink, we tested the effects of electrical stimulation of the brain. If it merely activated the rat, it should cause the dominant activity of drinking to become more vigorous. But if it had the effect of normal hunger, it should cause the animal to leave the water and go to food. That is what the rat did. In a considerably later test, we showed that the ESLH can motivate rats to learn to press the one of two bars that delivers food, and that when the opposite bar is made correct, it can motivate the rats to learn to reverse their habit (Coons, Levak, & Miller, 1965). Indiscriminate activation could not produce such results.

But all of the foregoing tests involved eating food. If the stimulation did elicit reflex gnawing it might be unpleasant to gnaw with nothing in the mouth, so a satiated rat might prefer to gnaw food rather than the apparatus or the air. We eliminated this alternative by showing that satiated rats that will not drink pure water when stimulated will start to lap up milk as soon as the stimulation is turned on and will stop when it is turned off. The behavior in this test shows that the response elicited by ESLH is not a specific set of movements, such as biting or drinking, but instead is a tendency to respond to a specific taste, that of food. In short, the correct response to electrical stimulation of the brain is defined by the sensory feedback (Miller, 1960). I have discussed other such responses elsewhere (Miller, 1959, pp. 248–252).

Having demonstrated that the stimulation had the other functional properties of hunger, we were now in a position to test a prediction from the drive-reduction hypothesis, namely, that turning off the stimulation should function as a reward. Coons and I did this by placing rats in the start of a simple T-maze, turning on the stimulation, and leaving it on until they reached the goal box on the correct side of the maze. At first they made errors, but they soon learned to run rapidly and directly to the correct side of the T-maze. This learning demonstrated that turning off the brain stimulation could serve as a reward, just as did the food which eventually terminated hunger (Miller, 1960; Coons, 1964). However, the results were not in unequivocal congruence with the drive-reduction hypothesis of reinforcement. A higher level of ESLH was required to motivate this learning than to motivate eating and the onset of the motivation served as a strong reward. You will remember that Coons' first observations of eating were in a strong-reward, weak-aversion area.

Was the reward effect of onset of ESLH a genuine part of the elicitation of hunger, or was it caused by activating a different mechanism? To answer this, Coons and I tested the effects of the anti-appetite drug, *d*-amphetamine (Miller, 1960). As might be expected, this drug raised the threshold for eating elicited by electrical stimulation of the brain and produced an even greater increase in the threshold for bar pressing for food elicited by ESLH. But, as might be expected from the previously cited results on methamphetamine, it lowered the threshold for bar pressing reinforced by ESLH. These opposite effects showed that the reward and eating were not different parts of the same simple unitary phenomenon. Later results by Gordon Ball (1969) indicated that the initial effects of ESLH were rewarding and hunger-reducing and the subsequent effects aversive and hunger-inducing. Ball has discovered additional inhibitory effects of rewarding brain stimulation (Ball, 1967).

To recapitulate, the experiments from my laboratory have found that the effect of electrical stimulation in the lateral hypothalamus has many of the properties of normal hunger: (a) It will motivate satiated rats to eat solid food or to drink liquid food; (b) it will motivate the learning and performance of food-seeking habits; (c) it will motivate a mildly thirsty rat to stop drinking water and go to the place where it has learned that food is hidden; (d) if strong enough, its offset functions as a reward; and (e) it is counteracted by the effects of *d*-amphetamine.

But how strong are the motivating effects of such stimulation? Tenen and I (1964) found that ESLH caused satiated rats to drink not only normal milk but also milk that was adulterated with quinine. Larger amounts of quinine were required to stop eating motivated by stronger electrical current, a result which seems to parallel the fact that larger amounts were also required to stop eating motivated by stronger hunger produced by longer periods of food deprivation. In the quinine test, the effects of ESLH were greater than those of 72 hours of food deprivation. Furthermore, the effects of ESLH summated positively with those of food deprivation.

In another experiment on the same topic, Steinbaum and Miller (1965) showed that during two one-hour periods each day ESLH was strong enough to overcome the normal food regulatory mechanisms and force rats to overeat enough so that they became markedly obese. As a control for the effects of electrical stimulation of the brain by itself, the experimental group was left without food for two one-hour periods per day without stimulation and a control group was given ESLH only during these two one-hour periods when no food was available. Each control animal was matched with an experimental animal, with both members of the pair receiving the same strength of stimulation.

This procedure worked well at first, but as we were increasing the strength of stimulation in order to force the experimental animals to eat more, we found that their control partners became so agitated that they threatened to bang their heads against the side of the apparatus hard enough to knock out their electrodes. Thus we were forced to stop increasing the strength of their stimulation. This observation indicated that the eating of the experimental rats had a marked calming effect which counteracted the exciting one of electrical stimulation of the brain. This fit in with our earlier observations that the taste of food can reduce hunger, and with Coons' earlier observation that having food available delays the rats' performance of a response that turns off electrical stimulation of the brain. Perhaps this calming effect of the taste and/or eating of food is the basis for the rewarding effect of food for a satiated rat motivated by ESLH. It also may be the reason why satiated animals given a series of tests show learning to eat better during the series.

If the consummatory response reduces the aversive effects of the ESLH, and if the ESLH elicits a number of drives because a number of different systems are stimulated, we would expect the animal to learn whichever kind of consummatory response—gnawing, eating, drinking—that was possible under the experimental conditions. But, as Valenstein points out in another article in this book, similar learning might produce the misleading appearance of specificity even if the initial arousal were not of a specific drive but of a more generalized nature. While everyone agrees that some learning of the type that I would call channeling (Miller, 1959, pp. 263–266) can occur, there is still considerable debate on the degree of specificity of drive circuits in the brain. Valenstein has presented evidence against specificity and Roberts (1969) for it. In normally elicited drives, there is a phenomenon of drive-generalization analogous to that of stimulus-generalization (Miller, 1948). Perhaps it will turn out that central drive circuits have certain elements in common and others that are specific.

You will remember that one of the original reasons for trying to elicit drives by direct electrical stimulation of the brain was to be able to suddenly elicit a drive such as hunger to see if it could be conditioned under this favorable circumstance. Coons and I made a number of unsuccessful attempts to condition hunger. We did observe some conditioned preparatory acts, such as approaching the food, but never conditioned eating. While we would not be so rash as to conclude that conditioning hunger is completely impossible, we are convinced that, if possible at all, it is a great deal more difficult than is conditioning fear. It is conceivable that our negative results came from using rats that were too thoroughly satiated. If I were doing it over, I would like to see whether or not conditioning could potentiate a weak hunger.

Another one of the original plans was to test for a possible rewarding effect of stimulation of the ventromedial nucleus of the hypothalamus. Stimulation in this area does seem to have a mildly rewarding initial effect, but this appears to be far weaker than its subsequent aversive one. If stimulating the ventromedial nucleus merely reduced the strength of hunger, we would not expect its effects to be aversive. Perhaps it is also eliciting unpleasant effects analogous to those from eating too much. One of my students, Frank Krasne (1962), has shown that the aversive effects of stimulation in this area are closely related to those of stopping eating and drinking. On the other hand, the offset of stimulation in the ventromedial nucleus will sometimes cause a transient "rebound" of eating in a satiated rat. One would scarcely expect this if aversiveness were the sole reason why stimulation of this nucleus stopped the rat from eating. The effects of electrical stimulation of the ventromedial nucleus obviously are fairly complex and certainly would benefit from further careful analysis.

CHEMICAL CODING OF BEHAVIOR IN THE BRAIN

The behavioral effects of electrical stimulation of the brain were highly encouraging, but they raised certain questions. Were they due to stimulating fibers of passage or to stimulating the synapses of a nucleus at which information was being integrated? Electrical stimulation excites both the fibers and the synapses, but the chemotransmitter normally involved in synaptic transmission, if it works at all, ought to affect only synapses. Furthermore, the effects of the chemotransmitter might conceivably be more selective, activating some circuits but not others. I was encouraged by the success of my own earlier work on the contrasting effects of hypertonic saline versus pure water in the third ventricle and by Alan Fisher's (1956) success in eliciting sexual and maternal behavior by minute injections of testosterone into the preoptic area. Thus, in a proposal to the National Science Foundation for work to start on July 1, 1958, I wrote: "In areas in which electrical stimulation or electrolytic lesions affect eating, what would be the effect of micro-injections via a permanently implanted needle of (a) presumptive transmitter substances, (b) presumptive inhibitor substances, (c) stimulants, (d) depressants, (e) amino acids, sugar, or insulin, (f) blood serum (or concentrated fractions) from hungry versus satiated animals?"

Some of the foregoing questions have not yet been answered, but I was extremely fortunate to have a highly talented, resourceful, and energetic graduate student, Sebastian P. Grossman, come to me soon thereafter with the idea he independently had developed of testing the effect of transmitter substances inserted via a chronic cannula into the brain. His excellent results are described later in this volume.

Grossman (1960) found that, when inserted via exactly the same cannula into the same region near the lateral hypothalamus of the rat, minute crystals of the cholinergic substances, acetylcholine or carbachol, will cause satiated rats to drink, while minute crystals of the adrenergic substances, norepinephrine or epinephrine, will cause them to eat. These results suggested the idea of chemical coding of behavior in the brain. After Grossman received his degree and left to continue his excellent work elsewhere, no one else in my laboratory could tap the crystals into the tip of the inner cannula in an accurate enough dosage to secure consistent results. Furthermore, we wanted to perform dose-response and time-response studies, so we switched from crystals to solutions (Miller, Gottesman, & Emery, 1964; Miller, 1965; Quartermain & Miller, 1966).

Since then, my laboratory has performed a series of pharmacological tests to secure additional evidence supporting the idea that the effects of chemo-stimulation are not an artifact, but do indeed represent physiological chemical coding of synaptic transmission. For example, we have administered centrally two different drugs, eserine and DFP, known to block the action of cholines-terase, the enzyme that destroys endogenous acetylcholine. Both of these elicited drinking, presumably by allowing the endogenous transmitter to accumulate at the synapses (Miller & Chien, 1968; Winson & Miller, 1970). Similarly, we have made an extensive series of tests involving various drugs known to have various effects on endogenous norepinephrine (Slangen & Miller, 1969). These tests and others (Booth, 1968) have shown that the eating elicited by norepinephrine has the properties that have been defined by work in the more easily accessible peripheral nervous system as an alpha-adrenergic effect.

Finally and most recently, Dr. Sarah F. Leibowitz (1970) in my laboratory has made the exciting discovery that the alpha-adrenergic receptors mediating the eating effect are complemented by beta-adrenergic receptors mediating a satiating effect. In a beautiful series of experiments, she has demonstrated that the classical agonists and antagonists known to affect alpha and beta receptors, respectively, in the periphery have analogous effects on central receptors, and that the alpha receptors, which apparently release hunger by exerting an inhibitory effect on the ventromedial nucleus, are located in that nucleus, whereas the beta receptors, which apparently exert their sating effect by inhibiting the lateral hypothalamus, are located there. Both types of receptors are located also in the perifornical area.

I shall conclude by citing only one example of how her conception of reciprocally inhibiting alpha and beta systems regulating hunger clarify some earlier puzzling results. You will remember that *d*-amphetamine is an anti-appetite drug and that systemic injections of it raise the threshold for eating elicited by electrical stimulation of the lateral hypothalamus. This effect has seemed to be incongruent with the eating elicited by central administration of norepinephrine, since both substances have a number of similar adrenergic effects. I had thought to resolve this paradox by considering two hypotheses: (a) that the peripheral effects of adrenergic stimulation might be opposite to the central ones and override them; or (b) that the amphetamine might be similar enough to norepinephrine to bind to the receptor, but not similar enough to activate it, serving like an imperfect key that jams the lock.

Attempts to check these hypotheses by central injections of amphetamine produced ambiguous results. But from studies of peripheral effects, it is known that, while norepinephrine has strong alpha but weak beta effects, amphetamine has weak alpha but strong beta ones. Thus, the idea of an alpha system responsible for eating and a beta one for satiation resolves the paradox.

Furthermore, Dr. Leibowitz (in press) has verified in satisfying detail the predictions that flow from her model. She has shown that *d*-amphetamine injected in the perifornical area, which has both alpha and beta receptors, manifests its dominant beta effect by reducing the amount of food eaten. But if it is preceded by a beta blocker, propranolol, its "submerged" weaker alpha effects are uncovered so that it will have the opposite effect of causing satiated rats to eat. If injected by itself into the ventromedial hypothalamus, which has only alpha receptors, it has a hunger-inducing effect; if injected by itself into the lateral hypothalamus, which has only beta receptors, it has the opposite effect, an anorexic one. This is but one example of the beautifully orderly relationships that have emerged from applying centrally facts and concepts that have been worked out by studies of peripheral alpha- and beta-adrenergic receptors. It is a fitting point at which to pause in a story which I hope will continue to unfold.

REFERENCES

Andersson, B. The effect of injections of hypertonic solutions into different parts of the hypothalamus of goats. *Acta Physiol. Scand.*, 1953, **28**, 188–201.

Bailey, C. J. The effectiveness of drives as cues. *J. Comp. Physiol. Psychol.*, 1955, **52**, 377–395.

Ball, G. G. Electrical self-stimulation of the brain and sensory inhibition. *Psychon. Sci.*, 1967, **8**, 489–490.

Ball, G. G. Electrically elicited eating and electrical self-stimulation of the brain: A comparison. *Commun. Behav. Biol.*, Part A, 1968, **1**, 299–303.

Berkun, N. M., Kessen, M. L., and Miller, N. E. Hunger-reducing effects of food by stomach fistula versus food by mouth measured by a consummatory response. *J. Comp. Physiol. Psychol.*, 1952, **45**, 550–554.

Booth, D. A. Mechanism of action of norepinephrine in eliciting an eating response on injection into the rat hypothalamus. *J. Pharmacol. Exp. Therap.,* 1968, **160**, 336–348.

Coons, E. E. Motivational correlations of eating elicited by electrical stimulation in the hypothalamic feeding area. Doctoral thesis, Yale University, 1964.

Coons, E. E., Levak, M., and Miller, N. E. Lateral hypothalamus: Learning of food-seeking response motivated by electrical stimulation. *Science,* 1965, **150**, 1320–1321.

Delgado, J. M. R., and Anand, B. K. Increase of food intake induced by electrical stimulation of the lateral hypothalamus. *Amer. J. Physiol.,* 1953, **172**, 162–168.

Dollard, J., and Miller, N. E. *Personality and Psychotherapy.* McGraw-Hill, New York, 1950.

Fisher, A. E. Maternal and sexual behavior induced by intracranial chemical stimulation. *Science,* 1956, **124**, 228–229.

Freud, S. *A General Introduction to Psychoanalysis* (G. S. Hall, translator). Liveright, New York, 1920.

Grossman, S. P. Eating or drinking in satiated rats elicited by adrenergic or cholinergic stimulation, respectively, of the lateral hypothalamus. *Science,* 1960, **132**, 301–302.

Hess, W. R. *Das Zwischenhirn: Syndrome, Lokalisationen, Funktionen.* Schwabe, Basel, 1949.

Knowles, W. B. Implanted electrodes for stimulating or recording from deep-lying brain structures. *Proc. Soc. Exp. Biol. Med.,* 1951, **76**, 315–320.

Kohn, M. Satiation of hunger from food injected directly into the stomach versus food ingested by mouth. *J. Comp. Physiol. Psychol.,* 1951, **44**, 412–422.

Krasne, F. B. General disruption resulting from electrical stimulus of ventromedial hypothalamus. *Science,* 1962, **138**, 822–823.

Leibowitz, S. F. Hypothalamic β-adrenergic "satiety" system antagonizes an α-adrenergic "hunger" system in the rat. *Nature,* 1970, **226**, 964.

Leibowitz, S. F. Reciprocal hunger-regulating circuits involving alpha- and beta-adrenergic receptors located, respectively, in the ventromedial and lateral hypothalamus. *Proc. Nat. Acad. Sci.,* 1970, **67**, 1063–1070.

Leibowitz, S. F. Central adrenergic receptors and the regulation of hunger and thirst. In *Neurotransmitters* (I. J. Kopin, editor). Williams and Wilkins, Baltimore, 1972.

Lilly, J. C. Injury and excitation by electric currents. A. The balanced pulse-pair waveform. In *Electrical Stimulation of the Brain* (D. E. Sheer, editor). Univ. of Texas Press, Austin, 1961. Pp. 60–64.

Masserman, J. H. Is the hypothalamus a center of emotion? *Psychosom. Med.,* 1941, **3**, 3–25.

Miller, N. E. Experimental studies of conflict. In *Personality and the Behavior Disorders* (J. V. McHunt, editor). Ronald Press, New York, 1944. Pp. 431–465.

Miller, N. E. Studies of fear as an acquirable drive: I. Fear as motivation and fear reduction as reinforcement in the learning of new responses. *J. Exp. Psychol.,* 1938, **38**, 89–101.

Miller, N. E. Theory and experiment relating psychoanalytic displacement to stimulus-response generalization. *J. Abnormal Social Psychol.*, 1948, **43**, 155–178.

Miller, N. E. Learnable drives and rewards. In *Handbook of Experimental Psychology* (S. S. Stevens, editor). John Wiley and Sons, New York, 1951. Pp. 435–472.

Miller, N. E., Richter, M. L., Bailey, C. J., and Southwick, J. B. "Thirst" induced or reduced, respectively, by minute injections of hypertonic NaCl or water into the ventricles of cats. Paper read at meetings of Eastern Psychological Association, New York City, 1955.

Miller, N. E. Experiments on motivation; Studies combining psychological, physiological, and pharmacological techniques. *Science,* 1957, **126**, 1271–1278.

Miller, N. E. Objective techniques for studying motivational effects of drugs on animals. In *Psychotropic Drugs* (S. Garattini and V. Ghetti, editors). Elsevier, Amsterdam, 1957. Pp. 83–103.

Miller, N. E. Central stimulation and other new approaches to motivation and reward. *Amer. Psychol.,* 1958, **13**, 100–108.

Miller, N. E. Liberalization of basic S-R concepts: Extensions to conflict behavior, motivation, and social learning. In *Psychology: A Study of a Science,* Study 1, Vol. 2 (S. Koch, editor). McGraw-Hill, New York, 1959. Pp. 196–292.

Miller, N. E. Some motivational effects of brain stimulation and drugs. *Federation Proc.,* 1960, **19**, 846–854.

Miller, N. E. Learning and performance motivated by direct stimulation of the brain. In *Electrical Stimulation of the Brain* (D. E. Sheer, editor). Univ. of Texas Press, Austin, 1961. Pp. 387–396.

Miller, N. E. Some reflections on the law of effect produce a new alternative to drive reduction. In *Nebraska Symposium on Motivation* (M. R. Jones, editor). Univ. of Nebraska Press, Lincoln, Nebr., 1963. Pp. 65–112.

Miller, N. E. Chemical coding of behavior in the brain. *Science,* 1965, **148**, 328–338.

Miller, N. E., Bailey, C. J., and Stevenson, J. A. F. Decreased "hunger" but increased food intake resulting from hypothalamic lesions. *Science,* 1950, **112**, 256–259.

Miller, N. E., and Chien, C. W. Drinking elicited by injecting eserine into preoptic area of rat brain. *Commun. Behav. Biol.,* Part A, 1968, **1**, 61–63.

Miller, N. E., Coons, E. E., Lewis, M., and Jensen, D. D. Electrode holders in chronic preparations. B. A simple technique for use with the rat. In *Electrical Stimulation of the Brain* (D. E. Sheer, editor). Univ. of Texas Press, Austin, 1961. Pp. 51–54.

Miller, N. E., and Dollard, J. *Social Learning and Imitation.* Yale Univ. Press, New Haven, 1941.

Miller, N. E., Gottesman, K. S., and Emery, N. Dose response to carbachol and norepinephrine in rat hypothalamus. *Amer. J. Physiol.,* 1964, **206**, 1384–1388.

Miller, N. E., Jensen, D. D., and Myers, A. K. Injury and excitation by electric current. B. A comparison of the Lilly waveform and the sixty-cycle sine wave. In *Electrical Stimulation of the Brain* (D. E. Sheer, editor). Univ. of Texas Press, Austin, 1961. Pp. 64–66.

Miller, N. E., and Kessen, M. L. Reward effects of food via stomach fistula compared with those of food via mouth. *J. Comp. Physiol. Psychol.,* 1952, **45,** 555–564.

Olds, J., and Milner, P. Positive reinforcement produced by electrical stimulation of septal area and other regions of rat brain. *J. Comp. Physiol. Psychol.,* 1954, **47,** 419–427.

Quartermain, D., and Miller, N. E. Sensory feedback in time response of drinking elicited by carbachol in preoptic area of rat. *J. Comp. Physiol. Psychol.,* 1966, **62,** 350–353.

Roberts, W. W. Rapid escape learning without avoidance learning under motivation aroused by hypothalamic stimulation. *J. Comp. Physiol. Psychol.,* 1958, **51,** 391–399. (a)

Roberts, W. W. Both rewarding and punishing effects from stimulation of posterior hypothalamus with same electrode at same intensity. *J. Comp. Physiol. Psychol.,* 1958, **51,** 400–407. (b)

Roberts, W. W. Are hypothalamic motivational mechanisms functionally and anatomically specific? *Brain, Behav., Evolution,* 1969, **2,** 317–342.

Slangen, J. L., and Miller, N. E. Pharmacological tests for the function of hypothalamic norepinephrine in eating behavior. *Physiol. Behav.,* 1969, **4,** 543–552.

Smith, O. A. Stimulation of lateral and medial hypothalamus and food intake in the rat. *Anat. Rec.,* 1956, **124,** 363–364.

Steinbaum, E. A., and Miller, N. E. Obesity from eating elicited by daily stimulation of hypothalamus. *Amer. J. Physiol.,* 1965, **208,** 1–5.

Teitelbaum, P. Random and food-directed activity in hyperphagic and normal rats. *J. Comp. Physiol. Psychol.,* 1957, **50,** 486–490.

Tenen, S. S., and Miller, N. E. Strength of electrical stimulation of lateral hypothalamus, food deprivation, and tolerance for quinine in food. *J. Comp. Physiol. Psychol.,* 1964, **58,** 55–62.

Winson, J., and Miller, N. E. Comparison of drinking elicited by eserine or DFP injected into preoptic area of rat brain. *J. Comp. Physiol. Psychol.,* 1970, **73,** 233–237.

Positive Reinforcement Produced by Electrical Stimulation of Septal Area and Other Regions of Rat Brain[1]

JAMES OLDS and PETER MILNER

McGill University

Stimuli have eliciting and reinforcing functions. In studying the former, one concentrates on the responses which come after the stimulus. In studying the latter, one looks mainly at the responses which precede it. In its reinforcing capacity, a stimulus increases, decreases, or leaves unchanged the frequency of preceding responses, and accordingly it is called a reward, a punishment, or a neutral stimulus (cf. Skinner, 1938).

Previous studies using chronic implantation of electrodes have tended to focus on the eliciting functions of electrical stimuli delivered to the brain (Delgado, 1952a, 1952b; Delgado & Anand, 1953; Dell, 1952; Gastaut, 1952; Hunter & Jasper, 1949; MacLean & Delgado, 1953; Rosvold & Delgado, 1953). The present study, on the other hand, has been concerned with the reinforcing function of the electrical stimulation.[2]

METHOD

General

Stimulation was carried out by means of chronically implanted electrodes which did not interfere with the health or free behavior of Ss to any appreciable extent. The Ss were 15 male hooded rats, weighing approximately

1. The research reported here was made possible by grants from the Rockefeller Foundation and the National Institute of Mental Health of the U.S. Public Health Service. The authors particularly wish to express their thanks to Professor D. O. Hebb, who provided germinal ideas for the research and who backed it with enthusiastic encouragement as well as laboratory facilities and funds. The authors are also grateful to Miss Joann Feindel, who performed the histological reconstructions reported here.
2. The present preliminary paper deals mainly with methods and behavioral results. A detailed report of the locus of positive, negative, and neutral reinforcing effects of electrical brain stimulation is being prepared by the first author.

James Olds and Peter Milner, "Positive Reinforcement Produced by Electrical Stimulation of Septal Area and Other Regions of Rat Brain," *The Journal of Comparative and Physiological Psychology,* 47 (6), 1954, 419–427. Copyright © 1954 by the American Psychological Association, and reproduced by permission.

250 gm. at the start of the experiment. Each *S* was tested in a Skinner box which delivered alternating current to the brain so long as a lever was depressed. The current was delivered over a loose lead, suspended from the ceiling, which connected the stimulator to the rat's electrode. The *S*s were given a total of 6 to 12 hr. of acquisition testing, and 1 to 2 hr. of extinction testing. During acquisition, the stimulator was turned on so that a response produced electrical stimulation; during extinction, the stimulator was turned off so that a response produced no electrical stimulation. Each *S* was given a percentage score denoting the proportion of his total acquisition time given to responding. This score could be compared with the animal's extinction score to determine whether the stimulation had a positive, negative, or neutral reinforcing effect. After testing, the animal was sacrificed. Its brain was frozen, sectioned, stained, and examined microscopically to determine which structure of the brain had been stimulated. This permitted correlation of acquisition scores with anatomical structures.

Electrode implantation

Electrodes are constructed by cementing a pair of enameled silver wires of 0.010-in. diameter into a Lucite block, as shown in Figure 1. The parts of the wires which penetrate the brain are cemented together to form a needle, and this is cut to the correct length to reach the desired structure in the brain. This length is determined from Krieg's rat brain atlas (1946) with slight modifications as found necessary by experience. The exposed cross section of the wire is the only part of the needle not insulated from the brain by enamel; stimulation therefore occurs only at the tip. Contact with the lead from the stimulator is made through two blobs of solder on the upper ends of the

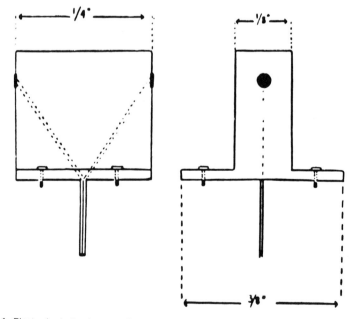

Figure 1. Electrode design (see text for detailed description).

electrode wires; these blobs make contact with the jaws of an alligator clip which has been modified to insulate the two jaws from one another. A light, flexible hearing-aid lead connects the clip to the voltage source.

The operation of implantation is performed with the rat under Nembutal anesthesia (0.88 cc/Kg) and held in a Johnson-Krieg stereotaxic instrument (Krieg, 1946). A midline incision is made in the scalp and the skin held out of the way by muscle retractors. A small hole is drilled in the skull with a dental burr at the point indicated by the stereotaxic instrument for the structure it is desired to stimulate. The electrode, which is clamped into the needle carrier of the instrument, is lowered until the flange of the Lucite block rests firmly on the skull. Four screw holes are then drilled in the skull through four fixing holes in the flange, and the electrode, still clamped firmly in the instrument, is fastened to the skull with jeweler's screws which exceed the diameter of the screw holes in the skull by 0.006 in. The electrode is then released from the clamp and the scalp wound closed with silk sutures. The skin is pulled tightly around the base of the Lucite block and kept well away from the contact plates. A recovery period of three days is allowed after the operation before testing. Figure 2 is an X-ray picture of an electrode in place.

Testing

The testing apparatus consisted of a large-levered Skinner box 11 in. long, 5 in. wide, and 12 in. high. The top was open to allow passage for the stimulating lead. The lever actuated a microswitch in the stimulating circuit so that when it was depressed, the rat received electrical stimulation. The current was ob-

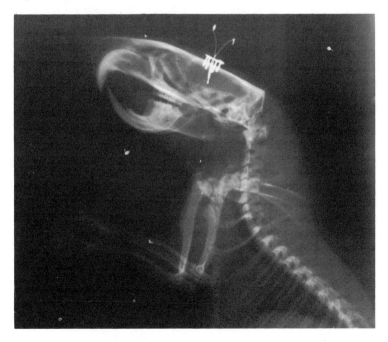

Figure 2. X ray showing electrode in place in intact animal. There are two wires insulated completely from each other, stimulating the brain with their tips.

tained from the 60-cycle power line, through a step-down transformer, and was adjustable between 0 and 10 v. r.m.s. by means of a variable potentiometer. In the experiments described here the stimulation continued as long as the lever was pressed, though for some tests a time-delay switch was incorporated which cut the current off after a predetermined interval if the rat continued to hold the lever down. Responses were recorded automatically on paper strip.

On the fourth day after the operation rats were given a pretesting session of about an hour in the boxes. Each rat was placed in the box and on the lever by *E* with the stimulus set at 0.5 v. During the hour, stimulation voltage was varied to determine the threshold of a "just noticeable" effect on the rat's behavior. If the animal did not respond regularly from the start, it was placed on the lever periodically (at about 5-min. intervals). Data collected on the first day were not used in later calculations. On subsequent days, *S*s were placed in the box for about 3 1/2 hr. a day; these were 3 hr. of acquisition and 1/2 hr. of extinction. During the former, the rats were allowed to stimulate themselves with a voltage which was just high enough to produce some noticeable response in the resting animal. As this threshold voltage fluctuated with the passage of time, *E* would make a determination of it every half hour, unless *S* was responding regularly. At the beginning of each acquisition period, and after each voltage test, the animal was placed on the lever once by *E*. During extinction periods, conditions were precisely the same except that a bar press produced no electrical stimulation. At the beginning of each extinction period, animals which were not responding regularly were placed on the lever once by *E*. At first, rats were tested in this way for four days, but as there appeared to be little difference between the results on different days, this period was reduced to three and then to two days for subsequent animals. Thus, the first rats had about 12 hr. of acquisition after pretesting, whereas later rats had about 6 hr. However, in computing the scores in our table, we have used only the first 6 hr. of acquisition for all animals, so the scores are strictly comparable. In behavioral curves, we have shown the full 12 hr. of acquisition on the earlier animals so as to illustrate the stability of the behavior over time.

At no time during the experiment were the rats deprived of food or water, and no reinforcement was used except the electrical stimulus.

Animals were scored on the percentage of time which they spent bar pressing regularly during acquisition. In order to find how much time the animal would spend in the absence of reward or punishment, a similar score was computed for periods of extinction. This extinction score provided a base line. When the acquisition score is above the extinction score, we have reward; when it is below the extinction score, we have punishment.

In order to determine percentage scores, periods when the animal was responding regularly (at least one response every 30 sec.) were counted as periods of responding; i.e., *intervals of 30 sec. or longer without a response were counted as periods of no responding.* The percentage scores were computed as the proportion of total acquisition or extinction time given to periods of responding.

Determination of locus

On completion of testing, animals were perfused with physiological saline, followed by 10 percent formalin. The brains were removed, and after further fixation in formalin for about a week, frozen sections 40 microns thick were cut through the region of the electrode track. These were stained with cresyl violet and the position of the electrode tip determined. Figure 3 is a photomicrograph showing the appearance of the electrode track in a stained and mounted brain section.

RESULTS

Locus

In Table 1, acquisition and extinction scores are correlated with electrode placements. Figure 4 presents the acquisition scores again, this time on three cross-sectional maps of the rat brain, one at the forebrain level, one at the thalamic level, and one at the midbrain level. The position of a score on the map indicates the electrode placement from which this acquisition score was obtained.

The highest scores are found together in the central portion of the forebrain. Beneath the *corpus callosum* and between the two lateral ventricles in section I of Figure 4, we find four acquisition scores ranging from 75 to 92 percent. This is the septal area. The *S*s which produced these scores are numbered 32, 34, M-1, and M-4 in Table 1. It will be noticed that while all of them spent more than 75 percent of their acquisition time responding, they all spent less than 22 percent of their extinction time responding. Thus the electrical stimulus in the septal area has an effect which is apparently equivalent to that of a conventional primary reward as far as the maintenance of a lever-pressing response is concerned.

If we move outside the septal area, either in the direction of the caudate nucleus (across the lateral ventricle) or in the direction of the *corpus callosum,* we find acquisition scores drop abruptly to levels of from 4 to 6 percent. These are definitely indications of neutral (neither rewarding nor punishing) effects.

However, above the *corpus callosum* in the cingulate cortex we find an acquisition score of 37 percent. As the extinction score in this case was 9 percent, we may say that stimulation was rewarding.

At the thalamic level (section II of Figure 4) we find a 36 percent acquisition score produced by an electrode placed again in the cingulate cortex, an 11 percent score produced by an electrode placed in the hippo-campus, a 71 percent score produced by an electrode placed exactly in the mammillothalamic tract, and a zero percent score produced by an electrode placed in the medial lemniscus. The zero denotes negative reinforcement.

At the midbrain level (section III of Figure 4) there are two zero scores produced by electrodes which are in the posterior portion of the medial geniculate bodies; here again the scores indicate a negative effect, as the corresponding extinction scores are 31 and 21 percent. There is an electrode deep in the medial, posterior tegmentum which produces a 2 percent score; this seems quite neutral, as the extinction score in this case is 1 percent. Finally, there is an electrode shown on this section which actually stands 1½ mm. anterior to the point where it is shown; it was between the red nucleus and the posterior commissure. It produced an acquisition score of 77 percent,

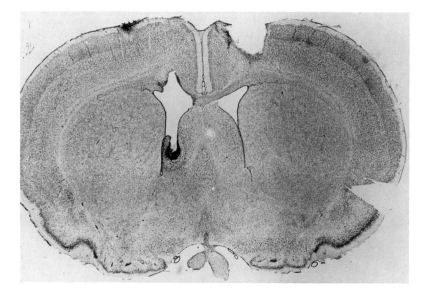

Figure 3. Photomicrograph showing the electrode track in a cresyl-violet–stained brain section. The section is 1 mm. in front of the anterior commissure. The electrode protruded through the lateral ventricle and its stimulating tip was in the septal area.

TABLE 1. ACQUISITION AND EXTINCTION SCORES FOR ALL ANI-
MALS TOGETHER WITH ELECTRODE PLACEMENTS AND
THRESHOLD VOLTAGES USED DURING ACQUISITION
TESTS.

Ani-mal's No.	Locus of Electrode	Stimulation Voltage r.m.s.	Percentage of Acquisition Time Spent Responding	Percentage of Extinction Time Spent Responding
32	septal	2.2 – 2.8	75	18
34	septal	1.4	92	6
M-1	septal	1.7 – 4.8	85	21
M-4	septal	2.3 – 4.8	88	13
40	c.c.	.7 – 1.1	6	3
41	caudate	.9 – 1.2	4	4
31	cingulate	1.8	37	9
82	cingulate	.5 – 1.8	36	10
36	hip.	.8 – 2.8	11	14
3	m.l.	.5	0	4
A-5	m.t.	1.4	71	9
6	m.g.	.5	0	31
11	m.g.	.5	0	21
17	teg.	.7	2	1
9	teg.	.5	77	81

KEY: *c.c., corpus callosum; hip.,* hippocampus; *m.l.,* medial lemniscus; *m.t.,* Mammil-lothalamic tract; *m.g.,* medial geniculate; *teg.,* tegmentum.

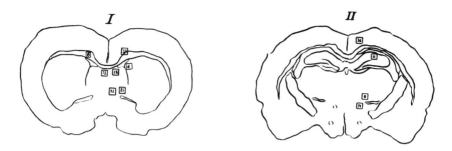

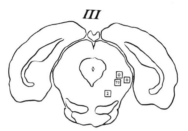

Figure 4. Maps of three sections, (I) through the forebrain, (II) through the thalamus, (III) through the midbrain of the rat. Boxed numbers give acquisition percentage scores produced by animals with electrodes stimulating at these points. On section I the acquisition scores 75, 88, 92, 85 fall in the septal forebrain area. On the same section there is a score of 4 in the caudate nucleus, a score of 6 in the white matter below the cortex, and a score of 37 in the medial (cingulate) cortex. On section II the acquisition score of 36 is in the medial (cingulate) cortex, 11 is in the hippocampus, 71 is in the mammillothalamic tract, and 0 is in the medial lemniscus. On section III the two zeroes are in the medial geniculate, 2 is in the tegmental reticular substance, 77 falls 2 mm. anterior to the section shown—it is between the posterior commissure and the red nucleus.

but an extinction score of 81 percent. This must be a rewarding placement, but the high extinction score makes it difficult to interpret.

Behavior

We turn our attention briefly to the behavioral data produced by the more rewarding electrode placements.

The graph in Figure 5 is a smoothed cumulative response curve illustrating the rate of responding of rat No. 32 (the lowest-scoring septal area rat) during acquisition and extinction. The animal gave a total of slightly over 3000 responses in the 12 hr. of acquisition. When the current was turned on, the animal responded at a rate of 285 responses an hour; when the current was turned off, the rate fell close to zero.

The graph in Figure 6 gives similar data on rat No. 34 (the highest-scoring septal rat). The animal stimulated itself over 7500 times in 12 hr. Its average

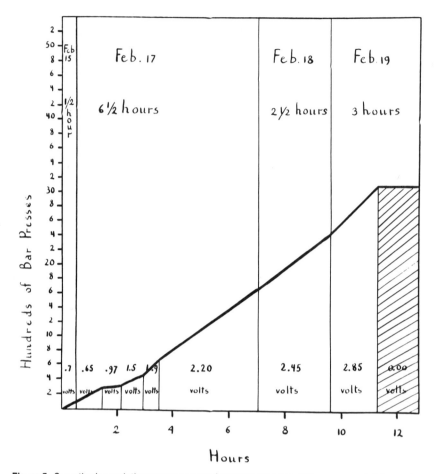

Figure 5. Smoothed cumulative response curve for rat No. 32. Cumulative response totals are given along the ordinate, and hours along the abscissa. The steepness of the slope indicates the response rate. Stimulating voltages are given between black lines. Cross hatching indicates extinction.

response rate during acquisition was 742 responses an hour; during extinction, practically zero.*

Figure 7 presents an unsmoothed cumulative response curve for one day of responding for rat No. A-5. This is to illustrate in detail the degree of control exercised by the electrical reward stimulus. While this rat was actually bar pressing, it did so at 1920 responses an hour; that is, about one response for every 2 sec. During the first period of the day it responded regularly while on acquisition, extinguished very rapidly when the current was turned off, and reconditioned readily when the current was turned on again. At reconditioning points, *E* gave *S* one stimulus to show that the current was turned on again, but *E* did not place *S* on the lever. During longer periods of acquisition, *S*

---

*Ed.: Subsequently, Olds and others have found posterior hypothalamic sites which would maintain self-stimulation at rates in excess of 5000 per hour.

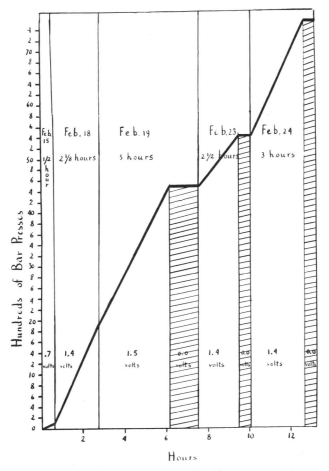

Figure 6. Smoothed cumulative response curve for rat No. 34

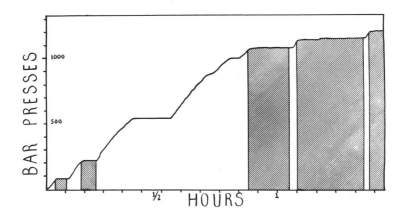

Figure 7. Unsmoothed cumulative response curve showing about ³/₄ hr. of acquisition and ³/₄ hr. extinction for rat No. A-5. Shading indicates extinction.

occasionally stopped responding for short periods, but in the long run *S* spent almost three quarters of its acquisition time responding. During the long period of extinction at the end of the day, there was very little responding, but *S* could be brought back to the lever quite quickly if a stimulus was delivered to show that the current had been turned on again.

DISCUSSION

It is clear that electrical stimulation in certain parts of the brain, particularly the septal area, produces acquisition and extinction curves which compare favorably with those produced by a conventional primary reward. With other electrode placements, the stimulation appears to be neutral or punishing.

Because the rewarding effect has been produced maximally by electrical stimulation in the septal area, but also in lesser degrees in the mammillothalamic tract and cingulate cortex, we are led to speculate that a system of structures previously attributed to the rhinencephalon may provide the locus for the reward phenomenon. However, as localization studies which will map the whole brain with respect to the reward and punishment dimension are continuing, we will not discuss in detail the problem of locus. We will use the term "reinforcing structures" in further discussion as a general name for the septal area and other structures which produce the reward phenomenon.

To provide an adequate canvass of the possible explanations for the rewarding effect would require considerably more argument than could possibly fit within the confines of a research paper. We have decided, therefore, to rule out briefly the possibility that the implantation produces pain which is reduced by electrical stimulation of reinforcing structures, and to confine further discussion to suggestions of ways the phenomenon may provide a methodological basis for study of physiological mechanisms of reward.

The possibility that the implantation produces some painful "drive stimulus" which is alleviated by electrical stimulation of reinforcing structures does not comport with the facts which we have observed. If there were some chronic, painful drive state, it would be indicated by emotional signs in the animal's daily behavior. Our *S*s, from the first day after the operation, are normally quiet, nonaggressive; they eat regularly, sleep regularly, gain weight. There is no evidence in their behavior to support the postulation of chronic pain. Septal preparations which have lived healthy and normal lives for months after the operation have given excellent response rates.

As there is no evidence of a painful condition preceding the electrical stimulation, and as the animals are given free access to food and water at all times except while actually in the Skinner boxes, there is no explicitly manipulated drive to be reduced by electrical stimulation. Barring the possibility that stimulation of a reinforcing structure specifically inhibits the "residual drive" state of the animal, or the alternative possibility that the first electrical stimulus has noxious aftereffects which are reduced by a second one, we have some evidence here for a primary rewarding effect which is not associated with the reduction of a primary drive state. It is perhaps fair in a discussion to report the "clinical impression" of the *E*s that the phenomenon represents strong pursuit of a positive stimulus rather than escape from some negative condition.

Should the latter interpretation prove correct, we have perhaps located a system within the brain whose peculiar function is to produce a rewarding effect on behavior. The location of such a system puts us in a position to collect information that may lead to a decision among conflicting theories of reward. By physiological studies, for example, we may find that the reinforcing structures act selectively on sensory or motor areas of the cortex. This would have relevance to current S-S versus S-R controversies (Hebb, 1949; Hull, 1943; Olds, 1954; Skinner, 1938).

Similarly, extirpation studies may show whether reinforcing structures have primarily a quieting or an activating effect on behavior; this would be relevant to activation versus negative feedback theories of reward (Deutsch, 1953; Olds, 1954; Seward, 1952; Wiener, 1949). A recent study by Brady and Nauta (1953) already suggests that the septal area is a quieting system, for its surgical removal produced an extremely active animal.

Such examples, we believe, make it reasonable to hope that the methodology reported here should have important consequences for physiological studies of mechanisms of reward.

SUMMARY

A preliminary study was made of rewarding effects produced by electrical stimulation of certain areas of the brain. In all cases rats were used and stimulation was by 60-cycle alternating current, with voltages ranging from 1/2 to 5 v. Bipolar needle electrodes were permanently implanted at various points in the brain. Animals were tested in Skinner boxes where they could stimulate themselves by pressing a lever. They received no other reward than the electrical stimulus in the course of the experiments. The primary findings may be listed as follows: (a) There are numerous places in the lower centers of the brain where electrical stimulation is rewarding in the sense that the experimental animal will stimulate itself in these places frequently and regularly for long periods of time if permitted to do so. (b) It is possible to obtain these results from as far back as the tegmentum, and as far forward as the septal area; from as far down as the subthalamus, and as far up as the cingulate gyrus of the cortex. (c) There are also sites in the lower centers where the effect is just the opposite: animals do everything possible to avoid stimulation. And there are neutral sites: animals do nothing to obtain or to avoid stimulation. (d) The reward results are obtained more dependably with electrode placements in some areas than others, the septal area being the most dependable to date. (e) In septal area preparations, the control exercised over the animal's behavior by means of this reward is extreme, possibly exceeding that exercised by any other reward previously used in animal experimentation.

The possibility that the reward results depended on some chronic painful consequences of the implantation operation was ruled out on the evidence that no physiological or behavioral signs of such pain could be found. The phenomenon was discussed as possibly laying a methodological foundation for a physiological study of the mechanisms of reward.

REFERENCES

Brady, J. V., & Nauta, W. J. H. Subcortical mechanisms in emotional behavior: Affective changes following septal forebrain lesions in the albino rat. *J. comp. physiol. Psychol.*, 1953, **46**, 339–346.

Delgado, J. M. R. Permanent implantation of multilead electrodes in the brain. *Yale J. Biol. Med.*, 1952, **24**, 351–358. (a)

Delgado, J. M. R. Responses evoked in waking cat by electrical stimulation of motor cortex. *Amer. J. Physiol.*, 1952, **171**, 436–446. (b)

Delgado, J. M. R., & Anand, B. K. Increase of food intake induced by electrical stimulation of the lateral hypothalamus. *Amer. J. Physiol.*, 1953, **172**, 162–168.

Dell, P. Correlations entre le système vegetatif et le système de la vie relation: Mesencephale, diencephale, et cortex cerebral *J. Physiol.* (Paris), 1952, **44**, 471–557.

Deutsch, J. A. A new type of behavior theory. *Brit. J. Psychol.*, 1953, **44**, 304–317.

Gastaut, H. Correlations entre le système nerveux vegetatif et le système de la vie de relation dans le rhinecephale. *J. Physiol.* (Paris), 1952, **44**, 431–470.

Hebb, D. O. *The organization of behavior.* New York: Wiley, 1949.

Hull, C. L. *Principles of behavior.* New York: Appleton-Century, 1943.

Hunter, J., & Jasper, H. H. Effects of thalamic stimulation in unanaesthetized animals. *EEG clin. Neurophysiol,* 1949, **1**, 305–324.

Krieg, W. J. S. Accurate placement of minute lesions in the brain of the albino rat. *Quart. Bull., Northwestern Univer. Med. School,* 1946, **20**, 199–208.

MacLean, P. D., & Delgado, J. M. R. Electrical and chemical stimulation of frontotemporal portion of limbic system in the waking animal. *EEG clin. Neurophysiol.,* 1953, **5**, 91–100.

Olds, J. A neural model for sign-gestalt theory.*Psychol. Rev.,* 1954, **61**, 59–72.

Rosvold, H. E., & Delgado, J. M. R. The effect on the behavior of monkeys of electrically stimulating or destroying small areas within the frontal lobes. *Amer. Psychologist,* 1953, **8**, 425–426. (Abstract)

Seward, J. P. Introduction to a theory of motivation in learning. *Psychol. Rev.,* 1952, **59**, 405–413.

Skinner, B. F. *The behavior of organisms.* New York: Appleton-Century, 1938.

Wiener, N. *Cybernetics.* New York: Wiley, 1949.

Commentary

JAMES OLDS

THE DISCOVERY OF REWARD SYSTEMS IN THE BRAIN

The discovery of rewarding effects induced by electrical stimulation of the brain occurred in the latter part of 1953. A rat was free to move around in a fairly large table-top enclosure (3 × 3 ft. or more). A pair of stimulating wires was planted deep in the brain and insulated except for the cross section of the tip. These were attached to a connector which was held rigidly to the skull, but which penetrated through the scalp to permit attachment of wires from the stimulator. This pair of fairly light, quite long wires was suspended from the ceiling by means of an elastic band which provided no more impediment to movement than a long, loose leash provides for a dog. I applied a brief train of 60-cycle sine-wave electrical current whenever the animal entered one corner of the enclosure. The animal did not stay away from that corner, but rather came back quickly after a brief sortie which followed the first stimulation and came back even more quickly after a briefer sortie which followed the second stimulation. By the time the third electrical stimulus had been applied the animal seemed indubitably to be "coming back for more."

Later this same rat furthered my view that the electrical stimulation was rewarding, by moving toward any part of the enclosure chosen by an independent observer, provided only that I turned on the switch which provided the electrical current whenever the animal took a step in the right direction. Still later the animal learned to run rapidly to that arm of an elevated T-maze in which electrical stimulation was regularly applied.

Attempts to repeat the experiment by implanting probes in similar places in other animals did not readily meet with success. Some animals evidenced a mild disposition to favor the stimulus, but other animals evidenced ambivalence or aversive reactions, and it soon became clear that a careful and systematic mapping would be required in order to find and exploit the exact brain area which had yielded the original phenomenon.

The self-stimulation experiment was developed in order to provide a quantitative dependent variable, a measure of reward, which might be correlated with the different brain points where electrical stimulation could be applied. In this experiment the animal was provided with a very large lever in a very small "Skinner box." The whole mechanism consisted of the box or enclosure, the pedal, an opening in the top of the box for the stimulating leads to pass through, and a very simple electrical stimulator which was activated by the animal's depression of the pedal. In early experiments stimulation lasted continuously while the pedal was depressed; in later experiments each pedal response produced a brief stimulus train (0.1 to 4 sec. in different experiments). Because a very small box was used, and because the large pedal was placed so that it would be depressed whenever the animal peered through the only aperture, initial response rates ranged as high as 60 responses in the first 10-minute period, even in cases when no reinforcement was used at all.

Because of this very high initial response rate, a very, very low pedal response rate could be taken as evidence of the aversive effects of the electrical brain stimulus, and very high rates (ranging from 200 responses to 1,000 responses in a 10-minute period) could be taken as evidence of rewarding effects induced by the electrical brain stimulus. The self-stimulation experiment provided the method needed for tracking the brain reward to its neuroanatomical substrate, and therefore it provided the basis for the reproduction of the original phenomenon, which is now regularly reproduced in many brain and behavior laboratories.

Most of us who study the phenomenon believe that the parts of the brain where rewarding effects can be induced by electrical stimulation are also involved in the control of behavior by normal rewards, just as we believe that the motor cortex where motor movements can be induced by electrical stimulation is involved in control of those same movements during normal behavior.

Before I review the significant consequences of this discovery, let me review the factors which caused the experiment to occur in the first place.

The tools, the situation, and the method of preparing the animal had more to do with the discovery of this effect than the ideas which were in my mind about how the brain might work. I think this will be the case regularly for our field until we come upon ideas which are easier to understand, communicate, and defend, than the data they are supposed to explain. Therefore the main question involved is: What caused me to be doing these things?

D. O. Hebb, by writing the "Organization of Behavior" (1949), had encouraged my natural tendency to speculate about neurophysiological mechanisms, even though my problem had been, up to this time, the explanation of mainly behavioral data. Richard L. Solomon, who had quite recently guided my thesis research, convinced me that if I wanted to talk about neurophysiological variables, they should be part of my subject matter. Conversely he suggested that if I was only observing behavior I should talk about behavior. As I was unwilling to give up ideas about brain mechanisms which seemed obscure but wonderful to me at the time, I went to Hebb's laboratory to study these things.

Hebb had brought together in the part of his laboratory where I worked behavioral methods applicable to the laboratory rat, neurosurgical methods applicable to the rat, and neurophysiological methods for electrically stimulating and recording from the rat brain during behaviorally meaningful processes. In support of these three main methods of study, he had also brought stereotaxic methods for placing probes and histological methods for verifying the placement of probes and surgical lesions. In retrospect, many of the techniques seem to have been done with just as much finesse as was necessary to the job, and no particular care for perfection of the technique beyond that point. This gave the behavior of Hebb's laboratory a free appearance, in contrast with that of the highly organized laboratories attacking more physiological aspects of similar problems in the nearby Montreal Neurological Institute.

Peter M. Milner and Seth K. Sharpless were Hebb's two graduate students involved in electrical stimulation and recording problems. Sharpless was working temporarily at the Montreal Neurological Institute with Herbert H. Jasper, where he was doing a thesis on habituation in the cat. Milner had developed his own version of the Hess (1948) and Delgado (1952) method for implanting probes to be used for electrical stimulation (and recording, too, for that matter) in the relatively freely behaving animal. Delgado's version of the Hess method was applicable to the cat, as was the original Hess method. Milner had developed a version applicable to the rat. He had also brought an excellent background in electrical engineering to bear upon the problems of electrical stimulation and recording, and had thereby greatly simplified methods.

Because Hebb spent much of his time hidden away in the back office writing a book, Sharpless and Milner provided most of my introduction to this new environment. With Sharpless I had intense, if not numerous, interactions over theories of brain function. Sharpless was very taken at the time with the writings of H. W. Magoun (1950), H. H. Jasper (1949), and D. B. Lindsley (1951) on the newly discovered arousal system. And he had developed sophisticated theoretical views about the control of motivated behavior by a brain arousal mechanism with a differentiated set of levels of output. Milner was undoubtedly working at that time on his theoretical reinterpretation of Hebb's concepts, but I do not remember having him as a partner in very many theoretical discussions. On the other hand, he immediately, cheerfully, and with enthusiasm, taught me how to handle his methods of electrode implantation, electrical stimulation, and electrical recording.

I quickly got involved in recording EEGs from electrodes as they were advanced through the brains of anesthetized animals in order to observe differences in spontaneous activity which could be recorded from different parts of the thalamus. I was particularly interested in differences that appeared as the probe penetrated through the interlaminar areas bounding the main thalamic nuclei.

Hebb's direct but unobtrusive intervention saved me from spending too much time on this kind of problem. He provided a senior honors student, Ralph S. Morison, who wanted to help with and participate in one of my experiments. I offered to put him to work on EEG maps of the thalamus, but Hebb demurred. By that I mean he answered without enthusiasm. So I suggested a second quasi-neurophysiological problem which received a similar reception. At this point I intimated that I also had in mind hanging wires from the ceiling and recording from and stimulating rats during behavior in a "Hebb-Williams" maze. This caused his eyes to light up in a very Hebbian way, and by this rather unloquacious interaction he modified my future to quite a considerable degree.

The list of things I would do with my rats in the Hebb-Williams maze proceeded to take shape in pencil scrawls on the back of an old envelope. There were some six or seven items on this list, and I do not remember whether the list was written in a burst of creative frenzy on one day, or slowly over a period of two or three weeks. In any event, the list was constructed on the basis of ideas derived from my recent interactions. One experiment was suggested by Milner's reading of Yoshii, who had recently recorded progressively aroused EEG waves from a rat as it approached the food compartment in a maze. There was also an experiment suggested by Sharpless' view that an animal aroused by electrical stimulation in the reticular formation might have its level of vigilance improved, and therefore might learn more rapidly to discriminate between cues at a choice point. A third idea, which Sharpless and

I had both discussed hopefully, was that an animal pointing tentatively at one stimulus and then at another (performing the Tolman vicarious trial-and-error response) might be induced to move toward one of the stimuli if during the tentative pointing a brain release mechanism could be electrically triggered. In my mind this experiment derived directly from a theory of reward set forth in my thesis; in Sharpless' mind it derived from the Magoun, Lindsley, and Jasper theory of arousal. Fourth, I wanted to determine whether the brain stimulus in any experiment might be aversive, as had recently been reported by Neal Miller verbally, and with movies, at meetings of the American Psychological Association.

Miller's title for that presentation had been "Reinforcement Induced by Electrical Brain Stimulation," or words similar to those. I had been at first greatly intrigued by the title, believing it to indicate positive reinforcement produced by brain stimulation. I was somewhat let down to find on further reading that the abstract and later the talk reported negative reinforcement which might be induced by stimulating even peripheral nerves.

In any event, it seemed that aversive effects induced by electrical brain stimulation would interfere with, obscure, or in other ways contaminate the outcome of experiments in which stimulation was to be applied at the choice point, either to capture attention or to release behavior. Therefore, even though the test for motivational effects of the stimulus was quite far down on my list of things to do, an arrow ran up the side of the envelope suggesting that it be done first. I believe the fact that the test seemed quite easy to perform influenced my judgment.

The neurophysiological model I had created in my thesis in 1952 on the basis of Tolman's cognitive theory of learning and Hebb's organizational theory of neuronal function yielded as one of its consequences the possibility that some brain stimulations might have positive or rewarding effects. Sad to say, I cannot remember the theoretical model (which was high in my mind whenever I held discussions with Sharpless) having any particular influence on my behavior as I was drawing up my penciled list. Similarly, I cannot remember any hope that Neal Miller's negative reinforcing centers would be matched by a discovery of positive reinforcing centers.

When I did proceed to test for possible aversive effects, I tested simultaneously for approach and avoidance in a relatively open situation, possibly because I had a dualistic attitude toward motivation. In any event, it was my good fortune that this rat which I tested grossly and without finesse did come back for more.

The probe, which was aimed for the midbrain reticular formation, missed its target by some 4 millimeters (which is roughly the whole longitudinal dimension of the rat diencephalon) and came to rest in a point which was probably near the anterior commissure, but which will never be very well specified because, as often happens with very precious brains, mistakes occurred in the histological preparation. The exact location, however, was not so important as was the fact that this was a very pronounced example of the phenomenon, and therefore it provided enough promise to point the way to a complete investigation.

After this fortunate event I learned that Hebb had previously suggested an experiment of a quite similar type to Milner. Thus, if this experiment had not "happened to me" in such an accidental fashion, it would likely have been more purposefully performed by someone else at roughly the same time in history. This could have been in Hebb's laboratory or elsewhere, because on the one hand the phenomenon was very clearly there in the brain (occupying perhaps as much as a quarter of the rat's brain tissue and even extending to the reticular formation point which was my initial target), and on the other hand, the methods of Hess had by then been brought together by people like Hebb and Miller with the behavioral problems generated by the psychologists. The question of reinforcement induced by electrical brain stimulation was being asked by Miller. And Skinner's method of measuring a positive reinforcing effect was a very prominent part of the psychological landscape at that time.

The initial observation led to studies which showed that electrical excitation in a restricted region of the central nervous system caused rats to work steadily at arbitrarily assigned tasks in order to obtain the electric stimulus (Olds & Milner, 1954). The behavior was easily reproducible from animal to animal, was sustained during extended periods of testing, and was not accompanied by any other obvious pathological signs. It seemed possible, therefore, to view this "self-stimulation" behavior in terms of an artificial activation of the brain's normal positive reinforcement mechanism. The discovery led to much research in my later laboratories at UCLA and the University of Michigan, and instigated parallel investigations in many other laboratories throughout the world.

BEHAVIORAL TESTS

At first much of this work was related to the question of whether we were being fooled by the data. Was this a psychologically valid reward or merely a sham, having the appearance but not the substance of a positive emotional effect? Experiments (Olds, 1956) showed that animals would run faster from trial to trial in a runway to get to a goal box where the brain was stimulated, and would improve performance in a maze, running faster and eliminating errors from trial to trial to arrive at the goal point where stimulation was administered. Twenty-three hours after a previous brain stimulation, they would run purposefully through the maze without errors and without dalliance. In other experiments (Olds, 1961) animals repeatedly crossed an electrified grid which applied aversive shocks to the feet to obtain rewards. When a choice between food and brain stimulation rewards was presented to hungry rats, they often chose the brain rewards and underwent the danger of starvation (Routtenberg & Lindy, 1965). In secondary reinforcement tests, the brain rewards imparted their rewarding properties to formerly neutral stimuli after repeated associations, much as food rewards did (Stein, 1958; Knott & Clayton, 1966). In ratio experiments, animals would press one bar many times to gain access to a second bar with which they could stimulate their brains (Pliskoff, Wright, & Hawkins, 1965). In extinction experiments, animals that had learned to press one of two pedals for brain reward continued to press that pedal in preference to the other for two days after the brain reward was discontinued (Koenig, 1967). All of these tests fostered a positive answer to the question of whether this was a psychologically valid reward.

This does not mean that there were not more problematic experiments along the way. At first animals seemed to "extinguish" too fast after the brain stimulus was withdrawn (Deutsch & Howarth, 1963). In other experiments, animals could not be induced to press a pedal many times for a single brain reward (Gallistel, 1964). Still other tests questioned whether a rat did not need priming by one brain reward within a one- or two-minute interval before it would work for further brain rewards (Wetzel, 1963). Another group of tests seemed to show that the brain stimulus might induce brain seizures with a concurrent reduction of pains (Porter, Conrad, & Brady, 1959). In each of these cases where one or a series of experiments strongly questioned the authenticity of the effect, further research involving either modification of experimental design or selection of different locations in the brain for the stimulating probes appeared to reverse or at least question the generality of the negative finding (Koenig, 1967; Pliskoff, Wright, & Hawkins, 1965; Scott, 1967; Bogacz, St. Laurent, & Olds, 1965).

ANATOMICAL STUDIES

Assuming that the brain stimulus was a "real" reward, other experiments were aimed at using the finding to help us toward an understanding of the workings of the reward mechanisms in the brain. The anatomical localization of the effect suggested some things about the function. A large anatomical system was involved, was clearly differentiated from other large systems of the brain, and was anatomically coherent and interconnected (Olds, 1956; Olds, Travis, & Schwing, 1960; Olds, M. E., & Olds, J., 1963). By itself this suggested a large role for this kind of mechanism in the organization of behavior, a relative separation of the processes mediating reward from at least some of the other processes in the brain, and a complexity that might be naively described by saying that there are many different kinds of reward, and rewards do many different kinds of things, but threads of unity or communication might mediate a harmony of effects. Homologous areas were implicated when similar experiments were carried out in rats, cats (Wilkinson & Peele, 1963), monkeys (Bursten & Delgado, 1958), human beings (Bishop, Elder, & Heath, 1963), and many other kinds of animals (Boyd & Gardner, 1962; Lilly & Miller, 1962; Stark & Boyd, 1963; Bruner, 1967). This made it likely that the experiments in lower animals would shed light on human brain functions and offered some hope that reports of direct experiences would help reveal the bases of the rewarding effects of brain stimulation. The centers were proportionally much larger in lower animals, which seemed to indicate that they perhaps played a smaller role in the control of higher behavior.

The anatomical system involved was composed almost entirely of centers having both phylogenetic and functional relation to the olfactory apparatus. The phylogeny therefore suggested that the reward mechanism might have evolved out of chemoreceptive, "homing" mechanisms placed in the forepart of the animal so that goals could be localized and pursued. The functional relations to chemoreception in advanced animals suggested that chemical messengers (both in the environment and in the blood) might be especially important in triggering the pursuit of rewards, guiding these pursuits, and mediating responses to actually presented rewards.

The view that genuine emotional effects were involved was compatible with early speculations, based partly on correlations of emotional changes in rabid (Papez, 1937) and temporal-lobectomized animals (Klüver & Bucy, 1937), both of which implicated the same olfactory-cortical structures that produced rewarding effects in self-stimulation experiments. Self-stimulation could also be obtained from related subcortical structures that had previously been shown to be involved in autonomic control and in the control of consummatory responses and other behaviors related to the basic drives (Stellar, 1954; Miller, 1958), and portions of the anatomically related "reticular" systems which had been shown to be involved in awakening and arousal mechanisms (Moruzzi & Magoun, 1949). The rewarding effects evoked from hypothalamic and other lower centers were far more intense than those evoked in paleocortical, olfactory centers (Olds, M. E., & Olds, J., 1963).

Further experiments showed that the overlap or interdigitation of neural reward with aversive and drive mechanisms was probably not fortuitous, but that physiological mechanisms of synergism and antagonism, or excitation and inhibition, were quite likely involved.

REWARD AND PUNISHMENT

The relations with aversive mechanisms were most interesting. Surprising as the neural reward observations seemed in 1953, in retrospect they appeared as a continuation of a long series of findings made by use of chronically implanted brain probes. Particularly they appeared continuous with findings of brain points where aversive behaviors could be stimulated, and where operant behavior could even be reinforced by a termination of brain stimulation. These were the findings of Neal Miller's group which I mentioned earlier. They were reported shortly before the rewarding observations were made and published the following year (Delgado, Roberts, & Miller, 1954).

Shortly afterwards, it was discovered that there were large areas of the brain where the electrical stimulus appeared to have the opposing effects of positive and negative reinforcement simultaneously (Roberts, 1958). Animals were either rewarded at the onset but aversively influenced by the continuation of a stimulus, or appeared to have mixed emotions in relation to all of the stimuli when probes were planted in some areas. In experiments with probes in these centers animals would pedal-press rapidly to stimulate the brain, but at the same time would try to escape from a situation in which the brain stimulus was available.

Mapping studies showed positive reinforcement to be correlated mainly with stimulation of rheincephalic and hypothalamic "emotion and drive mechanisms," and aversive reinforcement to be related mainly to nonspecific arousal mechanisms or nearby somesthetic centers of the midbrain and thalamus (Olds, M. E., & Olds, J., 1963). There was one particular set of areas which received fibers from one of the two opposing reinforcement systems and sent its fibers to the other. This included the midline nuclei of the hypothalamus and thalamus, which were related on the one hand to the rheincephalon via lateral hypothalamus and on the other hand to the nonspecific systems of the midbrain and thalamus. In at least one case and probably in others, stimulation of the input to a hypothalamic nucleus yielded reinforcement of one sign, and stimulation of the output from the same nucleus yielded reinforcement of the opposite sign. Stimulation of the nuclear mass itself yielded mixed or ambiguous positive-and-negative effects (Olds, M. E., & Olds, J., 1963).

The most likely hypothesis was, of course, that the nuclear masses of the

medial hypothalamus formed integrative switchboards where the two opposing emotional effects could interact to determine behavior. It was appealing to
suppose that these centers might give rise to a set of messages which would
reflect the integrated sum of the organism's emotional state at a given time, and
which would be effective in determining the probability of the organism's
getting into this condition a second time.

To test these theories, interaction studies were conducted in which
aversive and positive areas were simultaneously stimulated. There were also
lesion studies in which parts of one system or the other were destroyed. These
had interesting outcomes which not only permitted speculation about interactions and common denominators to continue, but provided some basis for
elaboration of this kind of model. For example, stimulation in one part of the
positive areas inhibited behavior evoked by stimulation at some of the aversive
points (Routtenberg & Olds, 1963). Stimulation at these same aversive points
inhibited behavior provoked by positive stimulation in the supposed "common denominator" area (Olds, M. E., & Olds, J., 1962). Furthermore, stimulation in this common denominator area had a facilitatory effect on operant
behavior, whether this was motivated by aversive or positive stimulation
elsewhere! Conversely, lesions at the aversive points often caused rewarding
effects induced by stimulation in the common denominator area to be
augmented (Olds, J., & Olds, M. E., 1964). Most interesting of all, lesions in
the common denominator area yielded losses of many different operant
behaviors. In one laboratory there were reports of these lateral hypothalamic
lesions resulting in the loss of both feeding and drinking behavior (Teitelbaum
& Epstein, 1962). In our laboratory there was the observation of the loss of
self-stimulation behavior (Olds, J., & Olds, M. E., 1964). In still another
laboratory there was the loss of conditioned avoidance behavior (Balinska,
Romaniut, & Wyrwicka, 1964)! In all of these cases lesions were placed at
approximately the same point in the lateral hypothalamic area, close to or in
the regions which had previously been found to be related to feeding,
drinking, or sexual behavior.

BASIC DRIVES

The lesion studies, with their concurrent effects on rewards, operant behaviors,
and consummatory responses, prepare the way for a discussion of the second
important series of interaction studies, those relating neural rewards to the
basic drives. The relation of hypothalamic centers to basic drives has been
studied repeatedly and thoroughly during the last 30 years (Brobeck, 1946;
Stellar, 1954; Teitelbaum & Epstein, 1962; Miller, 1958). Much has been
discovered, even though many aspects of the problem are still unresolved. In
some midline hypothalamic centers, lesions have been found to cause overeat-
ing and obesity (Brobeck, 1946). Here also electrical stimulation has sometimes been found to cause cessation of eating (Wyrwicka & Dobrzecka, 1960).
Therefore, one might have expected to find that stimulation in these regions
which terminated feeding would also terminate hunger, and that this stimulus
which terminated a drive would be drive reducing and rewarding. In fact, the
finding in this case was far more negative than positive. There were clearly
observed aversive effects of stimulating this part of hypothalamus (Krasne,
1962), and only ambiguous or totally questionable rewarding effects from

stimulating this same region (Olds, M. E., & Olds, J., 1963). In a more lateral area, lesions caused starvation (Anand & Brobeck, 1951). Here electrical stimulation caused animals to work for food and to eat it even though they were tested in a fully satiated condition (Miller, 1960). This electrical stimulus which caused the animal to respond as if it were very hungry might have been a drive-inducing stimulus and might therefore have been expected to have aversive properties. The findings were quite opposite from what might have been expected on the basis of this reasoning. Stimulation at these "feeding center" points was often quite rewarding, causing some of the highest rates of "self-stimulation" observed (Hoebel & Teitelbaum, 1962; Margules & Olds, 1962). Our first interpretation of this was that stimulation at these points might be mainly involved *not* in inducing drive, but in evoking the positive consummatory eating response. However, the fact that the stimulus caused not only eating of food when food was available, but also working for food when food was absent (Miller, 1960), belied the supposition that these were mere consummatory response centers and suggested that there was the induction by stimulation at these points of something very much like the hunger drive itself. The association of neural reward in its strongest form with brain points where basic drives were apparently induced or exacerbated was later confirmed by other experiments which found drinking and self-stimulation to be simultaneously induced by stimulation in nearby brain areas (Mogenson & Stevenson, 1966). Sexual responding and self-stimulation were also simultaneously induced by stimulation in a third set of brain centers (Caggiula & Hoebel, 1966). The so-called drinking, feeding, and sexual centers of the lateral hypothalamus are not clearly separated from one another, but the points of highest probability for the three different responses are generally believed to occupy different regions along an anterior-posterior line. In any event, a common denominator between many "drive-inducing" points was the fact that their stimulation was quite often rewarding to the animal.

In trying to make sense out of these data I have considered mainly facts about the set of feeding centers, because these were best known. Because stimulation in one area caused both cessation of eating and aversive behavior, while stimulation in a different area caused initiation of eating and positive motivational signs, it seemed that eating might be under a complex set of controls. Perhaps the condition of excessive satiety caused an aversive condition of the organism which brought eating to a halt. Prior to this the animal, in a middle condition (i.e., neither sated nor starved), would evidence eating as a positive feedback phenomenon; that is, eating would be rewarding and would induce further eating. What was missing was a center representing the other extreme from satiety, namely starvation. It seemed that we should find somewhere in the hypothalamus an area where stimulation would be aversive but would also induce eating. In recent research, I believe we have found this in dorsal parts of the medial hypothalamic area. Here, not far from the "lateral feeding center," both instrumental and consummatory feeding responses were induced by electrical stimulation. However, self-stimulation could not be induced; on the contrary, the animal evidenced aversive behavior to escape from this kind of stimulation. In another dorsal area not too far from this point, stimulation induced eating but had no reinforcing effect at all, neither positive nor negative. Our conclusion was that feeding might be under a tri- or quadra-partite control. It could be "bounded" at two ends by aversive mechanisms. It would commence as an escape reaction from dorsomedially mediated aversive, starvation symptoms. It would then continue as a positive reaction based on the laterally mediated positive stimulation emanating from the food objects. It would be terminated by ventromedially mediated aversive properties of excessive satiety which would punish continuation of the eating behavior, thereby causing it to terminate. The "drive" itself might be represented by a neutral common path triggered either by starvation or by food objects.

DRUG STUDIES

Because this was a highly differentiated system with interacting parts, and because messages in the brain are transmitted from neuron to neuron in chemical codes, the possibility of finding selective chemical messengers for the different parts of the interacting system seemed feasible. Were there special chemical triggers for the rewarding, aversive, and the several basic drive subdivisions of this supposed reinforcement mechanism? Close phylogenetic and functional relations of the tissues involved to the chemical-sensory, olfactory apparatus suggested that the answer might be yes. The known and postulated sensitivities of the hypothalamus to hormones and blood-borne nutrients such as glucose also suggested a positive answer. Finally, selective chemical stimulation studies in which different chemicals induced different consummatory responses at the same brain points also suggested that the answer might be positive (Grossman, 1960).

Experiments involving drug administration via normal routes during self-stimulation showed that the best-known chemical messenger, acetylcholine, was almost undoubtedly involved in one way or another (Stark & Boyd, 1963). When drugs were used which caused the active, neuroexcitatory form of this messenger to accumulate excessively in the brain, self-stimulation was impaired or totally counteracted. The effect was quite likely a consequence of the residual "unerased" acetylcholine in the brain, because it was counteracted by drugs such as atropine or scopolamine which are known to counteract the effects of actylcholine in the brain. Drugs which counteracted only the effects of acetylcholine outside of the central nervous system were not effective. These studies led to the belief that excesses of acetylcholine in the brain, at least in its free or active form, were inimical to the self-stimulation phenomenon.

Collateral studies utilizing similar methods have shown that the epinephrine-like compounds which are the prime opponents of acetylcholine in many reactions outside of the central nervous system are probably also involved. When drugs like chlorpromazine, which antagonized the influences of epinephrine-like compounds, were applied via normal pharmacological routes, self-stimulation behavior was impaired or abolished (Olds & Travis, 1960). Similar administration by normal routes of drugs which augmented or mimicked the effects of the epinephrine-like chemicals caused the rates to be augmented, or thresholds to be lowered (Stein, 1964; Poschel & Ninteman, 1963).

In other experiments chemicals related to acetylcholine or epinephrine were applied by means of implanted chemical stimulators directly in those parts of the lateral hypothalamus where electrical stimulation was rewarding (Olds, Yuwiler, Olds, & Yun, 1964). These studies clearly showed, when epinephrine or one of its close relatives was injected, results which were exactly the opposite of what might have been expected on the basis of the pharmacological experiments. Epinephrine, norepinephrine, and serotonin, when applied in these areas, caused a suppression of excitatory effects induced by simultaneous application of other excitatory chemicals. Further experiments showed that acetylcholine-like compounds, when directly applied in the lateral hypothalamus in similar experiments, also had the opposite effects from those which might have been predicted on the basis of the pharmacological studies. Two different acetylcholine-like compounds, carbamyl-choline and acetyl-carnatine, induced chemically stimulated excitatory effects much like those caused by withdrawing ionic calcium from interstitial fluid. Acetylcholine itself did not have these effects, but this was thought to be due to the fact that it was quickly inactivated by normal erasure mechanisms before its excitatory influences could be observed. Several hypotheses have been advanced to explain the apparent opposition between the implications of the pharmacological studies and the implications of the direct chemical stimulation studies, but the main questions are still unresolved.

In other experiments an interesting family of nonphysiological compounds, unrelated to either acetylcholine or epinephrine, were studied. All members of the family appeared to have special relations to self-stimulation behavior, either augmenting it selectively, or depressing other behaviors and selectively sparing self-stimulation. The compounds were interesting mainly because of their "popularity." Alcohol, for example, was on the list (St. Laurent & Olds, 1967), and the barbiturate compounds which are commonly used as sleeping pills (Olds & Travis, 1960), and also the mild tranquilizers such as meprobromate and chlordiazepoxide, whose trade names are Miltown and Librium (Olds, M. E., 1966). Alcohol was interesting in that doses which completely prostrated a rat were regularly counteracted by stimulation in self-stimulation centers. During the periods of counteraction, the animal had muscle tone, actively self-stimulated for as long as the electrical brain stimulus was available. As soon as the brain stimulus was made unavailable, however, the animal relapsed into a prostrate and atonic posture. During the drugged period, there was no similar arousing effect of aversive stimulation. The other drugs on the list had somewhat different patterns of effect; librium, for example, selectively augmented self-stimulation behavior in doses which slowed other behaviors. However, all these drugs had in common the fact that they selectively favored self-stimulation behavior.

LESION STUDIES

In studies aimed at finding brain areas critically involved in reinforcement, we repeatedly found that the lesions in the lateral hypothalamic fiber bundle impaired or abolished self-stimulation behavior provoked by other electrodes far away but in the same bundle (Olds, J., & Olds, M. E., 1964). And, as I mentioned earlier, lesions in this bundle have been found in other laboratories to abolish feeding and drinking and instrumental avoidance behaviors (Teitelbaum & Epstein, 1962; Balinska, Romaniut, & Wyrwicka, 1964). In fact, animals with bilateral lesions in these areas often died; I believe that the only reason our animals lived was that the lesions were placed only on the stimulated side of the brain, the other half remaining to support necessary feeding and drinking behaviors. In spite of this convergence of evidence, the view that medial forebrain bundle lesions halt self-stimulation and other voluntary behaviors is not generally accepted. This is because of experiments which showed that self-stimulation behavior induced with probes in one of the main anterior, subcortical nuclei of this system survived or recovered when animals had recovered from lateral hypothalamic lesions (Valenstein & Campbell, 1966). Concurring experiments seemed to show that self-stimulation via probes in the lateral hypothalamic bundle itself survived after lesions in other parts of that same bundle (Lorens, 1966). In relation to both of these experiments, my temptation is to speculate that the survival of the animal gave evidence for a recovery of function in some of the fibers of the lateral hypothalamic bundle. It therefore still seems possible to suppose that the lateral hypothalamic bundle is very importantly involved in, and perhaps even essential to, at least some of the positive reinforcement mechanisms. In spite of this confidence, I have no good idea yet which pathways out of this bundle toward other parts of the brain are important in mediating the various successive stages of the reinforcement process which stand between the brain stimulus in self-stimulation experiments and the organized behavioral output of the whole animal.

A set of recently reported experiments (Boyd & Gardner, 1967) suggested that there are three significant pathways passing out of the hypothalamus, one caudal through the midbrain, one frontward toward the rhinencephalon or neocortex, and one directly upward toward the thalamus. Lesions in any of these three caused marked attenuation but not total abnegation of hypothalamic self-stimulation behavior. These observations were most harmonious with the view that there are several different areas in the brain where reward traces might be stored or might cause critical neural events in behavior modification, and that all of these areas might function simultaneously and redundantly, providing perhaps a safety factor.

ELECTROPHYSIOLOGICAL STUDIES

Electrophysiological studies of the brain during rewarding brain stimulation and during the interstimulus intervals may also be expected to suggest which neural systems are primarily and secondarily involved. The first recording studies (Porter, Conrad, & Brady, 1959) were directed at the question of seizures. When probes were planted in some areas, self-stimulation was either accompanied or followed by abnormal electrical events which suggested that the behavior might be part of a seizure, or that the animal might be working as if the brain seizure were itself a goal. Later studies showed that drugs which prevented seizures caused improvement of self-stimulation (Reid, Gibson, Gledhill, & Porter, 1964), and that the highest rates of self-stimulation were obtained when probes were placed in areas where seizures were never provoked (Bogacz, St. Laurent, & Olds, 1964).

With a view to working out a different method which might demonstrate appropriate relations between "reward centers" and other parts of the brain, we have carried out a series of experiments in which we have tried to reward the animal for "making responses with its brain" (Olds, J., & Olds, M. E., 1961). In the first experiments the animal was anesthetized. The "reward" was an electrical brain stimulus applied by means of a probe shown by pretest to be in the appropriate areas of the lateral hypothalamus. In many cases, an apparently positive outcome of the experiment occurred as an artifact. The hypothalamic brain stimulation counteracted the barbiturate anesthesia which was used, thereby causing all neurons to fire more often. One way to surmout this problem was to correlate the reinforcing stimulus with rate reductions rather than rate increments. A second way was to record simultaneously from two neurons so that one could be used as a "wrong response" which, being unreinforced, would not increase in frequency to the degree shown by the reinforced response. A third method was to utilize a paralyzing agent such as curare rather than an anesthetizing agent such as a barbiturate. In the experiments along these three lines, it was found that rarely were neurons slowed by "rewarding" the animal for a slowing of neuron responses. In some experiments in which two neuron responses were recorded simultaneously by means of adjacent probes, it was possible to modify rates of neighboring neurons differentially by applying the brain stimulus first after active spiking exhibited by one of them, and later after similar spiking exhibited by the other (Olds, J., & Olds, M. E., 1964). More experimenting would have been required to make the results meaningful, and yet so many experiments had to be carried out to permit the observation of one positive case that the method was dropped because it was considered unfruitful.

Supposing that an animal that was neither anesthetized nor paralyzed with curare would be more capable of "voluntary" behavior, further experiments were carried out in freely behaving animals with chronically implanted microelectrodes (Olds, 1965, 1967). The operant response required was first that the animal stand quite still. While standing still the animal had to generate a patterned response of neuron action potentials. While several kinds of patterns were used in preliminary tests, it was in the end found most fruitful to require a high frequency pattern. Usually one of such high frequency was selected that it occurred only about once every fifteen minutes on a chance basis. Positive results in this experiment were all too frequent. Animals, it turned out, could stand still and during the quiet period maintain a heightened pattern of activity in many different neurons. It quickly became apparent that from the animal's viewpoint the responses being reinforced showed a great range, including the adoption of certain postures or certain orientation, and that quite often the response observed in the brain resulted from sensory feedback from these responses.

Some neuron responses which were derived from the hippocampus appeared to be modifiable with special ease in these experiments, even in cases where there was no obvious conditioning of a posture, orientation response, or low amplitude movement. There was not a sufficient canvass of other points in the brain to make it clear that the hippocampus had any monopoly on conditionable responses of this type. Exploration was not made in the neocortex, nor was there any careful exploration of the thalamus. Nevertheless, it is appealing to suppose that in some cases the changed rate was caused by a local "reinforcement" process in the hippocampus.

For lack of space I will not at this point go into special problems which arose in some of these experiments or into the operant and Pavlovian conditioning experiments that were done to clarify these problems. I will say that it now seems to me that while some hippocampal neurons appear to be under voluntary or operant control, others seem to be involved in representations (or anticipatory representations) of goal objects and still others behave as if they might be incorporated into temporary memory traces related to highly significant situations.

The organization of these three kinds of neurons into the beautiful gridlike structure of the hippocampus has made it an object of intensive study in our quest for an understanding of the mechanisms of reinforcement. The hope for success is fostered by the fact that stimulation of one of the main input pathways, and stimulation within the hippocampus itself, yields some rewarding effects. The hippocampus would not need to be the only home of a reinforcing mechanism to be an interesting focal point for these studies.

CURRENT BELIEFS AND THEORIES

Behavioral observation suggests that there are visceral rewards and sensory rewards, innate rewards and learned rewards, simple rewards and "organizational" rewards, rewards which are mainly related to drive reductions and others which are mainly related to emotional increments. All of these differences might account to some degree for the numerous areas where stimulation induces rewarding effects and for the different kinds of self-stimulation behavior obtained from different parts of the self-stimulation system. Because of the apparent focal point for self-stimulation in the posterior hypothalamus, I believe there is to some degree a confluence of the messages arising from diverse "rewards," a confluence upon one *or several different* final common control pathways. A final common pathway would derive and represent the algebraic sum of the motivational states of the animal at a given point in time and would bring this to bear on future behavioral possibilities. It would do this by means of learning mechanisms. Perhaps there would be one kind of learning mechanism in the cerebellum, another kind in the tectum, a different kind in the paleocortex or hippocampus, and still another sort in the neocortex.

As for the workings of these learning mechanisms, there are at least two respectable candidate theories for the explanation of the effect of rewards on behavior. One is the theory that rewards fix or stamp in stimulus response connections so that when the stimuli are presented again later there is more tendency for them to evoke the responses involved. It is as if the afferent and efferent of a synaptic relation, having discharged in the proper order, created a momentary trace which could then be fixed in a more permanent form by the immediately subsequent application of a reward stimulus. Interestingly, the concept, if turned naively into anatomy, requires a three-cross grid. That is, quite a large set of stimulus neurons would need to cross quite a large set of response neurons and then somehow a set of reward neurons would need to be in a position to reinforce all the synapses between stimulus and response elements.

The other theory is that the animal makes a recording of successive experiences in terms of their stimulus, response, and reinforcement components. Anatomically this theory implies a simpler grid, even though the information processing which occurs at the time of behavior is more complicated. A double-cross grid in which all stimulus, response, and motivational elements crossed in one direction, and memory elements crossed in the other, would suffice.

The brain contains many elegant, neuroanatomical grids. There is a three-cross grid in the cerebellum, and there are double-cross grids in the oldest and best-organized part of the cortex, which is the hippocampus. I cannot see any reason why both theories about reinforcement could not be true: one would be mainly involved in the learning of skilled motor movements and might in fact be carried out to some degree in the cerebellum; the other would be mainly involved in the memories of place-to-place behaviors and would have more to do with organizing planned and purposeful behaviors.

In the hippocampus the best-organized grid appears between the "dentate gyrus's mossy fibers" and the large pyramidal cells of the "CA-4 and CA-3 fields." In any given slice of the hippocampus (and there are many slices stacked like phonograph records) all of the mossy fibers appear to cross and synapse with all of the large CA-4 and CA-3 pyramidal neurons. The organization and appearance is quite similar to that in which the information channels cross the memory elements in the random access memory of a normal digital computer. The synapses involved are extremely complicated: very large endings emerge from the mossy fibers and are applied to specialized dendrites of the CA-4 and CA-3 neurons. What if these were modifiable, that is, resettable, synapses? In such a case the stimulus environment might be coded and transmitted as a pattern of firing in the mossy fibers. Successive pyramidal neurons in the CA-4 and CA-3 fields might then function as recording devices, recording successive experiences on the dendritic arborizations of successive neurons. A particular pattern of sensory input would reactivate the appropriate neurons (memories).

In order to have consequences the memory neurons would have to then reactivate the appropriate behaviors; and a single grid is not enough to get behavior. Because of the unidirectionality of neurons, it would be necessary for the motor and motivational aspects of the memory to be recorded, not along the dendrites of the memory elements (where they could never be activated by the memories), but rather along the axons of the memory elements. Interestingly, in the hippocampus a second grid exists in which the many axons of CA-3 and CA-4 neurons cross through the many dendrites of CA-1 elements. With the proviso of this second grid, a given CA-3 or CA-4 element could make a recording along its dendrites of the sensory code, and along its axon of the motor and motivational patterns which were correlated with a given experience.

The system might then function to a large degree like the random access memory of a computer. Recurrent experiences would reactivate appropriately matching memory elements, which would reactivate a string of successors. An appropriate motivational pattern recorded on a successor would cause the behavioral patterns "recorded" on the string of elements between the matching and the motivational memory to be converted into real behavior.

Of course, if memories were correlated in this way with individual neurons, there would not be enough elements for a very long string of memories; probably only enough for days or weeks, but not enough for the life of an animal. Therefore, if this kind of memory storage occurred in the hippocampus, it could only be of a very temporary nature. Interestingly, this speculation concurs with a growing body of evidence about the relations of the hippocampus to the temporary memory storage processes of the animal.

SUMMARY

An accidental observation led to the self-stimulation studies. The observation was not itself instigated by any self-conscious plan based on the theories surrounding us at the time. Subsequent behavioral investigations indicated that we were not fooled, that this was a psychologically valid reward. These studies also permitted us to suppose that this was an artificial activation of the brain's natural reinforcement mechanism, but this is still not proved. The "olfactory and chemoreceptive" nature of the stimulated tissues pointed to a possible relation of self-stimulation to homing reactions and hormones. The reward and punishment studies suggested negative interactions and a common pathway between two emotional mechanisms. The drive studies confirmed the strong relation of the phenomenon to the basic drives (supporting the view that real reward mechanisms were involved) and also suggested that a "drive" such as hunger might be a complex of (1) positive feedback, appetitive patterns, (2) negative "satiety" and "starvation" mechanisms for instigating or terminating the appetitive behavior, and (3) control mechanisms involved mainly with integrating the behaviors. Drug studies offered a contradiction between ideas generated by "intraperitoneal" studies and those generated by "intracerebral" studies of related drugs (the contradiction was particularly acute in relation to adrenergic and cholinergic compounds). The drug studies also indicated a positive relation between self-stimulation and certain "popular" drugs such as alcohol. Lesion studies emphasized first that we *do not yet even know where the somata of the self-stimulation neurons are* (as we stimulated mainly fibers), and second that projections in several directions from the self-stimulation point seem to mediate portions of the total self-stimulation behavior. Neurophysiological studies did not support the view that epileptiform effects caused by brain stimulation were likely at the root of self-stimulation. These studies did indicate that the hippocampus was an interesting focal point of electrical activity during behavioral learning and reinforcement.

The set of studies taken together triggered thoughts but did little to constrain them. Two viable theories of reinforcement (patterned after those of Hull and Toman) and others still to be evolved could be instantiated in the brain at the same time, one in the cerebellum involved mainly with the learning of skills and another in the hippocampus involved mainly with short-run purposeful actions.

REFERENCES

Anand, B., and Brobeck, J. R. Hypothalamic control of food intake in rats and cats. *Yale J. Biol. Med.*, 1951, **24**, 123–140.
Balinska, M., Romaniut, A., and Wyrwicka, W. Impairment of conditioned defensive reactions following lesions of the lateral hypothalamus in rabbit. *Acta Biol. Exper.*, 1964, **24**, 89–97.
Bishop, M. P., Elder, S. T., and Heath, R. G. Intracranial self-stimulation in man. *Science*, 1963, **140**, 394–396.
Bogacz, J., St. Laurent, J., and Olds, J. Dissociation of self-stimulation and epileptiform activity. *Electroenceph. clin. Neurophysiol.*, 1965, **19**, 75–87.
Boyd, E., and Gardner, L. Positive and negative reinforcement from in-

tracranial self-stimulation in teleosts. *Science,* 1962, **136,** 648.

Boyd, E. S., and Gardner, L. C. Effect of some brain lesions on intracranial self-stimulation in the rat. *Amer. J. Physiol.,* 1967, **213,** 1044–1052.

Brobeck, J. R. Mechanisms of the development of obesity in animals with hypothalamic lesions. *Physiol. Rev.,* 1946, **26,** 541–559.

Bruner, A. Self-stimulation in the rabbit: An anatomical map of stimulation effects. *J. comp. Neurol.,* 1967, **131,** 615–629.

Bursten, B., and Delgado, J. M. R. Positive reinforcement induced by intracranial stimulation in the monkey. *J. comp. physiol. Psychol.,* 1958, **51,** 6–10.

Caggiula, A. R., and Hoebel, B. G. "Copulation-reward site" in the posterior hypothalamus. *Science,* 1966, **153,** 1284–1285.

Delgado, J. M. R. Permanent implantation of multilead electrodes in the brain. *Yale J. Biol. Med.,* 1952, **24,** 351–358.

Delgado, J. M. R., Roberts, W. W., and Miller, N. E. Learning motivated by electrical stimulation of the brain. *Amer. J. Physiol.,* 1954, **179,** 587–593.

Deutsch, J. A., and Howarth, C. I. Some tests of a theory of intracranial self-stimulation. *Psych. Rev.,* 1963, **70,** 444–460.

Gallistel, C. R. Electric self-stimulation and its theoretical implications. *Psychol. Bull.,* 1964, **61,** 23–34.

Grossman, S. P. Eating or drinking elicited by direct adrenergic or cholinergic stimulation of hypothalamus. *Science,* 1960, **132,** 301–302.

Hebb, D. O. *The organization of behavior: A neuropsychological theory.* New York: Wiley, 1949.

Hess, W. R. *Die funktionelle Organisation des Vegativen Nervensystems.* Basel: Beno Schwabe and Co., 1948.

Hoebel, B. G., and Teitelbaum, P. Hypothalamic control of feeding and self-stimulation. *Science,* 1962, **135,** 375–377.

Jasper, H. H. Diffuse projection systems: The integrative action of the thalamic reticular system. *EEG clin. Neurophysiol.,* 1949, **1,** 405–419.

Kluver, H., and Bucy, P. C. Psychic blindness and other symptoms following bilateral temporal lobectomy in rhesus monkey. *Amer. J. Physiol.,* 1937, **119,** 352–353.

Knott, P. D., and Clayton, K. N. Durable secondary reinforcement using brain stimulation as the primary reinforcer. *J. comp. physiol. Psych.,* 1966, **61,** 151–153.

Koenig, I. D. V. The reinforcement value of intracranial stimulation and its interaction with arousal level. Unpublished doctoral dissertation, Univ. of Toronto, 1967. Cited in D. E. Berlyne, Arousal and reinforcement. In David Levine (Ed.), *Nebraska Symposium on Motivation,* 1967, 1–110.

Krasne, F. B. General disruption resulting from electrical stimulus of ventromedial hypothalamus. *Science,* 1962, **138,** 822–823.

Lilly, J. C., and Miller, A. M. Operant conditioning of the bottlenose dolphin with electrical stimulation of the brain. *J. comp. physiol. Psychol.,* 1962, **55,** 73–79.

Lindsley, D. B. Emotion. In S. S. Stevens (Ed.), *Handbook of experimental psychology.* New York: Wiley, 1951.

Lorens, S. A. Effect of lesions in the central nervous system on lateral hypothalamic self-stimulation in the rat. *J. comp. physiol. Psychol.,* 1966, **62,** 256–262.

Magoun, H. W. Caudal and cephalic influences of the brainstem reticular formation. *Physiol., Rev.,* 1950, **30,** 459–474.

Margules, D. L., and Olds, J. Identical "feeding" and "rewarding" systems in the lateral hypothalamus of rats. *Science,* 1962, **135,** 374–375.

Miller, N. E. Central stimulation and other new approaches to motivation and reward. *Amer. Psychol.,* 1958, **13,** 100–108.

Miller, N. E. Motivational effects of brain stimulation and drugs. *Fed. Proc.,* 1960, **19,** 846–854.

Mogenson, G. J., and Stevenson, J. A. F. Drinking and self-stimulation with electrical stimulation of the lateral hypothalamus. *Phys. and Behav.,* 1966, **1,** 251–254.

Moruzzi, G., and Magoun, H. W. Brainstem reticular formation and activation of the EEG. *Electroenceph. clin. Neurophysiol.,* 1949, **1,** 455–473.

Olds, J. A preliminary mapping of electric reinforcing effects in the rat brain. *J. comp. physiol. Psychol.,* 1956, **49,** 281–285.

Olds, J. Differential effects of drives and drugs on self-stimulation at different brain sites. In D. E. Sheer (Ed.), *Electrical Stimulation of the Brain.* Austin: Univ. of Texas Press, 1961.

Olds, J. Operant conditioning of single unit responses. Excerpta Medica International Congress Series No. 87. *Proceedings of the XXIII International Congress of Physiological Sciences,* Tokyo, 1965, 372–380.

Olds, J. The limbic system and behavioral reinforcement. In W. R. Adey and T. Tokozane (Eds.), *Progress in Brain Research: (Structure and Function of the Limbic System).* Amsterdam: Elsevier Publishing Co., 1967, **27,** 143–164.

Olds, J., and Milner, P. Positive reinforcement produced by electrical stimulation of septal area and other regions of rat brain. *J. comp. physiol. Psychol.,* 1954, **47,** 419–427.

Olds, J., and Olds, M. E. Interference and learning in paleocortical systems. In J. F. Delafresnaye (Ed.), *Brain mechanisms and learning.* Oxford: Blackwell Scientific Publications, 1961. Pp. 350–366.

Olds, J., and Olds, M. E. The mechanisms of voluntary behavior. In R. G. Heath (Ed.) *The role of pleasure in behavior.* New York: Hoeber Medical Division, Harper & Row, Publishers, 1964. Pp. 23–53.

Olds, J., and Travis, R. P. Effects of chlorpromazine, meprobamate, pentobarbital, and morphine on self-stimulation. *J. Pharmacol. Exp. Therap.,* 1960, **128,** 397–404.

Olds, J., Travis, R. P., and Schwing, R. C. Topographic organization of hypothalamic self-stimulation functions. *J. comp. physiol. Psychol.,* 1960, **53,** 23–32.

Olds, J., Yuwiler, A., Olds, M. E., and Yun, C. Neurohumors in hypothalamic substrates of reward. *Amer. J. Physiol.,* 1964, **207,** 242–254.

Olds, M. E. Facilitatory action of diazepam and chlordiazepoxide on hypothalamic reward behavior. *J. comp. physiol. Psychol.,* 1966, **62,** 136–140.

Olds, M. E., and Olds, J. Approach-escape interactions in rat brain. *Amer. J. Physiol.,* 1962, **203,** 803–810.

Olds, M. E., and Olds, J. Approach-avoidance analysis of rat diencephalon. *J. comp. Neurol.,* 1963, **120,** 259–295.

Papez, J. W. A proposed mechanism of emotion. *A. M. A. Neurol. Psychiat.,* 1937, **38**, 725–743.

Pliskoff, S. S., Wright, J. E., and Hawkins, D. T. Brain stimulation as a reinforcer: Intermittent schedules. *J. exp. Anal. Behav.,* 1965, **8**, 75–88.

Porter, R. W., Conrad, D., and Brady, J. V. Some neural and behavioral correlates of electrical self-stimulation in the limbic system. *J. Exptl. Anal. Behav.,* 1959, **2**, 43–55.

Poschel, P. H., and Ninteman, F. W. Norepinephrine: A possible excitatory neurohormone of the reward system. *Life Sci.,* 1963, **10**, 782–788.

Reid, L. D., Gibson, W. E., Gledhill, S. M., and Porter, P. B. Anticonvulsant drugs and self-stimulating behavior. *J. comp. physiol. Psychol.,* 1964, **57**, 353–356.

Roberts, W. W. Both rewarding and punishing effects from stimulation of posterior hypothalamus of cat with same electrode at same intensity. *J. comp. physiol. Psychol.,* 1958, **51**, 400–407.

Routtenberg, A., and Lindy, J. Effects of the availability of rewarding septal and hypothalamic stimulation on bar-pressing for food under conditions of deprivation. *J. comp. physiol. Psychol.,* 1965, **60**, 158–161.

Routtenberg, A., and Olds, J. The attenuation of response to an aversive brain stimulus by concurrent rewarding septal stimulation. *Fed. Proc.,* 1963, **22** (No. 2, Part I), 515 (abstract).

St. Laurent, J., and Olds, J. Alcohol and brain centers of positive reinforcement. In Ruth Fox (Ed.), *Alcoholism—behavioral research, therapeutic approaches.* New York: Springer Publishing Co., 1967. Pp. 80–101.

Scott, J. W. Brain stimulation reinforcement with distributed practice: Effects of electrode locus, previous experience, and stimulus intensity. *J. comp. physiol. Psychol.,* 1967, **63**, 175–183.

Stark, P., and Boyd, E. S. Effects of cholinergic drugs on hypothalamic self-stimulation response rates of dogs. *Amer. J. Physiol.,* 1963, **205**, 745–748.

Stein, L. Secondary reinforcement established with subcortical stimulation. *Science,* 1958, **127**, 466–467.

Stein, L. Amphetamine and neural reward mechanisms. In H. Steinberg, A. V. S. deReuck and J. Knight (Eds.), *Animal behavior and drug action.* Ciba Foundation Symposium, 1964. Boston: Little, Brown and Co., 1964. Pp. 91–113.

Stellar, E. The physiology of motivation. *Psychol. Rev.,* 1954, **61**, 5–22.

Teitelbaum, P., and Epstein, A. The lateral hypothalamic syndrome: Recovery of feeding and drinking after lateral hypothalamic lesions. *Psychol. Rev.,* 1962, **69**, 74–90.

Valenstein, E. S., and Campbell, J. F. Medial forebrain bundle-lateral hypothalamic area and reinforcing brain stimulation. *Amer. J. Physiol.,* 1966, **210**, 270–274.

Wetzel, M. C. Self-stimulation after-effects and runway performance in the rat. *J. comp. physiol. Psychol.,* 1963, **56**, 673–678.

Wilkinson, H. A., and Peele, T. L. Intracranial self-stimulation in cats. *J. comp. Neurol.,* 1963, **121**, 425–550.

Wyrwicka, W., and Dobrzecka, C. Relationship between feeding and satiation centers of the hypothalamus. *Science,* 1960, **132**, 805–806.

Direct Adrenergic and Cholinergic Stimulation of Hypothalamic Mechanisms[1, 2]

S. P. GROSSMAN

Department of Psychology, Yale University

The selective sensitivity of neural tissue to a variety of chemical agents has been known for some time. Chemical mediation of neural transmission in the peripheral nervous system has been firmly established, and the manifold effects which peripherally active neurohumors exert in the central nervous system have been attributed to a similar "transmitter" action. The evidence for this interpretation is at present largely inferential, and the possibility of neurochemical "coding" of functional systems, i.e., the differential sensitivity of neural elements to specific chemical substances, requires further study.

In the present series of experiments an attempt was made to approach this problem by investigating the behavioral effects of the peripherally active neurohumors, acetylcholine and norepinephrine, applied directly to an area of the hypothalamus that appears to contain neural elements active in the control of both food and water intake.

The choice of these agents was determined by a number of factors. Both have transmitter properties at peripheral synapses and are known to be distributed nonrandomly within the central nervous system, along with enzymes for their synthesis and destruction. The temporal relationships between the release and destruction of these humors meet the criteria for chemical mediators, and both have been shown to exert a great variety of central effects. Facilitory as well as inhibitory actions have been reported for both drugs at all levels of the neuraxis, the direction of the effects varying among different systems (Feldberg & Vogt, 1948; Vogt, 1957; Rothballer, 1959).

1. This study was supported by Public Health Service grants MY 647 and MY 2949. This paper is based on a dissertation presented to the Graduate School of Yale University in partial fulfillment of the requirements for the degree of Doctor of Philosophy; a preliminary report of the initial findings has been published *(Science, 132: 301, 1960).*
2. This research was undertaken during the tenure of a Public Health Service Predoctoral Research Fellowship.

The author expresses thanks to Dr. N. E. Miller for his continued guidance and support, and to Drs. J. P. Flynn, D. X. Freedman, and N. Giarman, whose constructive criticism and advice have greatly benefitted this project.

"Direct Adrenergic and Cholinergic Stimulation of Hypothalamic Mechanisms," by S. P. Grossman, from *American Journal of Physiology,* **202** (5), 1962, 872–882. Reprinted by permission.

The area chosen for this investigation is in the lateral hypothalamus, at the level of the ventromedial nuclei. Bilateral ablation of this region produces complete, although perhaps not permanent, aphagia in a variety of species (Anand & Brobeck, 1951a, 1951b; Teitelbaum & Stellar, 1954), whereas electrical stimulation (Bruegger, 1943; Delgado & Anand, 1953) or perfusion with hypertonic solutions (Larsson, 1955; Epstein, 1960) elicits eating in satiated animals. Miller (1957, 1960) has shown that the behavior evoked by electrical stimulation of this region appears to have many of the motivational properties of normal hunger.

Bilateral lesions in, or very close to, this area have also produced complete and permanent adipsia (Stevenson, Welt, & Orloff, 1950; Montemurro & Stevenson, 1938) and electrical stimulation (Anderson & McCann, 1955a, 1955b) as well as perfusion with hypertonic solutions (Anderson & McCann, 1955a, 1955b; Anderson, 1953) has been reported to elicit drinking in satiated animals. Ablation (Teitelbaum & Stellar, 1954) as well as electrical stimulation of this region (Bruegger, 1943; Delgado & Anand, 1953; Miller, 1960) frequently modifies both eating and drinking behavior.

These results suggest that this region of the hypothalamus contains neural elements active in the control of both food and water intake, but do not prove conclusively that the observed effects are results of the destruction or stimulation of localized cell concentrations rather than of fiber tracts which merely pass through this region.

Chemical stimulation of central structures by means of microinjections of chemicals in solution has been employed by a number of investigators. The interpretation of the experimental results that have been obtained with this technique is complicated, however, by the problem of excessive and uncontrolled diffusion. MacLean (1957a, 1957b) has shown that the use of chemicals in crystalline form minimizes spread and thus allows one to localize the affected neural elements more precisely, but this technique has not allowed repeated stimulation of a selected locus in a chronic animal because the guide provided for the stimulation implant did not penetrate into the brain itself. In the present study a double-walled cannula was developed that avoids this objection.

METHODS

Subjects

Thirty-six experimentally naive, male albino rats of the Sprague-Dawley strain (Holtzman Co., Madison, Wis.), approximately 90–120 days old at the time of the operation, were used. The animals were maintained on ad libitum food (Purina laboratory checkers) and water throughout the experiment. The same food and water were removed from the home cages and used for the test periods. Daily food and water consumption records were maintained.

Procedure

The general procedure of operation, testing, and histological verification remained constant in all experiments and will be summarized at this point.

Procedural variations, specific to a given experiment, will be discussed in the Results section of the particular study.

Construction of the Implant. The double-walled cannula, which was implanted in all animals, consisted of two modified syringe needles. The outer cannula was constructed of a standard no. 21 stainless steel syringe needle, the hub of which had been reduced on a lathe to an outside diameter of approximately 2.5 mm and a total length of approximately 5 mm and was threaded on the inside. The inner cannula was made of a standard no. 27 stainless steel needle, the hub of which was turned down to a 1.5 mm outside diameter and was threaded on the outside so as to screw into the outer cannula.

The needles were then cut so that the length of the cannulas themselves, i.e., exclusive of the hub, corresponded to the desired vertical stereotaxic coordinates. When tightly screwed together the tips of the two cannulas were flush with each other, and the hub of the inner needle protruded about 3–4 mm above that of the outer cannula. . . .

Operative Procedure. The double-walled cannula was implanted under Nembutal anesthesia (40 mg/kg) with a Johnson stereotaxic instrument into the hypothalamus of 36 albino rats, each of which weighed approximately 250–300 g at operation.

The design of this implant allowed the entire shaft of the cannulas to disappear below the skull, leaving only the reduced hub of the needle to protrude above the bone. Around this hub approximately 5–8 mm of dental cement were built up to secure the implant to the skull. . . .

Histology. All animals were sacrificed under heavy Nembutal anesthesia (60 mg/kg) and perfused with a 10 percent formalin solution. Since the tracts of the implants nearly reached the bottom of the brain, it was more convenient to cut the brain at an angle to the implant. Fifty-micron frozen sections were taken, and one of every group of three successive sections were selected at random for staining with Luxol blue and cresyl violet, according to a staining technique developed by Klüver and Barrera (1953).

Testing Procedure. In each separate experiment within a series of studies, successive treatments were administered in a counterbalanced sequence by means of a latin-square design. This variation of the complete factorial design systematically varies the order of drug administrations between subjects. Since the order of successive treatments is different for each animal, artifacts due to a possible interaction of drugs can be statistically assessed, and their effect on the combined results from a group of subjects is minimized.

There was a 24-hr interval between successive injections. This intertreatment interval was increased whenever there was reason to suspect a more prolonged effect of the experimental manipulation. In all but the first experiment, the animals were maintained and tested in a constant, temperature- and humidity-controlled environment.

To establish a control level separately for each experiment, the animals were sham stimulated (i.e., the inner cannula was removed, cleaned, and replaced as during chemical stimulation), and were then placed in the testing apparatus for 1 hr immediately before each experiment. All tests were conducted in the morning or early afternoon. None of the rats consumed measurable quantities (.5 g or 1 cc) of either food or water during any one of the prestimulation control periods, and additional control data on the intake of unstimulated animals indicate that both food and water consumption remained essentially zero throughout the morning and early afternoon. The control level for all effects is therefore virtually zero and is omitted from all figures.

For the purpose of stimulation, the inner cannula was unscrewed and cleaned in order to remove the .1–.2 mm crust of dried tissue fluid which formed at the tip of the inner cannula in the course of the intertreatment interval. Minute amounts (1–5 µg) of crystalline chemicals were then tapped into its tip before returning it to its usual position. The drug was then allowed to diffuse out of the cannula in order to avoid unnecessary tissue damage which would result from pushing the chemical out of the cannula by means of a stylus. Control data, obtained by microscopic analysis of the inner cannula, indicate that the minute amounts used in these studies diffused out of the cannula completely within 4–5 min, which corresponds fairly well to the latencies of the observed behavioral effects.

The quantities thus "injected" were estimated on the basis of both weight and volume (the height of the column of chemical inside the cannula). Variations in the molecular structure of the different chemical agents were not controlled. Although only relatively gross dose-response relationships could be obtained with this technique, it appeared suitable for the present purpose, since the effects observed in these experiments were reliably reproducible at relatively constant levels of magnitude in spite of slight variations in amount of stimulation. Since the concentration of the chemical at the tip of the inner cannula is always maximal, regardless of dosage, adding to the quantity of chemical inside this needle can only increase the extent of effective spread or prolong the duration of stimulation at a given site.

For all drugs used in the present series of experiments, an attempt was made to investigate gross dose-response relationships to ascertain: (a) the minimal dose required for the elicitation of some overt behavioral response (i.e., eating, drinking, changes in general activity, etc.); (b) the maximal dose tolerated (without evoking gross behavioral changes such as motor seizures or coma); and (c) the optimal dose for the elicitation of feeding or drinking behavior. Special care was exercised to vary the dosages of all control substances over a sufficient range to assure, within the limitations of the available techniques, that the observed failure of these agents to induce reliable food or water intake was not merely a function of dosage differences.

For the control and test periods the same food and water that were always available in the animals' home cages were transferred to the test boxes. Food intake was recorded by weighing the total amount of food in the test cages before and after a period of observation. Food lost through spillage was deducted from the total. Water intake was recorded by direct readings from graduated cylinders. The standard observation period in the present series of studies was 1 hr. The animals were tested when food and water satiated, but no special effort was made to obtain "super satiation" by special feeding schedules. . . .

RESULTS

Experiment 1

Double-walled cannulas were implanted in six albino rats with stereotaxic coordinates, from which Miller (1957, 1960) had obtained eating or drinking in response to electrical stimulation.

Three of these rats, with closely adjacent implant placements, showed a clear though relatively brief effect of the injection of crystalline acetylcholine chloride, vigorous drinking beginning 4–8 min after stimulation. This effect was greatly prolonged by the addition of small amounts of physostigmine sulfate, a cholinesterase inhibitor, to the injected acetylcholine. Control injections of equally minute amounts of physostigmine alone did not have a clear effect on water intake, suggesting that the dose was insufficient to inhibit enough cholinesterase to allow the accumulation of acetylcholine in concentrations adequate for stimulation of this system.

Since the drinking effect appeared to be limited primarily by the rapid rate of destruction of acetylcholine, carbamylcholine chloride (carbachol), a powerful parasympathomimetic agent which is not hydrolyzed by cholinesterase, was used with the expected result of greatly lengthening the drinking effect.

The injection of crystalline *l*-epinephrine bitartrate into the same loci in the same animals which had shown the cholinergic drinking effect produced a clear and prolonged eating effect which began after similar latencies. Levarterenol bitartrate (*l*-norepinephrine) produced an even more sustained and intense eating effect after comparable latencies.

Control for Nonspecific Activation. In order to control for the possibility of a general, nonspecific excitation of the neural elements in contact with the stimulating substances, strychnine sulfate was deposited in the hypothalamus of all animals.

A wide range of dosages, exceeding those used for the adrenergic and cholinergic substances, failed to elicit any overt behavioral changes, and no effect on subsequent food or water intake was recorded for either the standard 1-hr poststimulation period or the following 23-hr period. . . .

Experiment 2

Double-walled cannulas were implanted in 12 albino rats at constant coordinates derived from the results of the preceding study. The results of this experiment are summarized in Figure 1.

Effects of Adrenergic Stimulation. All the animals operated in the present study showed a reliable ($p < .0001$) eating effect after the injection of crystalline epinephrine, food consumption beginning 5–10 min after central stimulation and persisting with variable intensity for 20–40 min. The injection of norepinephrine into the same loci in the same 12 animals produced similar, although more persistent and pronounced, effects, beginning after comparable

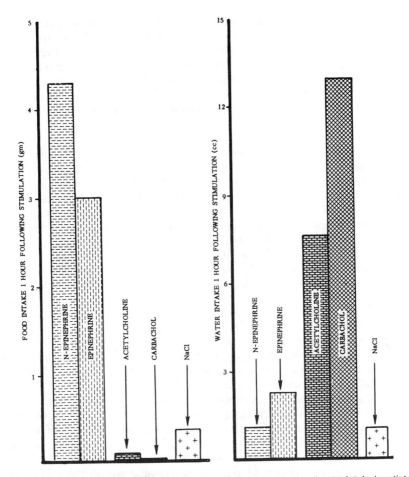

Figure 1. Effects of chemical stimulation of the hypothalamus on food and water intake in satiated animals during a 1-hr poststimulation period.

latencies. Total food consumption averaged 3.0 g after injection of epinephrine and 4.3 g after norepinephrine, with a range of 1.0–6.0 g and 2.0–11.0 g, respectively. This difference between the effects of the two adrenergic agents did not reach statistical significance in the present study, but was reliable ($p <$ .02) when data from seven additional animals (*exp. 3*) were added to the analysis.

Neither epinephrine nor norepinephrine induced drinking reliably, although 4 of the 12 animals tested consumed some water after the injection of epinephrine and 3 drank after norepinephrine. Since this water consumption occurred in all but one animal only near the end of the test period, after a considerable amount of dry food had been eaten, drinking appeared to be secondary to the consumption of dry food rather than a direct effect of the adrenergic stimulation.

In order to test this conclusion and to establish the specificity of the adrenergic effect, norepinephrine was deposited in six animals which had previously shown a pronounced eating effect. These animals were then tested in cages containing only water. For 30 min after norepinephrine stimulation none of the animals consumed any water, although four of them repeatedly approached the drinking tube to gnaw at it. When food was introduced all animals began to eat almost immediately, although total intake was, of course, lower than that normally observed after adrenergic stimulation, since the pellets were introduced into the test cages only toward the end of the period of effective stimulation.

Effects of Cholinergic Stimulation. The injection of acetylcholine (capped by physostigmine) into the identical loci in the same 12 animals which had shown the adrenergic eating effect reliably ($p <$ .001) resulted in drinking in all animals, the latency, duration, and magnitude of the effect being roughly comparable with those observed for eating. Carbachol again showed similar but more persistent and pronounced effects. Total water intake averaged 7.4 cc after injection of acetylcholine and 12.8 cc after injection of carbachol, with a range of 2.0–10.0 cc and 8.0–19.0 cc, respectively. This difference was statistically reliable ($p <$ .001). Neither substance reliably evoked eating in these animals, only one rat eating 1.0 g after injection of acetylcholine.

Dose-Response Relationships. Because of the relative crudeness of the measuring techniques used, only gross dose-response relationships could be investigated. Both adrenergic and cholinergic agents produced reliable and repeatable effects at relatively constant levels of magnitude over a fairly wide range of dosages (1–5 μg). Doses smaller than 1 μg either were not effective at all or produced only small and unreliable effects.

Increasing the amount of adrenergic stimulation beyond the optimal dose of 3–5 μg, either by increasing the quantity of a single injection or by repeating the stimulation before the effects of a previous injection had worn off, reduced or abolished the eating effect, and induced hypoactivity, somnolence, and general refractoriness to any form of sensory stimulation.

Increasing the amount of cholinergic stimulation, on the other hand, produced immediate and pronounced hyperactivity and increased reactivity to sensory stimulation, as well as excessive grooming, licking, and sniffing, followed by slowly developing motor seizures which persisted for 30–50 min. Even when an overdose did not elicit the seizure activity, drinking was strongly reduced or abolished.

That the failure of higher dosages to produce the eating and drinking effects may not be due primarily to these side effects on general activity is suggested by the fact that even relatively small doses (5–8 μg), which evoked only minor changes in overt motor activity, failed to elicit the consummatory behavior.

The significant differences between the effectiveness of carbachol and acetylcholine and of norepinephrine and epinephrine do not appear to be attributable to dosage variations, because an "optimal" dose was established for each drug which was used throughout these experiments.

Long-term Effects. The daily consumption records suggest that the amount of food or water consumed during the 1-hr observation period immediately following chemical stimulation was consumed in addition to the animal's normal daily intake. This conclusion is supported, at least for the adrenergic eating effect, by an increased body weight on the day after stimulation. These effects were not statistically reliable in this experiment due to temperature and humidity fluctuations which caused excessive variability in the data.

Control for Osmotic Stimulation. The results of the present series of studies demonstrate clearly a differential effect of adrenergic and cholinergic stimulation, but do not prove that these effects are due to the sympathomimetic and parasympathomimetic properties of norepinephrine and acetylcholine, respectively, rather than to one or more of the many "side effects" which these drugs are known to produce.

The first question to be raised concerns the effects of osmotic stimulation which occur as a by-product of the injection of hypertonic solutions. To control for this factor, crystalline NaCl, in quantities comparable with those used with the adrenergic and cholinergic substances, was deposited in the same points that had shown the eating and drinking effects. All the animals tested responded to this treatment with varying degrees of hyperactivity, but only 3 of the 12 animals consumed any food or water. Since this effect was so much smaller than those evoked by adrenergic and cholinergic stimulation ($p < .001$) and failed to be specific to either eating or drinking, the factor of osmotic stimulation does not appear to play an important role in the determination of the specific adrenergic and cholinergic effects.

Experiment 3

Replication of Adrenergic and Cholinergic Effects. In the third series of experiments the selective effects of adrenergic and cholinergic stimulation on the eating and drinking mechanisms, respectively, were fully replicated in 11 additional animals. The average magnitude of the effects corresponded very closely to those of the first experiment, the mean values being 4.3 g and 12.8 cc for the first study, and 4.4 g and 12.0 cc for the second. . . .

Long-term Effects. In this second series of studies it was possible to provide constant levels of temperature and humidity by air conditioning. The data summarized in Figure 2 indicate that the total water intake for the 24-hr period immediately following cholinergic stimulation was significantly greater ($p < .001$) than that of a normal control period immediately preceding stimulation. The additional intake was significantly greater ($p < .001$) than the amount consumed during the 1-hr observation period that immediately followed stimulation, and was reliable ($p < .001$) even when the water consumed during that first 1-hr period was deducted from the daily total. Food intake did not appear to be affected either primarily by the cholinergic stimulation or secondarily by the excessive water consumption.

The injection of norepinephrine, on the other hand, showed precisely the opposite effect. Total water consumption during the 24-hr period following adrenergic stimulation was entirely normal in spite of the fact that food intake for this same period showed a highly significant ($p < .001$) increase over the control level. This additional food intake was significantly greater ($p < .001$) than the amount consumed during the 1-hr observation period immediately

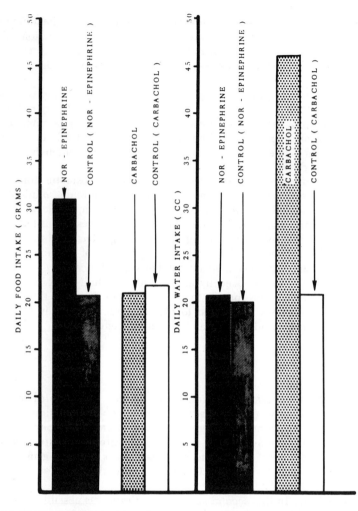

Figure 2. Effects of adrenergic and cholinergic stimulation of the hypothalamus on food and water intake during a 24-hr poststimulation period. Control levels were determined during a 24-hr period preceding each stimulation.
Figure 3. (not reprinted).

following stimulation, and was reliable ($p < .001$) even when the amount eaten during that 1-hr test period was deducted from the total.

Although the conspicuous effects of both adrenergic and cholinergic stimulation appeared to wear off within the 1-hr observation period, a residual differential effect remained, and was reflected in the increased intake during the following 23-hr period. We do not, unfortunately, know how far into the 23-hr period this residual effect extended. Both food and water intake returned to normal during the following 24 hr. . . .

Motivational Qualities of the Stimulation Effects. To investigate the motivational properties of the behavior evoked by chemical stimulation, 11 animals were preoperatively trained to press one bar for food and another for water on different reinforcement schedules, with variable intervals averaging one reward per 30 sec. The test situation required a spatial discrimination between the two bars that were mounted side by side on one end of an operant conditioning apparatus.

The results of the postoperative tests are summarized in Figure 4. The injection of norepinephrine in satiated animals resulted in a highly significant ($p < .001$) increase in the rate of bar-pressing for food without reliably raising the level of performance on the water bar above the prestimulation control level.

Cholinergic stimulation, on the other hand, resulted in a reliable ($p < .001$) increment of performance on the water bar without significantly increasing the number of bar presses for food.

Effects of Chemical Stimulation on Normal Hunger and Thirst. To secure evidence on the possible central interaction between the two drives, norepine-

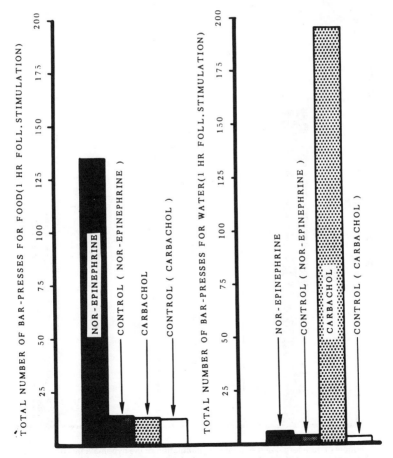

Figure 4. Effects of adrenergic and cholinergic stimulation of the hypothalamus of satiated rats on rate of bar-pressing for food and water rewards on a 30-sec variable-interval schedule. Control levels were determined during a 1-hr period preceding each stimulation.

phrine and carbachol were injected in 24-hr food- or water-deprived animals. Figure 5 summarizes the results of the complete design.

Rats which had been fasted for 24 hr and made "thirsty" by the injection of carbachol ate little or no food during a 30-min observation period without water, beginning 10 min after stimulation. Only 3 of the 11 animals tested consumed any food at all after cholinergic stimulation. The difference between the control intake and that following the injection of carbachol was highly significant ($p < .001$).

Similarly, animals deprived of water for 24 hr drank little or no water when made "hungry" by the injection of norepinephrine. Although 8 of the 11 animals tested drank some water after adrenergic stimulation, the average water intake was significantly smaller ($p < .01$) than that of a control test. Only water was available in both tests.

When "24-hr-hungry" rats were made more hungry by the injection of norepinephrine, they ate significantly more food ($p < .001$) than they did during the control period. When "24-hr-thirsty" animals were made more

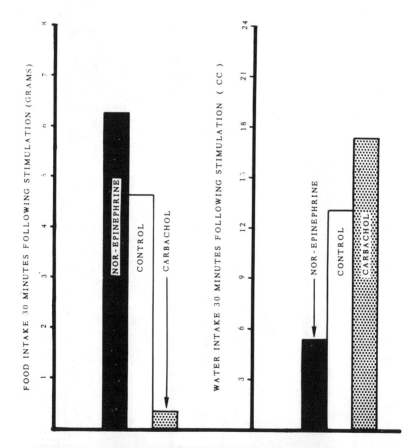

Figure 5. Effects of adrenergic and cholinergic stimulation of the hypothalamus on food and water intake of 24-hr food- or water-deprived animals, during a 30-min observation period beginning 10 min after stimulation. Control levels were determined on a preceding control test without central stimulation.

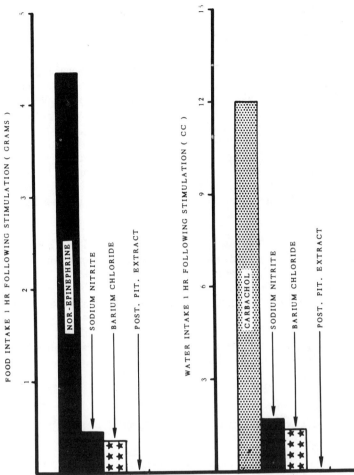

Figure 6. Effects of centrally administered vasodilator and vasoconstrictor agents on food and water intake in satiated animals during a 1-hr poststimulation period, compared with effects of adrenergic and cholinergic stimulation of the same points on a preceding control test.

thirsty by the injection of carbachol, they drank significantly more water ($p <$ .001) than they did during the control period.

Control for Vasomotor Effects. Both adrenergic and cholinergic substances are known to have pronounced effects on the vascular system which might excite or inhibit neighboring neural tissue. To control for this factor, sodium nitrite and barium chloride, powerful vasodilator agents, and posterior pituitary extract, a vasoconstrictor, were applied locally to all animals in a counterbalanced sequence in quantities comparable with those used with the adrenergic and cholinergic drugs.

That the epinephrine-induced eating effect observed in the present experiments is probably independent of the vascular effects of the adrenergic agents is shown by the failure of posterior pituitary extract to elicit eating or drinking in any one of the 11 animals tested. All animals showed a slight tendency toward hypoactivity and decreased reactivity to sensory stimulation, which was, however, in no instance severe enough to account for the observed failure of the drug to affect food intake.

The cholinergic drinking effect similarly does not appear to be based on the vasodilatation which is incident to the injection of acetylcholine or carbachol, since control injections of sodium nitrite and barium chloride failed to replicate the characteristically selective effects on water intake. A pronounced increase in general activity, as well as mild motor seizures similar to those observed after an overdose of carbachol, were observed in some animals after both injections. During the period of hyperactivity both eating and drinking appeared briefly in 3 of the 11 animals tested. This effect was statistically unreliable and significantly smaller ($p < .001$) than those of adrenergic and cholinergic stimulations, and failed to be specific to either eating or drinking.

Control for Local pH Changes. Changes in the local acid-base composition of the stimulated region could conceivably exert significant and differential effects on the surrounding neural tissue.

To control for this factor, the pH values of all substances used in the present studies were established, both in supersaturated solution and in brain homogenate.

Adrenergic and cholinergic substances of varying pH values were effective in eliciting eating and drinking, respectively, whereas control substances of identical or similar pH values consistently failed to evoke comparable results. . . .

HISTOLOGICAL VERIFICATION OF INTENDED PLACEMENTS

A coordinate system, based on the de Groot (1959a, 1959b) atlas of the rat brain, schematically summarizes in Figure 7 the results of the histological examination of a total of 47 placements (33 positive and 14 negative). This distribution includes all 36 animals used in the present study as well as 13 additional rats (8 positive and 5 negative cases). Inspection of Figure 7 indicates no clear anatomical separation of the neural elements which regulate feeding and drinking behavior, respectively. . . .

Although many of the positive points correspond well to the "lateral hypothalamic feeding area" described in the literature (Anand & Brobeck, 1951a, 1951b; Teitelbaum & Stellar, 1954), many of the more medial and dorsal placements are considerably removed from this area and correspond more closely to the "drinking area" described by Anderson and McCann (Anderson & McCann, 1955a, 1955b; Anderson, 1953).

An indication of the extent of spread or diffusion of the injected chemicals can be obtained from a study of the distribution of positive and negative points in Figure 7. It is recognized that these placements were taken from different animals; nevertheless, the extremely close proximity of positive and negative cases indicates that the effective diffusion was relatively small.

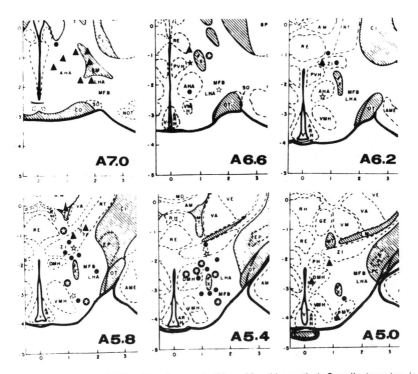

Figure 7. Localization of 47 implant placements (33 positive, 14 negative). Coordinate system is based on the de Groot (1959a, 1959b) atlas of the rat brain. *Filled circles* indicate consistently good effects of both adrenergic and cholinergic stimulation; *white stars* inside *filled circles* indicate consistently excellent effects of both adrenergic and cholinergic stimulation; *white stars* represent predominantly cholinergic effects; *black stars* represent predominantly adrenergic placements; *black triangles* indicate negative placements.

DISCUSSION AND CONCLUSIONS

The results of the present series of studies demonstrate clearly that the placement of adrenergic substances into a circumscribed region of the diencephalon elicits specific changes in one type of motivated behavior (food intake), while the placement of cholinergic agents into the same area of the hypothalamus evokes pronounced changes in a different type of motivated activity (water intake).

The behavior which is elicited by the injection of these chemicals appears to have many of the specific motivational properties of normal hunger and thirst, since satiated animals will work to obtain food or water following the injection of the appropriate substance, in spite of the fact that their efforts are only infrequently rewarded.

The motivational effects which these two groups of chemicals elicit from the same region of the midbrain appear to be, at least to some extent, antagonistic. Adrenergic substances elicit food intake in satiated animals but inhibit drinking in thirsty rats, whereas cholinergic substances evoke vigorous drinking in satiated animals but inhibit food intake in the hungry animal. These results suggest that the well-known tendency of thirst to inhibit eating may, at least partially, be a central neural effect, perhaps analogous to reciprocal inhibition, as suggested by Miller (1960), rather than a purely peripheral effect of dehydration such as dryness of the mouth and throat.

These inhibitory effects appear to be highly specific, since hungry animals apparently were made even more hungry by the injection of norepinephrine, and thirsty animals consumed significantly more water after the injection of carbachol.

The principal question to be raised with regard to the observed effects of chemical stimulation concerns the neural and/or chemical mechanisms responsible for the elicitation of the pronounced behavioral changes.

In view of the fact that both acetylcholine and norepinephrine have well-documented neurohumoral functions in the peripheral nervous system, it is tempting to consider the observed central effects of these drugs as due to a similar transmitter action. Before this notion can be entertained, however, a number of problems and alternate possibilities must be considered.

Considerable evidence has been accumulated suggesting a neurohumoral action of acetylcholine in the central nervous system. The existence of a comparable adrenergic mechanism, however, has not yet been satisfactorily demonstrated. These catecholamines apparently do not cross the blood-brain barrier in detectable amounts, so that the systemic administration of these drugs cannot be expected to have a direct effect on central neural elements. The few studies in which adrenergic solutions have been injected directly into the brain have not provided adequate control over diffusion, so that only a very gross localization of the observed effects has been possible.

The use of crystalline chemicals in the present series of experiments has reduced the problem of uncontrolled spread considerably, although the exact extent of effective diffusion can only be estimated on the basis of the anatomical distribution of positive and negative placements. This analysis depends necessarily on a composite picture, based on histological data from many animals. It nevertheless appears clear that the effective spread must be quite limited, since both positive and negative placements occur in very close proximity.

The fact that none of the placements attempted in any of the experiments showed either the cholinergic or the adrenergic effect alone suggests further that the effective spread of carbachol and norepinephrine was not, in fact, significantly different. Placements very closely adjacent to points from which both highly positive eating and drinking effects could be obtained were entirely negative with respect to both drugs.

Since the crystalline drugs were tamped into the inner cannula, and since neural tissue in direct contact with any foreign body, such as the metal cannula, almost invariably shows some necrosis and recession, it appears unlikely that any active neural elements were in direct contact with the stimulating substance before a considerable amount of dilution had taken place. It is nevertheless probable that normal neural tissue in the immediate vicinity of the implant tip was exposed to nonphysiological concentrations of the stimulating agents. This fact may be responsible for the observed motor effects and abnormal EEG pictures seen after the injection of overdoses of both adrenergic and cholinergic substances, since the area of nonphysiological stimulation undoubtedly was increased by the presence of larger quantities of the crystalline substances.

It does not seem likely that the observed effects of the smaller doses of these substances on food and water intake could be due to the inactivation or abnormal functioning of these neural elements since: (a) almost identical effects have been elicited from this portion of the midbrain with minimal-current electrical stimulation; (b) the behavior elicited by the injection of these chemicals appeared in all respects "normal"; and (c) EEG recordings taken from the tip of the implant failed to show any gross changes in the electrical activity of the affected region, such as one might expect if seizure activity were induced by the introduction of the chemicals. It should parenthetically be noted that the injection of chemicals in solution does not, per se, guarantee that physiological concentrations will be active at the site of stimulation, because the rates of destruction and diffusion of the different chemicals remain largely unknown.

Assuming then that the observed effects are due to the excitation or inhibition of neural elements within a reasonable distance from the implant tip, and that this neural activity is within normal limits, the contention remains to be supported that this activation is, in fact, due to the neurohumoral properties of the adrenergic and cholinergic substances rather than to one of the many side effects which these chemicals are known to produce in peripheral structures.

In the following discussion of the control experiments which were performed in an attempt to obtain evidence on this question, it should be borne in mind that we are concerned with the effects of drugs on neural tissue which is probably not in direct contact with the crystalline chemical itself, but is sufficiently removed from the point of application to provide physiological concentrations of the two neurohumors used in this study.

While differential solubility and diffusion of some of the control substances cannot be ruled out, so that initially "comparable" amounts or osmotic pressures may, in fact, not result in comparable effects at the point of effective stimulation, this fact is at least partially controlled by the use of a wide range of dosages for each drug implanted in these experiments. While it is not intended to prove the null hypothesis, i.e., demonstrate beyond any doubt that a particular substance could not, under any circumstances, produce effects comparable to those observed after adrenergic or cholinergic stimulation, an attempt was made to rule out this possibility for a sufficiently wide range of dosages to make such an interpretation highly unlikely.

The first of our control experiments was concerned with the possibility of nonspecific neural activation similar to that produced by the topical application of a variety of chemical agents to the surface of the cortex.

The drug chosen for this purpose was strychnine sulfate, which has been used extensively as a tool in physiological neuronography (Dusser de Barenne, 1933; Frankenhaeuser, 1951) and has been shown to evoke extremely violent rage reactions, similar to those seen following electrical stimulation, when injected into the medial hypothalamus (Fulton, 1950). Strychnine appears to act primarily at synaptic junctions and activates cell bodies or dendrites with which it is in contact without having a noticeable effect on adjacent fibers (De Groot, 1959a). The mechanism of strychnine action has been variously explained and may involve a selective blockade of inhibitory synapses (Bradley, Easton, & Eccles, 1953; Grundfest, 1957).

In the present study no overt behavioral effects of the injection of strychnine were observed, and no effect on subsequent food or water intake was recorded for either the standard 1-hr poststimulation period or the following 23-hr period. Although these results argue strongly against a general activation factor, they should not be interpreted as negative evidence as far as the cholinergic nature of the acetylcholine stimulation effect is concerned, since it appears extremely unlikely that the activating action of strychnine is in any way related to the inactivation of cholinesterase which Nachmansohn (1938) has demonstrated in vitro, because atropine has been shown to exert no influence on strychnine action (Wescoe & Green, 1948).

The second question to be raised concerns the effects of osmotic stimulation which occur as a by-product of the injection of hypertonic solutions. This problem is particularly relevant in the present context, since Larsson (1955) has reported pronounced hyperphagia in satiated animals after microinjections of hypertonic salt and sugar solutions into an area just 'caudal to the optic chiasma, and similar results have recently been reported by Epstein (1960). Anderson and McCann (1955a, 1955b) have reported excessive drinking as well as increased food intake in goats after microinjections of hypertonic saline into the same general area.

Since the specific osmotic pressure changes produced by crystalline chemicals are a function of their solubility and rate of diffusion, it was not possible to duplicate the specific osmotic effects of carbachol and norepinephrine at the site of stimulation. It was found, however, that the placement of various dosages of pure NaCl, designed to cause maximal osmotic stimulation, failed to duplicate the specific effects of the adrenergic and cholinergic agents. Furthermore, none of the control substances which were used in our experiments produced any consistent effects on food and water intake, in spite of the fact that their osmotic effects undoubtedly varied considerably. . . .

The results of the present series of experiments can best be summarized by the postulation of two anatomically overlapping systems of neural elements at the level of the hypothalamus, which participate in the regulation of food and water intake, and appear to be selectively sensitive to adrenergic and cholinergic stimulation, respectively. The differential excitation and inhibition of a single neural mechanism appears unlikely, in spite of the fact that all placements showed both effects, since the relative magnitude of the eating and drinking effects, though constant in a given animal, varied considerably between subjects.

The results of our control experiments on the effects of nonspecific activation, osmotic stimulation, vasomotor effects, and local changes of the acid-base composition of the stimulated region support the notion that the observed effects may be due to a neurohumoral action of the cholinergic and adrenergic substances. Further experiments, using specific antagonists of acetylcholine and norepinephrine, are in progress to obtain further evidence on this point.

REFERENCES

Anand, B. K., and J. R. Brobeck. *Proc. Soc. Exptl. Biol.,* **77**: 323, 1951. (a)

Anand, B. K., and J. R. Brobeck. *Yale J. Biol. and Med.,* **24**: 123, 1951. (b)

Anderson, B., and S. M. McCann. *J. Physiol., London,* **129**: 44, 1955. (a)

Anderson, B., and S. M. McCann. *Acta Physiol. Scand.,* **33**: 333, 1955. (b)

Anderson, B. *Acta Physiol. Scand.,* **28**: 188, 1953.

Bradley, K., D. M. Easton, and J. C. Eccles. *J. Physiol., London,* **122**: 474, 1953.

Bruegger, M. *Helv. Physiol. et Pharmacol. Acta,* **1**: 183, 1943.

De Groot, J. *J. Comp. Neurol.,* **113**: 389, 1959. (a)

De Groot, J. *Trans. Roy. Neth. Acad. Sci.,* **52**: 1, 1959.(b)

Delgado, J. M. R., and B. K. Anand. *Am. J. Physiol.,* **172**: 162, 1953.

Dusser de Barenne, J. G. *Physiol. Revs.,* **13**: 325, 1933.

Epstein, A. N. *Am. J. Physiol.,* **199**: 969, 1960.

Feldberg, W., and M. Vogt. *J. Physiol., London,* **107**: 372, 1948.

Frankenhaeuser, B. *J. Neurophysiol.,* **14**: 73, 1951.

Fulton, J. F. In *A textbook of physiology,* ed. J. F. Fulton. Philadelphia: Saunders, 1950. Pp. 232–244.

Grundfest, H. *Ann. N.Y. Acad. Sci.,* **66**: 537, 1957.

Klüver, H., and E. A. Barrera. *J. Neuropathol. Exptl. Neurol.,* **12**: 400, 1953.

Larsson. S. *Acta Physiol. Scand.,* **32**: 1, 1955.

MacLean, P. D. *A.M.A. Arch. Neurol. Psychiat.,* **78**: 113, 1957. (a)

MacLean, P. D. *A.M.A. Arch. Neurol. Psychiat.,* **78**: 128, 1957. (b)

Miller, N. E. *Science,* **126**: 1271, 1957.

Miller, N. E. *Federation Proc.,* **19**: 846, 1960.

Montemurro, D. G., and J. A. F. Stevenson. *Yale J. Biol. and Med.,* **28**: 396, 1938.

Nachmansohn, D. *Compt. rend. soc. biol.,* **129**: 941, 1938.

Rothballer, A. B. *Pharmacol. Revs.,* **11**: 494, 1959.

Sokoloff, L. *Pharmacol. Revs.,* **11**: 1, 1959.

Stevenson, J. A., L. G. Welt, and J. Orloff. *Am. J. Physiol.,* **161**: 35, 1950.

Teitelbaum, P., and E. Stellar. *Science,* **120**: 894, 1954.

Vogt, M. *Brit. Med. Bull.,* **13**: 166, 1957.

Wescoe, W. C., and R. E. Green. *J. Pharmacol. Exptl. Therap.,* **94**: 78, 1948.

Commentary*

S. P. GROSSMAN

The systematic application of intracranial drug injection techniques to the study of brain-behavior relationships has a brief but eventful history. A few exploratory investigations were reported in the middle fifties, but most of the evidence which suggests that pharmacological means of facilitating or inhibit-

Preparation of this manuscript was supported by Grant MH–10130 from the United States Public Health Service.

*Ed.: As Dr. Grossman's original material was the first to be completed, it may have been most affected by subsequent scientific progress during the inevitable delays involved in a multiple-authored publication.

ing the activity of restricted portions of the brain may produce more selective behavioral effects than traditional surgical or electrophysiological procedures dates back only a few years.

My own interest in the potential usefulness of microinjection procedures was first aroused in the winter of 1958 when, as a graduate student in Neal Miller's laboratory, I found myself confronted by a problem which seemed impervious to solution by traditional approaches. I was interested then, as well as now, in brain mechanisms which control basic biological drive states. Stellar's (1954) model of the central organization of motivational influences, which suggests that every biological drive state reflects the activity of specific hypothalamic "centers," had been proposed a few years earlier, offering a rather tidy solution to a difficult conceptual problem. Since the hypothalamic center hypothesis rests primarily on evidence related to hunger and thirst, it seemed important to demonstrate that anatomically distinct and functionally independent "centers" did indeed regulate food and water intake. The literature on this point was not entirely convincing. Damage to the lateral hypothalamus of a variety of species had been shown to produce long-term inhibitory influences on food intake (aphagia), but this was invariably accompanied by an equally complete inhibition of water intake (adipsia). In fact, the animals eventually recovered the ability to regulate food intake in accordance with biological requirements, but never recovered regulatory control over water intake, suggesting that the lateral hypothalamus might indeed contain a drinking "center," but only part of whatever mechanism regulates food intake.

Feeding behavior in response to electrical stimulation of the hypothalamus had been reported in the cat (Bruegger, 1943), but when a colleague of mine, Ted Coons, attempted to replicate these observations in the rat, it appeared that the nature of the animal's response to lateral hypothalamic stimulation was significantly influenced by environmental factors. Feeding typically occurred if the rat was surrounded by bits of food during the experiment. However, stimulation of the same points often evoked drinking, particularly when the animal was in the immediate vicinity of the drinking tube. (Dr. Coons has subsequently found a few electrode placements which permit the elicitation of feeding but not drinking, but these appear to be quite rare. Dr. Valenstein's recent work in this area suggests, furthermore, that even these apparently specific responses to electrical stimulation of the lateral hypothalamus may change, often dramatically, in the course of an experiment.) It seemed that neither electrical stimulation nor ablation techniques produced sufficiently selective effects to permit the detailed study of the hypothalamic feeding and drinking "centers" which I had in mind. What, then, could I do?

As luck would have it, I was also studying the pharmacological reactions which occur when nerve cells react to stimulation and pass information on to other cells. The basic mechanisms of this information processing system are simple. Once the stimulation threshold of a cell is reached, an explosive electrochemical reaction takes place. This reaction is then propagated to the most distant projection of the cell, the axon terminal. Here the electrochemical disturbance triggers the release of minute quantities of neurohumoral substances which diffuse across the narrow synaptic gap that separates the axon termination from the body of the next cell. This transmitter substance interacts with specific receptor sites on the surface of the postsynaptic cell membrane and evokes electrochemical reactions which, in turn, may be propagated. The transmitter substance is then rapidly destroyed to permit the transmission of subsequent bits of information (nerve cells are capable of transmitting at least 1000 such "impulses" per second).

What caught my attention in particular was the possibility that different nerve cells might use different transmitter substances. Neuropharmacologists still do not know for sure precisely how many different transmitter substances may be used by cells in the brain, but there is fairly good evidence for at least four or five substances and excellent evidence for two of them. (The nerves of the sympathetic division of the peripheral autonomic nervous system use a different transmitter, norepinephrine, than other peripheral nerves, which use acetylcholine. Even in 1958 there was pretty good evidence to suggest that these two transmitters might also be active in the brain.) Since the complex organization of biological organisms rarely permits fortuitous accidents, it seemed possible that the neurohumoral specificity of certain brain cells might be used to prevent "cross-talk" between geographically overlapping but functionally distinct neural pathways. If this were true, a prime candidate for such a pharmacological "coding" seemed to be the feeding and drinking "centers" which appeared to coexist anatomically in the lateral hypothalamus. I consequently decided to see whether microinjections of the two transmitter substances into this region of the brain might permit a selective activation of the feeding or drinking mechanisms. What happened is described in the preceding article.

What has happened since these initial observations supported my hunch that the brain might use a system of pharmacological "codes" to maintain functional specificity in the face of extensive geographic overlap? Many investigators have used the technique successfully to investigate a broad spectrum of neuropsychological and neuropharmacological problems. Though young, the field has become too large to be reviewed here. Let me therefore give you only some examples, taken mainly from my own laboratory.

THE CENTRAL REPRESENTATION OF HUNGER AND THIRST

It is perhaps ironic that a series of experiments designed to demonstrate the existence of restricted hypothalamic "centers" have instead led to the discovery of extensive extrahypothalamic influences on feeding and drinking behavior. Even in my original paper it was clear that the distribution of norepinephrine- and carbachol-positive sites was not restricted to the lateral hypothalamus. Indeed, some of the very best placements were outside the hypothalamus itself, in the subthalamic region, as can be seen by referring to Figure 7 in the article. Experiments in my own (Grossman, 1964a, 1964b) and other laboratories (Fisher & Coury, 1962; Wagner & DeGroot, 1963; Miller, 1965) have since shown that carbachol-sensitive points can be found in a number of subcortical and limbic structures (notably the anterior hypothalamus, preoptic area, medial septal area, cingulate gyrus, and dorsal hippocampus) and that cholinergic stimulation of many of the extrahypothalamic areas often produces larger drinking effects with shorter latencies than comparable stimulation of the hypothalamus itself.

Coury (1967) has recently reported that many of the extrahypothalamic carbachol sites also respond positively to norepinephrine and has suggested that food and water intake might be regulated by two generally parallel neural pathways which maintain their pharmacological specificity throughout their course. Booth (1967), on the other hand, finds a more restricted distribution of norepinephrine-sensitive sites, including the preoptic area, lateral septal area, and ventral thalamus, which may correspond to the distribution field of the stria medullaris—one of the major projections from the amygdala. My own data agree with those of Booth, but it may be premature to draw boundaries around the feeding and drinking systems. The available data do suggest that all currently known aspects of the "thirst circuit" respond preferentially to cholinergic stimulation, whereas components of the hunger circuit appear to respond to norepinephrine. Whether this generalization turns out to be true or not, we seem to have a useful tool at hand which permits the selective activation or inactivation of functionally rather than purely geographically defined pathways in the brain.

What about areas of the brain which have been implicated in the regulation of food or water intake by ablation or electrical stimulation studies? Are they all part of the pharmacologically defined circuits? The answer seems to be a qualified "yes," with perhaps one major exception. The carbachol- and norepinephrine-sensitive sites coincide rather nicely with most of the sites from which appetitive behaviors can be elicited by electrical stimulation (Robinson, 1964).

Some years ago we seemed to have come across an exception to this rule when we found that chemical stimulation of the amygdaloid complex did not elicit food or water intake in sated animals at implantation sites which did respond to electrical stimulation. We were about to terminate our experiments when fortune, in the guise of a forgetful graduate student, smiled. The student forgot to feed and water the animals entrusted to his care and all the animals ate and drank heartily during our stimulation tests on the next day. When we discovered the reason for their behavior, I was about to discard the data and terminate the experiment when I noticed that the animals that had received norepinephrine before the experiment had eaten a good deal more than normal animals do following 24-hour food deprivation. When we checked further, we found that the carbachol-treated animals had similarly drunk much greater quantities of water than could be explained on the basis of their deprivation schedule. A formal replication of the accidental experiment proved my observations to be correct; although chemical stimulation of the amygdala did not elicit food or water intake in sated animals, it very markedly potentiated feeding or drinking behavior in animals that have been food or water deprived.

The one apparent exception to the pharmacological "coding" of the hunger and thirst circuits is the ventromedial hypothalamus, which functions in Stellar's model as a satiety center for feeding behavior. Feeding as well as drinking responses to chemical stimulation of this region have been reported (Wagner & DeGroot, 1963), but the latency of these reactions is typically quite long, suggesting that the drug may have to diffuse to a distant site. Furthermore, many totally negative sites in and around the ventromedial nucleus exist (Grossman, 1966a; Margules & Stein, 1969), and the positive direction of the effects (one would expect inhibitory reactions from a satiety center) suggest that this region may not be part of the pharmacologically defined feeding and drinking circuits. This may be the proverbial exception to the rule, but the results of some of our experiments suggest an alternative explanation.

It has long been known that rats with ventromedial lesions overeat only when the diet is palatable and that they starve to death rather than accept food which is slightly bitter or otherwise unpleasant. These animals also do not work as hard as normal rats for food rewards, particularly when the effort required is fairly high (Miller et al., 1960). When I investigated the behavioral reactions to drug injections into the ventromedial hypothalamus (Grossman, 1966a), I found that this apparently paradoxical pattern of effects could also be obtained by atropine injections, which selectively block cholinergic pathways. When we conducted routine tests to demonstrate the specificity of the observed behavioral changes, we found that atropine injections, as well as small ventromedial lesions, also reduced the animals' willingness to work for water rewards. Subsequent (unpublished) observations have suggested that atropine injections into the ventromedial hypothalamus also produce exaggerated reactions to saccharin or quinine adulteration of the water supply.

When viewed in conjunction with Krasne's (1962) observation that electrical stimulation of the ventromedial area seems to inhibit all ongoing activity, our results suggest that this region of the brain may act not specifically as a satiety center, but perhaps as a source of inhibitory influences which affect behavior regardless of its motivation. This is, of course, at present merely speculation, but it would account rather nicely for the fact that this region does not seem to respond selectively to adrenergic substances, as do other portions of the neural circuit which regulate food intake. Our hypothesis receives some support from the well-known fact (Wheatley, 1944) that lesions in the ventromedial area produce a state of hyperirritability and viciousness as well as excessive reactions to painful grid shock (Grossman, 1966a).

NONSPECIFIC MOTIVATIONAL SYSTEMS

Encouraged by the success of our investigations of the feeding and drinking circuits, I decided some years ago to apply the intracranial drug administration technique to a problem which has intrigued psychologists and physiologists for many years. A good deal of behavior can be attributed to the organism's attempts to reduce specific "drive" stimuli (such as the sensations attendant on food or water deprivation) which may or may not directly reflect a biological need state. It is clear, however, that not all behavior can conveniently be explained in terms of specific drive stimulation, and that the threshold of responding to particular stimuli varies widely, independent of the status of the related drive.

Physiologists have used notions such as "arousal," "activation," or "generalized energy" (Pavlov, 1927; Cannon, 1929) to account for the observed fluctuations in the organism's reactivity to internal as well as external stimulation. The related psychological concept of "nonspecific drive" has been used extensively by such theorists as Hull (1943), Malmo (1959), and Brown (1961), and some (Hebb, 1955; Lindsley, 1957; Miller et al., 1960) have attempted to account for all behavior within the framework of such "arousal" or "activation" theories.

Arousal theories have flourished since the pioneering research of Magoun and his associates demonstrated that the reticular formation of the brainstem appears to be the anatomical substrate for physiological processes which seem to be related to the psychologist's concept of arousal or nonspecific activation. Electrical stimulation of the midbrain reticular formation was shown to produce behavioral as well as electrophysiological arousal (Moruzzi & Magoun, 1949) and destruction of this region resulted in somnolence and a complete lack of reactivity to sensory input, although the sensory pathways to higher cortical areas appeared to function normally (Lindsley et al., 1949, 1950). Other aspects of the reticular formation have been shown to control sensory input to the higher centers of integration by modulating receptor functions as well as transmission properties all along the sensory pathways (Granit, 1955; Hagbarth & Kerr, 1954). Even the organism's output—i.e., the motor system—appears to be controlled to a large extent by reticular influences (Magoun & Rhines, 1946; Lindsley et al., 1949).

On the basis of this information, Lindsley (1957) has proposed an arousal theory of motivation which suggests that all motivational states are composed of (a) a general state of arousal which is related to the activity of the midbrain reticular formation and affects cortical reactivity via extrathalamic projections, and (b) a specific alerting response to those stimuli in the environment which are specifically related to the arousal. The nonspecific thalamic projections of the thalamus were thought to mediate this specific alerting response.

It has been difficult to test Lindsley's theory empirically and to study the role of reticular functions in motivation because it has been all but impossible to obtain graded responses to damage or stimulation of the reticular formation. Large lesions produce essentially complete coma and electrical stimulation of a sleeping animal results in arousal. However, small lesions or electrical stimulation in the awake animal rarely produce sufficient changes in arousal to affect overt behavior in most test situations.

I have attempted to provide some relevant information by injecting neurohumoral substances into various aspects of the reticular formation. The pattern of results is complex and much remains to be accomplished before we can confidently interpret all of our observations. It is clear, however, that the microinjection technique provides a convenient tool for activating or inactivating portions of the reticular formation at several levels of the brainstem and that the effects are, at least in some instances, peculiar to functionally distinct aspects of the reticular formation.

It seemed that the nonspecific thalamic projection system might be the ideal place to start our investigation if it indeed mediated specific alerting reactions, as Lindsley's hypothesis suggested. We therefore implanted cannulas into two prominent aspects of the nonspecific thalamic system, the midline nuclei and the dorsolateral reticular nuclei.

The initial experiments (Grossman et al., 1965) demonstrated that carbachol injections into both of these regions depressed locomotor activity and exploratory behavior in an open field. The food or water intake of deprived animals appeared to be unaffected by the injections, but the animals' rate of bar-pressing for food rewards decreased dramatically. Further tests showed that the carbachol-treated animals readily learned and performed a simple hurdle-jumping response to escape from painful footshock, but failed to learn the simple association required to avoid the painful shock by responding to a visual warning signal.

This apparently complex pattern of results is plausible if carbachol injections, either by stimulating an inhibitory system or by inhibiting an excitatory influence, raise the organism's threshold of responding to sensory input. When such stimulation is intense (as is the case following 24 hours of food or water deprivation or in the shock-escape experiment), the signals exceed the increased threshold and the animal responds normally, particularly when the response required to remove the stimulation is simple. When the drive stimulation is relatively weak (as in the exploratory test or the avoidance situation) or the required response complex (such as lever-pressing), the animal fails to respond.

In a subsequent series of experiments, we (Grossman & Peters, 1966) attempted to support such an interpretation by modifying the activity of the nonspecific thalamic projection system in a different way. Microinjections of the cholinolytic blocking agent atropine into the midline nuclei of the thalamus produced the expected result—a pattern of behavioral facilitation which was in all instances opposite that seen after injections of carbachol into the same sites. Similar atropine injections into the dorsolateral reticular nuclei of the thalamus failed, however, to produce similar facilitatory effects. To our surprise, these injections delayed the acquisition of avoidance (but not escape) responses in the double-grill shuttle box and interfered with the acquisition of food-rewarded brightness discriminations (without significantly inhibiting food and water intake in deprived animals). This pattern of results is, of course, remarkably similar to that seen after carbachol injections.

We were initially dismayed by the finding that a drug thought to *inhibit* a portion of the nonspecific thalamic projection system should have the same behavioral effects as a drug known to *stimulate* it, and were about to give up this line of investigation when one of my students pointed out that the apparent paradox in the pattern of our results might indeed be predicted by contemporary arousal theories (Berlyne, 1960; Hebb, 1955; Hunt, 1963). It is generally accepted that the efficiency of behavior is nonmonotonically related to arousal and that the shape of this function approximates an inverted U (i.e., performance is best within a range of moderate arousal and falls off as activation is increased or decreased). Let's see how such a notion applies to our findings:

Animals attempting to learn a novel appetitive or avoidance response are undoubtedly operating very near the upper end of the optimal arousal region. Carbachol-induced stimulation of an arousal-related mechanism may well push the animal beyond this border and thus cause a disruption of performance. A similar explanation may account for the disruption in open-field exploratory activity, since this type of test is known to induce a good deal of fear in rats. Feeding and drinking measured in the animal's home cage, on the other hand, would not be expected to give rise to a high level of arousal and thus would show little disruption when the reactivity level was increased by carbachol injections.

When atropine is injected into the midline nuclei, mechanisms related to arousal level may be inhibited to the extent that the animal's reactivity is shifted from the descending limb to a more optimal portion of the arousal spectrum. Similar injections into the dorsolateral reticular nuclei may have produced inhibitory influences strong enough to push the animal's performance past the optimal region and further down on the left, ascending limb of that curve, thus resulting in poorer performance.

To make this interpretation plausible, one must assume that the differences between the reactions of the two injection sites are quantitative rather than qualitative. This assumption is supported by the observation that the carbachol-induced inhibition of behavior in aversive as well as appetitive test situations was always significantly greater when the drug was applied to the reticular nuclei. This observation saves the suggested interpretation from being pure sophistry, but the underlying dilemma is unfortunately inherent in all investigations of reticular functions. Since we have no independent measure of "arousal," it is always possible that an experimental manipulation may have produced its behavioral effects by shifting the organism's level of arousal to the right or to the left of the inverted-U function. Only when the experiments are repeated in situations of widely different inherent arousal value can one hope to arrive at a reasonable interpretation. We encountered this problem again in the next series of experiments which attempted to investigate the influence of lower portions of the arousal system.

The first of these experiments (Grossman, 1966b) showed that small bilateral lesions in the midbrain reticular formation did not modify locomotor activity, but impaired the acquisition of a simple shuttle-box avoidance (but not escape) response. Carbachol injections into this portion of the reticular formation seemed to increase the animals' levels of reactivity or arousal, but the resultant behavioral changes were difficult to predict. When the injections were given just before each daily training session, the animals appeared capable of adjusting to the increased reactivity level and even made use of it, as shown in a consistent improvement in their learning scores in the avoidance situation. However, the same injections interfered with learning when given only once or repeated infrequently.

Since arousal might be particularly relevant to an escape-avoidance situation, we (Grossman & Grossman, 1966) next trained rats to press a lever or to perform simple brightness discriminations in a T-maze to obtain food rewards. Bilateral lesions in the midbrain reliably improved the animals' performances in both test situations, enhancing response speeds as well as the accuracy of the discriminations. Carbachol injections before each daily training or testing session reversed this pattern. The animals appeared distractible and unable or unwilling to concentrate on the problem at hand.

This pattern of effects can, once more, be explained on the basis of the U-shaped relationship between arousal and performance, but our understanding of the relevant variables is inadequate to permit predictions except in the limited cases illustrated below. Small lesions in the midbrain reticular formation appeared to have raised the general response threshold to environmental stimulation and thus lowered the efficiency of behavior in the escape-avoidance situation, where arousal is directly relevant. The same decrease in arousal may have produced an improvement in performance in the appetitive learning situations, partly because the animals' emotional reactions to handling were reduced and partly because relatively weak (because nonreinforced) tendencies to respond to irrelevant aspects of the environment may have fallen below the raised response threshold while the continually strengthened tendency to react to the cues which signaled reinforcement became more distinct. This differential effect should have become larger and larger as training progressed, a prediction which was borne out by our data. Carbachol should have produced opposite effects in all test situations to the extent that its stimulating effect decreased the organism's response threshold.

I am always uncomfortable when the outcome of a series of experiments, though logically acceptable, cannot be predicted *a priori.* I therefore attempted more recently (Grossman, 1968) to prove that at least some simple predictions could be made within the theoretical framework which we had used earlier to interpret our findings. It seemed that an increase in arousal or reactivity should be beneficial only in situations where there are few distracting stimuli and the inherent level of arousal is low. I tested this prediction in three experiments which used identical shuttle-box avoidance paradigms, but varied the level of grid shock used. In agreement with my prediction, carbachol facilitated the acquisition of avoidance responses in the low-shock situation but produced disruptive effects in the high-shock situation. Perhaps the most interesting observations were, however, made in the medium-shock situation. As a group the animals showed no significant reaction to carbachol, but this turned out to be an artifact of the pooling of data from very different animals. When the performances of individual animals were correlated with their aversion thresholds for electric footshock (i.e., the minimal intensity required to reliably obtain such signs of emotionality as squealing, jumping, defecating, urinating, etc.), it turned out that rats with very low thresholds showed disruptive reactions to carbachol in the avoidance situation and consequently performed very poorly, whereas rats with high-shock thresholds performed better than one would have predicted (a rather nice confirmation of our prediction). Atropine injections produced opposite shock-dependent effects in all three avoidance situations. This blocking agent also reduced the animals' rates of responding for food or water rewards in a two-lever operant situation and depressed response latencies in a brightness discrimination test—a pattern of results which, once more, supports the suggested interpretation.

Perhaps the most intriguing finding from this series of experiments was made in the course of subsequent routine tests for pharmacological specificity. Our standard tests for pH, vasomotor, and osmotic factors turned out negative, supporting our expectation that the behavioral effects might be due to a specific neurohumoral action of the drugs. However, when we tested other possible neurohumors, we found that norepinephrine injections produced marked behavioral effects which seemed in some instances similar to those of carbachol, in other instances opposite. Much like carbachol, norepinephrine interfered with the acquisition and performance of conditioned responses in all of our appetitive tests, suggesting at first glance that the midbrain reticular formation might have adrenergic as well as cholinergic links and that the pharmacological distinctions might not reflect a functional division. However, a closer look at the topography of the behavior of the norepinephrine-treated animals suggested an alternative hypothesis. It seemed that the norepine-phrine-treated animals were distinctly hypoactive and hyporeactive in all of our test situations and performed poorly because their responses to even fairly intense stimulation were depressed. Although their performances in all formal test situations showed the same depression previously seen after carbachol injections, this depression seemed to have a very different cause.

This interpretation accounted nicely for our observations without necessitating the assumption that adrenergic and cholinergic components of the reticular formation might be functionally equivalent, but we were dissatisfied with it because it rested entirely on "clinical" observations. We therefore scouted around for behavioral tests which might be differentially affected by an increase or decrease in reactivity or arousal. The most obvious prediction, based on the shock-dependent effects of carbachol, was that norepinephrine should improve avoidance behavior in high-shock situations in which a decrease in reactivity might be expected to prevent some of the disruptive reactions to pain, and impair performance in low-shock situations. When we trained norepinephrine-treated animals in our double-grill box, this pattern of results (which is directly opposite that seen after carbachol) did indeed emerge. Our interpretation was further supported by the observation that carbachol injections increased locomotor activity, whereas norepinephrine decreased it. We also obtained some electrophysiological data in support of this interpretation. Norepinephrine injections into the midbrain reticular formation significantly increased the probability of high-voltage, slow activity in all cortical leads, whereas carbachol produced a sharp increase in the probability of low-voltage, fast activity.

The overall pattern of reactions to adrenergic and cholinergic stimulation of the midbrain suggests that the reticular formation may, at this level, contain (a) a cholinergic component which exerts excitatory influences on cortical activity and the organism's level of reactivity to the environment, and (b) an adrenergic component which may produce opposite, inhibitory influences. This is, of course, still mostly conjecture, but it seems that none of the available alternative hypotheses can account as readily for our data. We are presently trying to learn more about this interesting mechanism by observing behavioral and electrophysiological responses to drug injections into lower portions of the brainstem.

CHOLINERGIC COMPONENTS OF THE LIMBIC SYSTEM AND INHIBITION

Lesions in the septal area produce a bewildering variety of behavioral changes, including such apparently diverse items as hyperemotionality, photophobia, facilitation or inhibition of avoidance behavior (depending on the nature of the test situation), and changes in extinction or reversal behavior (see McCleary, 1966, for a review of this literature). Rather unsuccessful attempts have been made to interpret these behavioral effects in terms of a common mechanism such as "reactive inhibition" or "response perseveration," but it has become increasingly clear that the septal area contains functionally independent neural systems which are, at least to some extent, anatomically coexistent. We are currently engaged in a series of experiments designed to dissociate some of these functions by means of pharmacological techniques. The story is as yet incomplete, but some encouraging progress has been made.

The first of these investigations (Grossman, 1964b) demonstrated that cholinergic stimulation of the septal area of rats completely prevented the learning of avoidance (but not escape) responses in a shuttle box and significantly impaired performance of previously acquired lever-pressing responses. The cholinergic blocking agent, atropine, produced opposite facilitatory effects.

More recently, we (Hamilton et al., 1968) have found that atropine injections into the medial septal area of rats produce a deficit in passive avoidance behavior (i.e., the animals returned to eat at a food dish which had been electrified on the preceding trial) and retard the extinction of an avoidance response. However, the atropine-treated cats learned a one-way avoidance response normally and reversed a position habit as rapidly as our controls. Both of these tests reliably showed the effects of large as well as small septal lesions, suggesting that the atropine injections may have spared the neural pathways which affect the behavior in these test situations.

In the course of these investigations we made some puzzling observations. Since septal lesions facilitate acquisition of a shuttle-box avoidance response but impair passive avoidance, we thought it might be interesting to test the effects of intraseptal atropine injections in a situation which contained both active and passive avoidance responses. We trained cats to eat their daily ration in the test apparatus. Next a flashing light was presented and a shelf projected out of one of the walls of the apparatus. This was followed after 10 seconds by grid shock. Both the CS and UCS were terminated 5 seconds after the cat jumped onto the shelf. The animals soon learned to respond to the light CS, but then found themselves unable to eat unless they returned to the place where they had been shocked.

We (Hamilton & Grossman, 1969) found that atropine-treated cats did not show a passive avoidance deficit in this situation (i.e., they returned to the food no sooner than normals). More surprising yet, they were significantly *poorer* than controls in learning the simple avoidance response—a deficit which seemed in direct conflict with our previous observation that intraseptal atropine injections *facilitated* acquisition in the shuttle box. It seemed possible that the presence of food (and conflict) might be the important variable, so we trained another group of cats on the shelf-jumping avoidance response without this complication. The pattern of results did not change—atropine-treated animals were clearly inferior to normals. Baffled but unwilling to give up just yet, we modified the task so that the animals had to use the shelf as a lever rather than a jump-platform (on the hypothesis that the nature of the response may be the important variable). Still the same result—atropine produced marked deficits.

We finally decided to see whether the apparently paradoxical result might be peculiar to cholinergic blockade. Hamilton (1969) ran through the entire sequence of experiments once more, using cats with electrolytic or surgical lesions of the septal area. To our further bafflement, the animals also learned each of the avoidance responses more slowly than normals and were, in fact, indistinguishable from the atropine-treated cats. It seems, then, that the nature of the influence of the septal area on avoidance learning is much more complicated and situation dependent than anyone had thought. To follow the atropine story a little further, we (Hamilton & Grossman, 1969) compared atropine and septal lesion effects in the traditional shuttle box and found almost identical *facilitatory* effects.

Kelsey and I (1969) have successfully used the atropine injection technique to rule out some possible explanations of the typical shuttle-box facilitation. Since septal lesions produce marked photophobia as well as an increase in locomotor activity, it has been suggested that the facilitation seen in the shuttle box (where the CS typically is a light and increased activity would be helpful) may be due to either or both of these factors. We found, however, that intraseptal injections of low doses of atropine produce neither photophobia nor hyperactivity, but clear evidence of facilitation in the shuttle box—a clear refutation of the suggested hypothesis.

Since there is some question about the cross-species generality of some central drug effects, we (Hamilton & Grossman, unpublished) have recently looked at the effects of intraseptal drug administration in another species. Monkeys trained in a Sidman-avoidance paradigm to press a lever at least once every 20 seconds to avoid painful tailshock performed poorly if at all following intraseptal injections of carbachol (which inhibit lever-pressing and shuttle-box avoidance in the rat), particularly when the animals were tested just after they had begun to master this difficult task. Atropine injections produced small but consistent facilitatory effects.

Many experiments remain to be done before we can completely unravel the complexities of the septal influence on avoidance behavior, but it seems that, once more, intracranial drug injections may provide one of the tools needed to obtain behavioral effects distinct enough to suggest manageable interpretation.

WHERE IS THE FIELD GOING?

Due to the nature of my theoretical orientation and interests, I have generally applied the intracranial injection technique to questions about the central substrate of motivational processes. This is not, of course, a limitation of the technique, and more and more investigators are applying it to their own spheres of interest. Microinjections are being used increasingly to study the relationship of particular brain areas to memory, learning, or recall, and a wide variety of pharmacological agents are used to produce facilitatory or inhibitory effects in these studies. Agents which interfere with neurohumoral transmission (Deutsch, 1966), inhibit protein synthesis (Flexner et al., 1963), or nonspecifically inhibit or facilitate neural activity (Grossman & Mountford, 1964; Grossman, 1969) have been used in these experiments. Aside from providing an often more selective means of activation or inactivation of functionally defined pathways, the microinjection techniques produce long-lasting (relative to electrical stimulation) effects which are, however, unlike those of lesions, reversible. Moreover, the nature of the injection procedure makes it possible to monitor the electrical activity of the directly affected region throughout, an advantage which should become increasingly useful as we perfect techniques for recording the activity of single cells in unrestrained animals.

The microinjection technique has, however, some problems of its own. Most vexing, perhaps, is the question of anatomical specificity—i.e., just how far the injected materials spread. This question is complicated and probably has no single answer because diffusion is determined by such variables as mode of injection, quantity of injection, and nature (i.e., molecular size, solubility, etc.) of the drug itself.

There are several techniques for administering drugs intracranially. The most widely used microinjection procedure consists of the administration, under pressure, of drugs in solution. The time-course of the injection is typically in terms of seconds and the injection consequently produces marked pressure gradients and mechanical deformation of the tissue surrounding the cannula implant. The microinfusion procedure attempts to circumvent this problem by injecting the same small quantities of solution over a period of minutes or even hours. This technique unfortunately requires some degree of immobilization and is thus not always useful in behavioral research. The third, crystalline application technique, which I have favored in my own work, permits the drug to go into solution in the brain, using the extracellular fluids as the solvent.

Several dye-diffusion studies (MacLean, 1957; Myers, 1966) have shown that the microinjection procedure produces fairly extensive diffusion, particularly when quantities greater than 0.5 microliters are employed. The problem seems to stem, at least in part, from the fact that the cannula implant produces a tissue reaction all along its extent. This leaves a space between the cannula and the surrounding tissue and the injected fluids tend to follow this "path of least resistance." More recent experiments, relying on injections of hydrochloric acid (Rech, 1968) or potassium chloride (Hull, 1967) to produce abnormal staining reactions, have generally supported the dye-diffusion studies in showing that quantities of 1 to 2 microliters tend to diffuse to a sphere of about 1 to 2 millimeters. This is not, in many applications, an unacceptable spread of the drug, but it is not clear that these estimates are in any way representative of the *effective* spread of other drugs. It is quite clear that the molecular size, solubility, and other physicochemical properties of a drug determine its transport through the nervous system and one must therefore view the results of the diffusion studies with caution.

It is clear, on the basis of the dye-diffusion as well as more recent autoradiographic studies (Michael, 1962), that the implantation of drugs in crystalline form produces significantly less diffusion, but just how much effective distribution of the drug is still open to question. An analysis of the distribution of positive and negative carbachol points in the hypothalamus and other portions of the limbic system appears to provide rather convincing proof that this drug remains fairly well localized to a sphere of less than 1 mm. We are currently conducting some microelectrode studies which have confirmed this pattern of spread. A microelectrode apparently must be within about 1 mm of the tip of the cannula implant to record significant changes in cellular activity in response to carbachol injections. So far, our experiments suggest that this is also true for most of the other drugs which we have used in past experiments.

There is a puzzling experimental finding which has led to the suggestion that some drugs, notably atropine, may diffuse very widely throughout much of the brain following local application. Levitt and Fisher (1967) reported that the application of atropine to most, if not all, carbachol "drinking" sites in the limbic system could block the drinking reaction to carbachol at other, often distant sites. The most obvious explanation of this effect would seem to be that atropine diffuses to the site of carbachol application and thus blocks the response to it. However, as is so often the case, the most obvious explanation does not seem to be the correct one. To prove this, I, in collaboration with Dr. Walter Stumpf, have repeated the atropine-blocking experiment using radioactively labeled atropine. We injected carbachol into the medial septal area and waited until the animal began to drink. Next we injected labeled atropine into the lateral hypothalamus and waited until it exerted its blocking effect. When the animal ceased to drink it was killed by immersion in liquid nitrogen, and its brain was removed and sectioned. The brain slices were then placed onto a photographic emulsion and kept in a dark closet for several months. When retrieved, we could follow the atropine diffusion because the radioactivity had exposed some of the photographic emulsion. In these tests it seemed that the radioactivity remained confined to a sphere of about 1 to 1.5 mm from the cannula. None appeared in the septal area where carbachol had been injected. Just how that block comes about is still a mystery which we are presently attempting to solve by cutting afferent and efferent pathways to and from the carbachol injection site, but it seems that the postulated direct atropine action can be ruled out.

These experiments do not remove the problem of diffusion entirely from consideration, and one must always keep in mind that such factors as vicinity of blood vessels, ventricles, or brain surface may result in different and possibly extensive diffusion patterns. Our results do suggest, however, that the application of drugs, particularly in crystalline form, can produce quite restricted effects on neural functions. It therefore continues to be the technique of choice in much of my own research, even though it does not provide very good estimates of dosage and active concentration. The dosage problem does not seem to be a serious problem because most of the behavioral effects which have so far been identified occur over a fairly wide range of dosages. The matter of concentration is potentially a more serious problem since the concentration at the tip of our implant is undoubtedly not physiological. In practice, even that does not seem to be a prohibitive factor, since we find in all instances that we obtain essentially identical results from the application of drugs in crystalline form and from the slow infusion of lower concentrations of the same drug in solution.

Finally, it should be pointed out that important species differences may exist with respect to the neuropharmacological properties of particular neural pathways and mechanisms. In the rabbit, for instance, carbachol injections into the hypothalamus elicit drinking from some sites and feeding from others (Sommer et al., 1967), suggesting that both systems may be cholinergic in this species. The monkey, on the other hand, eats in response to adrenergic stimulation but seems to show only inhibitory reactions to carbachol, even at low dosages (Myers, 1969). The most puzzling species, however, may be the cat. Microinjections of adrenergic substances into the hypothalamus and brainstem of cats typically produce behavioral coma, whereas cholinergic drugs induce rage and attack behavior (Hernández-Peón et al., 1963; Myers, 1964; McPhail & Miller, 1968). Sleep and emotional reactions are sometimes seen in the rat, particularly when higher doses are used, and it appears possible that norepinephrine may activate pathways related to sleep as well as feeding in both species, and that carbachol similarly activates not only the thirst circuit but also pathways related to emotional behavior. For some as yet unknown reason, sleep and attack may dominate in the cat, food and water intake in the rat.

REFERENCES

Berlyne, D. E. *Conflict Arousal and Curiosity.* New York: McGraw-Hill, 1960.
Booth, D. A. Localization of the adrenergic feeding system in rat diencephalon. *Science,* **158**, 515–517, 1967.

Brown, J. S. *The Motivation of Behavior.* New York: McGraw Hill, 1961.

Bruegger, M. Fresstrieb als hypothalamisches Symptom. *Helv. physiol. pharmacol. Acta,* 1: 183–198, 1943.

Cannon, W. B. *Bodily Changes in Pain, Hunger, Fear, and Rage.* (Rev. ed.) New York: Appleton, 1929. Originally published in 1915.

Coury, J. N. Neural correlates of food and water intake. *Science,* 156: 1763–1765, 1967.

Deutsch, J. A. Substrates of learning and memory. *Dis. nerv. Syst.,* 27: 20–24, 1966.

Fisher, A. E., & Coury, J. N. Cholinergic tracing of a central neural circuit underlying the thirst drive. *Science,* 138: 691–693, 1962.

Flexner, J. B., Flexner, L. B., & Stellar, E. Memory in mice as affected by intracerebral puromycin. *Science,* 141: 57–59, 1963.

Granit, R. *Receptors and Sensory Perception.* New Haven, Conn.: Yale Univ. Press, 1955.

Grossman, S. P. Behavioral effects of chemical stimulation of the ventral amygdala. *J. comp. physiol. Psychol.,* 57: 29–36, 1964. (a)

Grossman, S. P. Effects of chemical stimulation of the septal area on motivation. *J. comp. physiol. Psychol.,* 58: 194–200, 1964. (b)

Grossman, S. P. The VMH: A center for affective reactions, satiety, or both. *Physiol. & Behav.,* 1: 1–10, 1966. (a)

Grossman, S. P. Acquisition and performance of avoidance responses during chemical stimulation of the midbrain reticular formation. *J. comp. physiol. Psychol.,* 61: 42–49, 1966. (b)

Grossman, S. P. Behavioral and electroencephalographic effects of microinjections of neurohumors into the midbrain reticular formation. *Physiol. & Behav.,* 3: 777–787, 1968.

Grossman, S. P. Facilitation of learning following intracranial injections of pentylenetetrazol. *Physiol. & Behav.,* 4: 625–628, 1969.

Grossman, S. P., & Grossman, Lore. Effects of chemical stimulation of the midbrain reticular formation on appetitive behavior. *J. comp. physiol. Psychol.,* 61: 333–338, 1966.

Grossman, S. P., & Mountford, H. Effects of chemical stimulation of the dorsal hippocampus on learning and performance. *Amer. J. Physiol.,* 207: 1387–1393, 1964.

Grossman, S. P., & Peters, R. Acquisition of appetitive and avoidance habits following atropine-induced blocking of the thalamic reticular formation. *J. comp. physiol. Psychol.,* 61: 325–332, 1966.

Grossman, S. P., Freedman, P., Peters, R., & Willer, H. Behavioral effects of cholinergic stimulation of the thalamic reticular formation. *J. comp. physiol. Psychol.,* 59: 57–65, 1965.

Hagbarth, K. E., & Kerr, D. I. B. Central influences on spinal afferent conduction. *J. Neurophysiol.,* 17: 295, 1954.

Hamilton, L. W. Active avoidance impairment following septal lesions in cats. *J. comp. physiol. Psychol.,* 69: 420–431, 1969.

Hamilton, L. W., & Grossman, S. P. Behavioral changes following disruption of central cholinergic pathways. *J. comp. physiol. Psychol.,* 69: 76–82, 1969.

Hamilton, L. W., McCleary, R. A., & Grossman, S. P. Behavioral effects of cholinergic septal blockade in the cat. *J. comp. physiol. Psychol.*, **66**: 563–568, 1968.

Hebb, D. O. Drives and the C.N.S. (conceptual nervous system). *Psychol. Rev.*, **62**: 243–254, 1955.

Hernández-Peón, R., Chávez-Ibarra, G., Morgane, P., & Timo-Iaria, C. Limbic cholinergic pathways involved in sleep and emotional behavior. *Exp. Neurol.*, **8**: 93–111, 1963.

Hull, C. L. *Principles of Behavior.* New York: Appleton-Century, 1943.

Hull, C. D., Buchwald, N. A., & Ling, G. Effects of direct cholinergic stimulation of forebrain structures. *Brain Res.*, **6**: 22–35, 1967.

Hunt, J. McV. Motivation inherent in information processing and action. In *Motivation and Social Interaction: Cognitive Determinants* (Harvey, O. J., ed.). New York: Ronald Press, 1963.

Kelsey, J. E., & Grossman, S. P. Cholinergic blockade and lesions in the ventromedial septum of the rat. *Physiol. & Behav.*, **4**: 837–845, 1969.

Krasne, F. B. General disruption resulting from electrical stimulation of ventromedial hypothalamus. *Science,* **138**: 822–823, 1962.

Levitt, F. A., & Fisher, A. E. Failure of central anticholinergic brain stimulation to block natural thirst. *Physiol. & Behav.*, **2**: 425–428, 1967.

Lindsley, D. B. Psychophysiology and motivation. In *Nebraska Symposium on Motivation: 1957* (Jones, M. R., ed.). Lincoln: Univ. of Nebraska Press, 1957. Pp. 44–105.

Lindsley, D. B., Bowden, J., & Magoun, H. W. Effect upon the EEG of acute injury to the brainstem activating system. *EEG clin. Neurophysiol.*, **1**: 475–486, 1949.

Lindsley, D. B., Schreiner, L. H., Knowles, W. B., & Magoun, H. W. Behavioral and EEG changes following chronic brainstem lesions in the cat. *EEG clin. Neurophysiol.*, **2**: 483–498, 1950.

MacLean, P. D. Chemical and electrical stimulation of hippocampus in unrestrained animals. I. Methods and electroencephalographic findings. *Arch. Neurol.*, **78**: 113–127, 1957.

Magoun, H. W., & Rhines, R. An inhibitory mechanism in the bulbar reticular formation. *J. Neurophysiol.*, **9**: 165–171, 1946.

Malmo, R. B. Activation: A neuropsychological dimension. *Psychol. Rev.*, **66**: 367–386, 1959.

Margules, D. L., & Stein, L. Cholinergic synapses in the ventromedial hypothalamus for the suppression of operant behavior by punishment and satiety. *J. comp. physiol. Psychol.*, **67**: 327–335, 1969.

McCleary, R. A. Response modulating functions of the limbic system: initiation and suppression. In *Progress in Physiological Psychology* (Stellar, E., & Sprague, J. M., eds.). New York: Academic Press, 1966. Pp. 210–272.

McPhail, E. M., & Miller, N. E. Cholinergic brain stimulation in cats: Failure to obtain sleep. *J. comp. physiol. Psychol.*, **66**: 499–503, 1968.

Michael, R. P. Estrogen-sensitive neurons and sexual behavior in female cats. *Science,* **136**: 322–323, 1962.

Miller, G. A., Galanter, E., & Pribram, K. H. *Plans and the Structure of Behavior.* New York: Holt, 1960.

Miller, N. E. Chemical coding of behavior in the brain. *Science,* **148**: 328–338, 1965.

Moruzzi, G., & Magoun, H. W. Brainstem reticular formation and activation of the EEG. *EEG clin. Neurophysiol.,* 1: 455–473, 1949.

Myers, R. D. Modification of drinking patterns by chronic intracranial chemical infusion. In *Thirst—Proceedings of the First International Symposium on Thirst in the Regulation of Body Water* (Wayner, M. J., ed.). Elmsford, N.Y.: Pergamon Press, 1964. Pp. 533–552.

Myers, R. D. Injection of solutions into cerebral tissue: Relation between volume and diffusion. *Physiol. & Behav.,* 1: 171–174, 1966.

Myers, R. D. Chemical mechanisms in the hypothalamus mediating eating and drinking in the monkey. *Ann. N.Y. Acad. Sci.,* 157: 918–932, 1969.

Pavlov, I. *Conditioned Reflexes. An Investigation of the Physiological Activity of the Cerebral Cortex.* New York: Oxford Univ. Press, 1927.

Rech, R. H. The relevance of experiments involving injection of drugs into the brain. In *Importance of Fundamental Principles in Drug Evaluation* (Tedeschi, D. H., & Tedeschi, R. E., eds.). New York: Raven Press, 1968. Pp. 325–360.

Robinson, B. W. Forebrain alimentary responses: Some organizational principles. In *Thirst—First International Symposium on Thirst in the Regulation of Body Water* (Wayner, M. J., ed.). Elmsford, N.Y.: Pergamon Press, 1964.

Sommer, Sally R., Novin, D., & LeVine, M. Food and water intake after intrahypothalamic injections of carbachol in the rabbit. *Science,* 156: 983–984, 1967.

Stellar, E. The physiology of motivation. *Psychol. Rev.,* 61: 5–22, 1954.

Wagner, J. W., & DeGroot, J. Changes in feeding behavior after intracerebral injections in the rat. *Amer. J. Physiol.,* 204: 483–487, 1963.

Wheatley, M. D. The hypothalamus and affective behavior in cats: A study of the effects of experimental lesions with anatomic correlations. *Arch. Neurol. Psychiat. (Chicago),* 52: 296–316, 1944.

Motivational Properties of Hypothalamic Aggression in Cats[1]

WARREN W. ROBERTS

University of Minnesota

HAROLD O. KIESS

University of Illinois

Hess (1954), Hunsperger (1956), Masserman (1941), and other investigators have described aggressive behavior that can be elicited in the conscious cat by stimulation of the medial hypothalamus and mesencephalic central gray. This "affective defense" or "rage" reaction, which includes hissing, growling, retraction of ears, piloerection, and striking with the claws, closely resembles the normal behavior of cats in conflicts with animals of equal or larger size. Recently, Wasman and Flynn (1962) have obtained a second type of aggression from the lateral hypothalamus that they have termed "stalking attack" because of its resemblance to normal predatory hunting behavior. It lacks the prominent vocal and gestural display of the affective defense reaction and consists of locomotor activity and, when a prey object is sighted, a direct biting attack.

A number of studies have attempted to determine the behavioral properties of these centrally elicited aggressive responses. Masserman (1941) was unable to classically condition the affective defense reaction and concluded that it was only a motor automatism and was not effectively related to higher sensory, motivational, or associational systems. On the other hand, Hess's (1954) and Wasman and Flynn's (1962) observations that the overt attack components of both the affective defense and stalking responses were directed toward appropriate objects in the environment and were inhibited in an empty area indicate that the sensory systems do exert an important degree of control over the responses. . . .

1. This research was conducted at Syracuse University with support from Grant MY–3979 from the National Institute of Mental Health to the first author. A report of this study was presented at the American Psychological Association Convention in 1963 (Roberts & Kiess, 1963). The assistance of Katherine Tubbert and Janice Olszowka in performing the histology is gratefully acknowledged.

The purpose of the present study was to investigate the motivational properties of the hypothalamic attack responses using a different type of experiment, originally described by Miller (1959, p. 270) in another context, in which the reinforcing properties of the performance of attack could be separated from all other reinforcement produced by the stimulation. The stimulation was turned on in the start box of a Y-maze where the attack was prevented by the absence of attackable objects, and the cats were given an opportunity to learn an approach response to one of the arms where the reward was a rat that they could attack. By alternating free and forced trials to opposite arms, any reinforcing effects associated with the stimulation per se or its termination were equalized between the arms, leaving the performance of attack as the only differentiating feature. Cats that spontaneously attacked rats (only 7 percent of the total) were eliminated to make sure that the learning could not be due to spontaneous attack habits.

If the cats learned to go consistently to the arm containing the rat, it would mean that excitation of the hypothalamic attack mechanism: (a) confers positive reinforcing properties on performance of attack and (b) possesses motivational and cue properties sufficient to evoke subsequent performance of learned prey-procuring responses. If the cats learned to prefer the empty arm, it would mean that the performance of the attack response was negatively reinforcing.

METHODS

Subjects

Before surgery, 15 adult cats were tested for spontaneous aggression toward rats by leaving a hooded rat weighing about 350 gm in each cat's home cage for 24 hr. One cat attacked the rat and was eliminated, leaving seven females and seven males as the primary group for the present experiment. A second group of six cats used in exploratory work was added to the analysis correlating unlearned responses to stimulation with anatomical structures to provide a greater sampling of electrode locations.

Surgery

Multiple electrodes (Delgado, 1955) were implanted bilaterally in the anterior hypothalamus of each cat. They consisted of a cemented column of three insulated stainless-steel wires .254 mm in diameter. Each wire was 1.5 mm shorter than the next longer one, and the insulation was scraped for approximately .6 mm from the tip. . . .

Apparatus

The stimulator was a Grass Model S-4 set for a unidirectional pulse width of .2 msec and a frequency of 100 pps. Voltage and current were monitored with a calibrated oscilloscope. The stimulation was monopolar, with the brain electrode negative. The current was conducted to Ss through light wire leads attached to a harness. . . . At the end of each arm [of the Y maze] was a 38 cm. of lateral cul-de-sac where the rat was tethered   out of sight of the choice point.

Behavior tests

Preliminary Tests. One week after surgery, the unconditioned responses elicited by stimulation of the electrodes were observed in the observation box. Five males and four females that made relatively pure and sustained attacks on rats were selected for the maze training and given an average of nine additional attack trials in the straight alley to determine optimal voltages for use in the maze. After 5 sec of stimulation in the closed start box, the door was opened to give access to the rat which was tethered first 127 cm, then 190 cm from the start box. Ten seconds later, the stimulation was turned off by a motor-driven potentiometer that gradually reduced the voltage to zero over a 15-sec period. The purpose of the slow termination was to minimize any possible reinforcing property associated with the end of the stimulation. The voltage was varied on successive trials until the level producing maximally persistent and intense attack was determined.

The rats included both hooded and albino strains and weighed about 300–400 gm. Because several cats in preliminary work manifested some fear of rats that counterattacked vigorously, the rats' incisors were severed at gum level and they were quieted with subanesthetic pentobarbital.

Maze Test. . . . On odd-numbered trials, Ss were allowed a free choice between the two arms. On even-numbered trials, the arm chosen on the preceding free trial was blocked with a transparent door, causing S to enter the other arm. This was done to equalize the amount of stimulation and number of stimulus terminations associated with each arm.

At the start of a trial, the stimulation was administered for 5 sec before the start-box door was opened. When S entered one of the goal arms, a door was closed behind him and he interrupted a photoelectric beam that started a timer which allowed 10 sec more of stimulation and then started the motor-driven potentiometer that turned the stimulation off slowly over 15 sec. After the trial, S was placed in a detention box for an intertrial interval of approximately 2 min. Four free and four forced trials were given daily. When the criterion of 9 correct out of 10 free trials was reached, the rat was switched to the other arm and a minimum of 40 additional trials was administered to test for habit reversal. Response times were obtained automatically with a .01-sec clock started by a Microswitch on the start-box door and stopped by the interruption of the photoelectric beam. . . .

Conditioned Attack Test. After the maze training, Ss were tested in the maze without stimulation to determine whether attack behavior had been conditioned to the maze cues and whether the learned locomotor approach response would generalize to the nonstimulated state. Two free-choice trials were given with the same procedure as in the training, except that rats were placed in both arms, Ss were 16-hr food-deprived, and E timed the duration of close visual attention to the rat, defined as prolonged direction of the head toward the rat from a distance of less than 38 cm.

Hunger Test. After 2 days of training to eat in the test box, Ss were deprived of food for 48 hr and placed in the box with a bowl of food and a rat. While Ss were in the process of eating, the stimulation was turned on for 15 sec, and E timed the latency of stopping eating, the latency of attack, and the duration of attack and of eating. Four trials were administered.

Anatomy

At the conclusion of testing, Ss were anesthetized and perfused with 10 percent formalin. A reference cut was made in the stereotaxic frontal plane to guide the sectioning. The upper tip of each multiple electrode was marked by the Prussian blue staining method. Alternate frozen sections were stained with neutral red and cresyl violet. Localization in the atlas of Jasper and Ajmone-Marsan (1954) was performed without knowledge of the responses elicited by particular points.

RESULTS

Behavior toward rats without stimulation

None of the 14 Ss prepared with electrodes attacked the rat during the pretest for spontaneous attack habits. When the rats were first placed in their cages, Ss displayed a mixture of investigatory behavior and cautious avoidance. After a few minutes, most Ss lost interest, but continued to avoid close proximity to the rats. Several Ss playfully pawed and nosed the rats at first, but by the end of the period avoided them, probably because of counterattacks by the rats, which were observed in one case and inferred from evidence of bites in other cases.

Unconditioned responses to stimulation

Both the affective and stalking attack patterns described by Wasman and Flynn (1962) were observed. In several cases, they were obtained in the same animal when different electrode points were stimulated. One pattern was characterized primarily by striking with the paw and affective display, the other by biting and a much smaller amount of affective display. . . .

The clawing attack was more delayed, less consistent, and less sustained than the biting attack. The Ss did not direct their locomotion toward the rat, as in the case of biting attack, but struck briefly only when they happened to walk near a rat. For this reason, only points evoking biting attack were used in the maze training. Four of these points also elicited hissing, but in two cases the hissing threshold was above the voltage level used in the maze test.

While attacking in the maze, four *S*s directed their initial bites consistently at the head and neck, one seized the midsection, and the remaining four grasped any part of the body indiscriminately. Five *S*s made repeated brief bites that were shifted considerably in location, while four continued to bite the same spot, but alternately relaxed and tightened their jaws as in the "killing bite" described by Leyhausen (1960). Eight *S*s used their paws to hold the rat or to pinion it to the floor, while the ninth seized it at the start with his teeth and carried it while he walked around the arm for the remainder of the trial.

Maze learning

Original Training. All nine *S*s learned to go consistently on free trials to the arm containing the rat. By a conservative two-tailed sign test, this outcome was significant beyond the .01 level. The median number of errors on free-choice trials was only 2.0 (range 0–12). The median number of free and forced trials to criterion (including the 20 criterion trials) was 30 (range 20–44).

There was a significant reduction in response times for entering the arm containing the rat (3.0 sec on the first trial, .7 sec on the last five criterion trials; $t = 2.85$, $df = 8$, $p = .02$). The much smaller difference between the response times for entering the empty arm, 2.2 sec and 1.7 sec, was not significant ($t = .67$). The response times on the last five criterion trials were significantly faster for the arm containing the rat than for the empty arm ($t = 2.58$, $df = 8$, $p = .03$). The mean duration of attack was 7.4 sec. . . .

Reversal Training. The reversal task proved to be much more difficult than the initial learning. Two *S*s succeeded in reversing their habits, reaching criterion in 34 and 50 trials. A third almost achieved criterion at one point with a score of eight correct out of nine trials. A fourth, whose first electrode was accidentally damaged, reversed in 44 trials when another electrode on the same side of the brain . . . was substituted. The remaining five *S*s continued to enter the originally correct side on 93 percent of the reversal free trials.

Test for conditioned attack

On the two trials in the maze without stimulation, there were no conditioned attack responses, and *S*s ignored the rat most of the time. The mean duration of close visual attention to the rat was only 4 sec on the first trial and 0 sec on the second trial.

The median times for the locomotor response were exceedingly slow (81 and 96 sec), and the choice of arm showed a partial generalization decrement from the performance on the training trials. On the first trial seven out of nine *S*s chose the arm preferred at the end of training, and on the second five chose the preferred arm. Four *S*s behaved in an anxious manner, resisting placement in the start box, meowing, and attempting to escape from the goal arm.

Hunger test

This procedure tested whether the centrally elicited readiness for attack could compete successfully with ongoing feeding behavior motivated by normal hunger. When the stimulation was turned on while Ss were eating, they stopped with a median latency of .3 sec, attacked in 6.3 sec, and maintained the attack for a median duration of 4.7 sec. Most of the time not spent in attacking was taken up with locomotion around the box. None of the Ss returned to eating while the stimulation was on, but most took a bite while passing the food on one or two trials. These were quick, seizing bites like those administered to the rats, were not accompanied by licking, chewing, or swallowing, and appeared to be generalized biting attacks.

Anatomical findings

. . . Figure 2 presents summary diagrams of the locations of the electrodes in the 14 Ss of the present study and 6 additional Ss used in preliminary work. Although it was not the purpose of the present research to explore the hypothalamus thoroughly, some degree of anatomical differentiation is apparent. The greatest number of biting attack points were located in the dorsomedial and anterior lateral hypothalamus. The points eliciting pure affective display without attack were located in the ventromedial area, while the majority of those evoking clawing attack together with affective display were placed near the border between the biting attack and affective display zones. Since some locomotion or "flight" behavior accompanied stimulation of most points, it was omitted from the diagrams in the interest of clarity.

DISCUSSION

The learning evidenced in the maze indicates that when a readiness for predatory attack is aroused in cats by hypothalamic stimulation, the overt performance of the attack becomes positively reinforcing. The absence of attack when stimulation was not administered, both in the pretest for spontaneous aggression before the surgery and in the test for conditioned attack after the maze training, rules out any possibility that the learning might have been due to spontaneous attack tendencies. Since the durations and frequencies of termination of the stimulation were kept equal in the two goal arms throughout training, any reinforcing property of the stimulation per se or of its termination (Brown & Cohen, 1959; Cohen et al., 1957; Roberts, 1958) could not have produced the learned preference for the arm containing the rat.

Although the clawing attack accompanying the affective defense reaction was not tested in the maze, its poor persistence and strong dependence on chance proximity to the rat indicates that its performance possessed little or no reward effect. In view of the general adaptive function of threat displays such as hissing and piloerection in minimizing mutually injurious fighting between peers (Eibl-Eibesfeldt, 1961), it would be expected that attack associated with such displays would be more purely defensive and lack the rewarding properties of beneficial predatory aggression.

Although the motor discharge or the sensory feedback from the response may have acted directly to strengthen the learned associations, a second

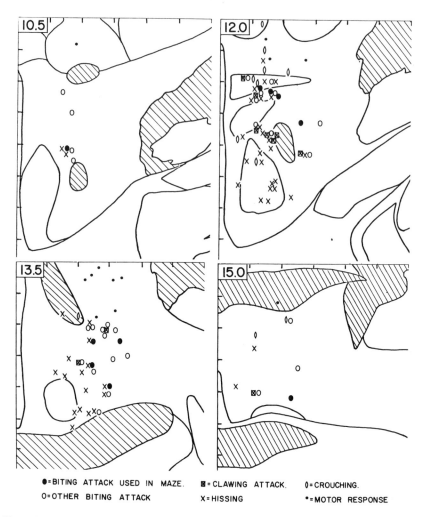

●=BITING ATTACK USED IN MAZE.   ◼=CLAWING ATTACK.   0=CROUCHING.
O=OTHER BITING ATTACK   X=HISSING   *=MOTOR RESPONSE

Figure 1 (not reprinted).
Figure 2. Locations of electrode points in hypothalamus and preoptic area are plotted on frontal plane diagrams located 10.5 to 15.0 mm anterior to interaural zero of stereotaxic instrument (Jasper & Ajmone-Marsan, 1954). (Points that evoked mixed responses are shown by multiple symbols. Omitted are a number of points that were in the optic chiasm or the vascular tissue beneath the hypothalamus or were poorly localized in the histology.)

possibility is that they may have generated the reinforcement by reducing a general frustration drive aroused when the strong readiness for attack was blocked in the start box by the absence of an attack object (Miller, 1959). As Miller has suggested, the latter hypothesis could be differentiated from the former by testing whether the magnitude of the reinforcement was an increasing function of the delay from the onset of the brain stimulation to the performance of the response.

The exceedingly slow locomotor response times in the maze when the stimulation was omitted in the conditioned attack test indicate that the central readiness for attack produced by the stimulation possessed motivational and cue properties of salient importance in the evocation of the instrumental locomotor response. The finding that hungry *S*s would switch from eating to attacking when stimulated demonstrates that these motivational and cue properties were specific enough and strong enough to overcome a normally dominant competing response. This finding also rules out the possibility that the attack might have been a secondary consequence of centrally induced hunger, which would be expected to intensify the eating rather than shift the behavior to attack.

The absence of conditioned attack in the maze is somewhat puzzling in view of *S*s' extensive attack experience with stimulation, but it parallels Masserman's (1941) inability to condition the affective defense response. Whether this was due to a defect of generalization from the stimulated state, to interference from fear conditioned to the rats or the general maze cues, or to a true absence of conditioning cannot be concluded from the present data. Whatever the explanation, the finding that a highly effective mechanism for aggression can exist in the brains of animals that do not use it, but would if given appropriate early training (Kuo, 1930), demonstrates that experience is an important determinant of the conditions for utilization of such central behavior mechanisms.

The fact that relatively crude electrical stimulation can arouse this complex response readiness without interrupting its coordination with sensory, motivational, and associational mechanisms indicates that this hypothalamic area is a strategic point where relatively simple neural or hormonal input, varying only in gross magnitude, could modulate the strength of the general mood or readiness for predatory aggression. The possibility that the hypothalamus may be a nodal control point for aggression is supported by reports that indicate that aggressive responses are more integrated and directed when elicited from the hypothalamus than from other areas such as the amygdala (Akert, 1961, p. 292; DeMolina & Hunsperger, 1959; MacLean & Delgado, 1953; Ursin & Kaada, 1960) and mesencephalon (Hunsperger, 1956). It is also consistent with DeMolina and Hunsperger's (1962) evidence that the amygdala has only a unilateral projection to the efferent motor components of the affective defense mechanism, while the hypothalamus has a bilateral projection.

The locomotor activity accompanying the readiness for predatory attack resembled the appetitive or searching behavior that occurs when a motive has been aroused but suitable goal objects are absent. However, the locomotor tendency frequently competed with and interrupted the performance of attack when a rat was present, indicating that the locomotion was independently potentiated in its own right and not just a consequence of lack of a prey object.

REFERENCES

Akert, K. Diencephalon. In D. E. Sheer (Ed.), *Electrical stimulation of the brain.* Austin: Univer. Texas Press, 1961. Pp. 288–301.

Brown, G. W., & Cohen, B. D. Avoidance and approach learning motivated by stimulation of identical hypothalamic loci. *Amer. J. Physiol.,* 1959, **197,** 153–157.

Cohen, B. D., Brown, G. W., & Brown, M. L. Avoidance learning motivated by hypothalamic stimulation. *J. exp. Psychol.*, 1957, **53**, 228–233.

Delgado, J. M. R. Evaluation of permanent implantation of electrodes within the brain. *EEG clin. Neurophysiol.*, 1955, **7**, 637–644.

DeMolina, A. F., & Hunsperger, R. W. Central representation of affective reactions in forebrain and brainstem: Electrical stimulation of amygdala, stria terminalis, and adjacent structures. *J. Physiol., London,* 1959, **145**, 251–265.

DeMolina, A. F., & Hunsperger, R. W. Organization of the subcortical system governing defense and flight reactions in the cat. *J. Physiol., London,* 1962, **160**, 200–213.

Eibl-Eibesfeldt, I. The fighting behavior of animals. *Scient. American,* 1961, **205**, 112–122.

Hess, W. R. *Das Zwischenhirn: Syndrome, Lokalisationen, Funktionen.* (2nd ed.) Basel: Schwabe, 1954.

Hunsperger, R. W. Affektreaktionen auf electrische Reizung im Hirnstamm der Katze. *Helv. physiol. acta,* 1956, **14**, 70–92.

Jasper, H. H., & Ajmone-Marsan, C. *A stereotaxic atlas of the diencephalon of the cat.* Ottawa: National Research Council of Canada, 1954.

Kuo, Z. Y. The genesis of the cat's responses to the rat. *J. comp. Psychol.*, 1930, **11**, 1–35.

Leyhausen, P. *Verhaltenstudien an Katzen.* Berlin: Parey, 1960.

MacLean, P. D., & Delgado, J. M. R. Electrical and chemical stimulation of frontotemporal portion of limbic system in the waking animal. *EEG clin. Neurophysiol.*, 1953, **5**, 91–100.

Masserman, J. H. Is the hypothalamus a centre of emotion? *Psychosom. Med.,* 1941, **3**, 1–25.

Miller, N. E. Liberalization of basic S-R concepts: Extensions to conflict behavior, motivation, and social learning. In S. Koch (Ed.), *Psychology: A study of a science.* Vol. 2. *General systematic formulations, learning, and special processes.* New York: McGraw-Hill, 1959. Pp. 196–292.

Roberts, W. W. Both rewarding and punishing effects from stimulation of hypothalamus of cat with same electrode at same intensity. *J. comp. physiol. Psychol.*, 1958, **51**, 400–407.

Roberts, W. W. Fear-like behavior elicited from dorsomedial thalamus of cat. *J. comp. physiol. Psychol.*, 1962, **55**, 191–197.

Roberts, W. W., & Kiess, H. O. Positive reinforcing property of performance of attack potentiated by stimulation of cat hypothalamus. *Amer. Psychologist,* 1963, **18**, 426. (Abstract)

Ursin, H., & Kaada, B. R. Functional localization within the amygdaloid complex in the cat. *EEG clin. Neurophysiol.*, 1960, **12**, 1–20.

Wasman, M., & Flynn, J. P. Directed attack elicited from hypothalamus. *AMA Arch. Neurol.*, 1962, **6**, 220–227.

Commentary

WARREN W. ROBERTS

A wide variety of largely unlearned adaptive behaviors that are important in survival and reproduction can be induced by localized stimulation of certain brain structures, including the midbrain, thalamus, rhinencephalon, and especially the hypothalamic-preoptic region. The behaviors include eating, drinking, male mating behavior, defensive threat, biting attack, escape-like locomotion, crouching, grooming, exploratory activity, gnawing, sleep, hoarding, burrowing, and certain components of nest-building and maternal behavior (for references, see Roberts, 1970). Because of their striking intensity, relatively stereotyped form, and specific anatomical localization, these centrally induced responses constitute some of the strongest evidence for the existence of specialized neurological mechanisms for bioadaptive behaviors. The study reprinted in this book shows that the performance of one of these responses, biting attack, is not an emotionally neutral motor response, but is sufficiently rewarding or pleasureable to animals that they will learn a new maze habit in order to obtain an attackable object.

My interest in centrally induced behaviors began when I was a graduate student in Neal E. Miller's laboratory at Yale. Our first study using brain stimulation is also included in this book (p. 44). During this experiment and additional exploratory studies, which were mainly concerned with aversive learning and the drives of pain, fear, hunger, and thirst, I was deeply impressed by a number of response patterns that closely resembled the natural aggressive or fearful behavior of cats. These included the defensive threat or "affective defense" originally discovered by W. R. Hess in 1928, which consisted of hissing, growling, piloerection, flattening of the ears, pupilodilation, clawing, and biting; a flight response that consisted of vigorous locomotion and climbing around the test box; and a crouching or skulking pattern that consisted of crouching mixed with intermittent locomotion in a low slinking posture. The responses were highly stimulus bound, ceasing almost immediately after termination of the stimulation. Their intensity was closely graded to the current level, varied little from trial to trial at a given current level, and at strong currents was more vigorous and persistent than spontaneous behaviors. These characteristics led me to presume that the stimulated structures had powerful and probably innately organized projections to the motor mechanisms for the behaviors.

Later studies of the flight and crouching responses, which resembled normal fear behavior, were concerned with the negative and positive reinforcing properties of the onset and termination of the stimulation that produced the responses (Roberts, 1958a, 1958b, 1962). When stimulation that elicited crouching was used as the aversive stimulus in active avoidance training, the animals learned to escape and avoid efficiently, indicating that the stimulation was purely aversive. Stimulation that evoked the flight pattern produced similarly rapid learning of escape responses, but failed to cause significant avoidance in a large number of additional trials. This paradoxical separation of escape and avoidance learning was attributed to a transient positive reinforcing effect at the onset of stimulation that rewarded animals for not avoiding, followed by a transition to an aversive state that rewarded them for turning off the stimulation. The initial reward effect was confirmed by vigorous bar pressing or accurate choice of a particular maze arm when each response was followed by a short duration of stimulation. The delayed aversive or punishing effect was confirmed by the appearance of conflict hesitation and finally response cessation in bar pressing and maze tests when the fixed duration of stimulation was lengthened appreciably.

A problem that bothered me in these studies was the possibility that the reinforcing effects of the onset and termination of the stimulation might be due not to the neuronal mechanisms that produced the observable crouching and flight responses, but to unrelated mechanisms located in the same region that were simultaneously excited by the nonspecific stimulation. It was not until the experiment reprinted in this book, and another that was executed immediately before it (Roberts & Carey, 1965), that a method for separating stimulation-related reward from response-related reward became clear to me.

The study reprinted in this book originated as an extension of a study of the rewarding properties of gnawing elicited by electrical stimulation of the hypothalamus in rats (Roberts & Carey, 1965). In the fall of 1961, my research assistant, Robert Carey, and I were engaged in some exploratory work on the rewarding and punishing effects of hypothalamic stimulation in rats. Soon after we began testing, Carey came to me with great concern because the stimulation caused one of our first two rats to gnaw so intensely on exposed edges of our laboriously constructed maze that he threatened serious damage to the apparatus. The animal's vigor, persistence, and adaptiveness to the conformation of the slightly projecting edges was so impressive that the empathic thought occurred to me that the activity must be somehow rewarding or pleasurable to be maintained so intensely and persistently. Since the animal and a suitable maze were immediately available, we decided to test the hypothesis. All exposed edges in the maze were armored with sheet metal so that the only gnawable object was a cleated board that was placed in one arm as the reward. The brain stimulation was turned on when the rat was placed in the start box, and turned off 30 seconds after he entered either arm. The animal increasingly favored the arm containing the gnawing board until he reached the criterion of learning in 38 trials. When the gnawing board was switched to the other arm, he reversed his preference in 137 trials. Subsequently we replicated this result in six more animals, and extended the findings to a more difficult problem, brightness discrimination.

While we were completing the study of gnawing in rats, I began to think about possible extensions of our findings to other responses and species, and their relevance to the interaction between innately organized and learned behaviors. Thus, my earlier interest in the reinforcing properties of stimulation *per se* shifted to the reward associated with performance of innately organized or species-typical behaviors, which appeared to be more clearly and directly related to natural adaptive behavior processes. At about this time, Wasman and Flynn (1962) published their report of quiet biting attack elicited from the hypothalamus of cats, which offered an ideal opportunity for testing the generality of response-related reward because it involved a different movement pattern, different adaptive function, and a high degree of object-specificity.

COMMENTS ON STUDY

The possibility that the attack was a reflexive response to centrally elicited pain (Ulrich & Azrin, 1962) is unlikely because pain-elicited attack persists for about 10 to 30 sec after the termination of pain, while hypothalamically induced attack ceases almost immediately after the end of the stimulation. Also, the hissing and growling that cats very consistently emit in the presence of pain was never elicited by half of the electrodes that induced biting attack, and in the remaining cases had a significantly higher threshold than attack.

Hutchinson and Renfrew (1966), who found a perfect correlation of hypothalamically induced attack and eating, suggested that the attack might be a learned food-procuring response acquired during uncontrolled prelaboratory experience. However, attack and eating have not been obtained together as consistently in our own laboratory or in that of J. P. Flynn (Flynn, Vanegas, Foote, & Edwards, 1970), and the suggestion that hypothalamically induced attack might be a learned food-procuring response appears to be ruled out by the finding that cats raised in isolation from other cats and prey objects displayed all of the basic components of attack during their first stimulation trial in the presence of rats (Roberts & Bergquist, 1968). Experience may have a supplementary role, since the isolated animals were less persistent and less discriminating between attack objects than normal cats.

The reward associated with centrally induced bioadaptive behaviors could be due to either the motor discharge of the responses or the sensory feedback from interaction with the goal object or goal situation. Because of the usual interdependence of these two factors, their relative roles in reinforcement are hard to assess directly except in special cases. However, a number of considerations favor sensory input as the main source of reward. First, many rewards result from sensory stimulation in the absence of apparent consummatory behavior. For example, the sound of adult chaffinch song produced by a tape recorder is rewarding for young chaffinches (Stevenson, 1969). Stimulation of warmth receptors is rewarding for hypothermic animals, and stimulation of cold receptors for hyperthermic animals. H. F. Harlow's studies of young monkeys raised with artificial mother surrogates strongly suggest that the gentle tactile stimulation provided by fur is rewarding, and the visual stimulus of a chick seen through a transparent window is rewarding for another chick (Sarty, 1968).

A second consideration favoring sensory feedback as the source of most reinforcement is the greater effectiveness that it would have in limiting the behavior to appropriate objects and in directing learned habits toward biologically significant ends. If the efferent discharge of bioadaptive responses were rewarding, performance of responses with inappropriate objects or even no objects at all ("vacuum activities" of ethology) would be reinforced, and learned habits would be directed toward maximization of responses rather than achievement of functionally adaptive interaction with appropriate objects. On the other hand, evolutionary selection of strategic consummatory stimuli as unlearned rewards would tend to insure the appropriateness of object choices and learned habits.

ADAPTIVE FUNCTIONS OF RESPONSE-ASSOCIATED REWARD

The finding in the attack and gnawing studies that the performance of centrally induced consummatory responses can be rewarding was replicated with a third behavior in a third species, the preintromission portion of male mating behavior in opossums, which consisted of mounting, rubbing the chin in the fur, sexual biting of the nape, and intermittent relaxing (Roberts, Steinberg, & Means, 1967). This male-type mating pattern was elicited by brain stimulation in females as readily as in males, and the fastest learner in the maze happened to be a female. However, neither intact nor spayed females treated with testosterone ever evidenced any of these behaviors spontaneously in tests with receptive females, although males tested with the same receptive females readily did so. This indicates that most of the brain connections for male mating behavior and for the reward associated with it develop during ontogeny in both male and female brains, but are not activated in females, possibly because of lower sensitivity to testosterone.

Other investigators have found that similar reward properties are associated with centrally induced eating and drinking (Andersson, Larsson, & Persson, 1960; Wyrwicka, Dobrzecka, & Tarnecki, 1960), and with naturally induced attack, threat, running, burrowing, exploring, hoarding, maternal behavior, and preejaculatory mating responses, as well as with the obvious cases of eating, drinking, and ejaculation (Kagan & Berkun, 1954; King & Weisman, 1964; Montgomery, 1954; Myer & White, 1965; Richelle, 1967; Simmons, 1924; Thompson, 1963; Whalen, 1961). Thus it appears that a wide range of centrally and naturally induced bioadaptive behaviors are accompanied by reward, although there are probably some exceptions. Additional reward effects are associated with the reduction of aversive states such as pain or the malaise caused by dietary deficiencies (Garcia, Ervin, Yorke, & Koelling, 1967).

Rewarding sensory input from bioadaptive behaviors would be expected to improve the effectiveness of the innately organized components of the behaviors by engendering a number of different kinds of learning and related motivational processes whose relative importance would depend on particular circumstances. Most obvious is learning of instrumental responses, such as foraging and manipulatory habits, that assist in procuring objects or situations needed for performance of the behaviors. A second type of learning is improvement or elaboration of innately organized behaviors, such as polishing of landing techniques and complex aerial maneuvers during the early flights of young birds, or improved spatial orientation of copulation by males during initial experience with females. A third type of learning is the improved ordering of innately organized response components whose effectiveness depends on an optimal sequence that is not specified innately, as is the case with the gathering, carrying, and arranging components of nest construction. To the extent that rewarding sensory feedback is dependent on a particular sequence, that order would be strengthened. A fourth type of learning is the conditioning of learned and innately organized responses to the special cues of locally available goal objects or goal situations, such as particular mates, foods, or nest locations. A fifth type of learning is the acquisition of memories of previous rewards ("incentive motivation," "reward expectancies") which are specific to particular rewards and can exert both directive and energizing effects on overt behaviors (Trapold, 1970). A sixth contribution of response-related rewards is short-term positive feedback from performance that strengthens and maintains the behavior for bouts of appreciable length until satiation or other shut-off factors take effect, thus preventing rapid oscillation between behaviors of similar strength. A seventh function of reward associated with innately organized behaviors may be to protect the behaviors against excessive suppression by the punishing effects of inappropriately directed or timed responses resulting in pain, fear, nausea, bitter tastes, discomfort vocalizations of young, or other aversive states.

Some of the types of learning listed above, especially 1, 4, 5, and 6, may well play an important role in the "modifiability" of performance of hypothalamically potentiated behaviors described by Valenstein, Cox, and Kakolewski (1968, 1969, 1970). Learning of approach responses, reward expectancies, and conditioned consummatory responses for a particular goal object on the first few stimulation trials would increase the probability of performance of consummatory responses with that object to the exclusion of other consummatory responses potentiated by stimulation of overlapping or adjacent mechanisms. Several examples of such stereotyped approach habits have been described by Valenstein et al. (1968; 1969, pp. 263–265, 270). Subsequent withdrawal of the goal object for the initially dominant response would permit practice of other responses, and development of similar supporting habits that would enable the late emerging responses to compete more effectively with the initially dominant response after restoration of its goal object (Roberts, 1969).

OTHER STUDIES OF CENTRALLY INDUCED RESPONSES

Following completion of our experiments on the rewarding properties of centrally induced gnawing and attack, we decided to study a representative of the primitive mammalian levels from which rats, cats, and other "higher" mammals evolved. We picked the opossum, a marsupial, because it is probably the least specialized of existing primitive mammals.

We found that a number of complex behaviors could be induced by stimulation of the hypothalamic-preoptic region, including male mating behavior, quiet biting attack, defensive threat, eating, grooming, exploratory behavior, and escape-like activity. Each behavior pattern, except for generalized investigatory behavior consisting of looking around, sniffing, and locomotion, was obtained from a limited portion of the hypothalamic-preoptic region. There was some partial overlap of the effective zones for some behavior patterns, especially in the preoptic region, but most zones differed from others in at least part of their distribution. The greatest amount of overlap was between the mating and grooming responses, but when more specific thermal stimulation was applied in a later experiment (Roberts, Bergquist, & Robinson, 1969), grooming was elicited without mating, indicating that the two behaviors were not due to activation of a single mechanism, but were obtained together because of the nonspecific action of electrical stimulation.

Most of the behavior patterns consisted of a number of separable elements. For example, the threat pattern consisted of opening the mouth wide, growling, swinging the head slowly from side to side, and backing, usually into a corner. Since most previous descriptions of elicited behaviors tended to emphasize complete response patterns, we were surprised to find that only 20 percent of the electrodes that elicited mating, biting attack, threat, or grooming produced complete patterns, while 80 percent produced various incomplete subsets of elements that were highly reproducible for particular electrodes, but differed between electrodes. Hess and Brugger (1943) have reported similar variation in the completeness of the affective defense response of the cat. From these and related findings, we concluded that (a) the electrical field of a single electrode directly excites only a small fraction of the cells in hypothalamic-preoptic behavior mechanisms, (b) there is relatively little synaptic spread between neurons controlling different response elements within hypothalamic-preoptic mechanisms, (c) hypothalamic efferents project separately to independent sensorimotor (often reflex-like) mechanisms for individual elements of response patterns, and (d) the small zone of direct electrical excitation samples these efferents probabilistically. Thus, the tendency of animals to display complete response patterns under natural conditions must be due to integrative connections in structures that project to the hypothalamic-preoptic region, or to neural or humoral input to the hypothalamic-preoptic mechanisms that act nonspecifically on neurons controlling different components of a given pattern.

One of my students, Ernest Bergquist (1970), has traced the hypothalamic efferent path that produces motivational responses in the opossum into the midbrain. He found that mating, attack, threat, eating, grooming, and investigation induced by hypothalamic stimulation could be abolished or their thresholds markedly elevated by lesions at the border between the posterior hypothalamus and midbrain. Following unilateral lesions, the blockage was limited to responses elicited by stimulation on the same side of the brain as the lesion, which rules out nonspecific debilitation. The critical descending path for all of the responses except threat was the medial forebrain bundle, while threat was impaired only by more medial lesions in the vicinity of the periventricular system. Lesions located anterior or lateral to the stimulation electrodes did not affect the elicited responses, indicating that the descending paths are not only essential but also sufficient in the absence of anterior or lateral connections.

Another student, Gary Berntson (1972), has very recently localized the output pathways for hypothalamic aggressive responses in cats at the level of the posterior midbrain. He found that destruction of a medial tegmental zone blocked biting attack induced by hypothalamic stimulation, while damage to a lateral tegmental zone produced vigorous and persistent spontaneous biting attack in the absence of brain stimulation. Figure 1 shows the location of these areas. The medial zone corresponds fairly closely with the area where Flynn (1967) elicited attack by midbrain stimulation, and appears to be a way station between the hypothalamus and lower sensorimotor mechanisms for attack. The spontaneous attack that followed lateral lesions appeared very soon after the lesions were made, indicating that the area normally exerts a tonic inhibitory influence on attack. Additional evidence suggested that the lateral area is probably not intercalated in the pathway between the hypothalamus and sensorimotor mechanism, but exerts a separate inhibitory influence on the attack system below the midbrain level. The hissing and growling components of the threat pattern were blocked by lesions that interrupted any part of a

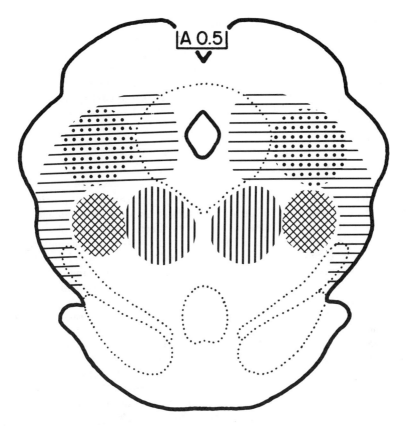

Figure 1. Schematic diagram of critical areas where lesions altered hypothalamic aggressive responses in cats. Biting attack and associated biting reflexes were blocked by destruction of vertically hatched area, while release of spontaneous attack and associated reflexes was produced by lesions of cross-hatched area. Lesions that interrupted any level of the pathway represented by horizontal hatching blocked hissing and growling. Lesions that included dotted area blocked ear-flattening component of threat. Courtesy of Gary G. Berntson.

pathway that extended laterally from the central grey to the ventrolateral border of the midbrain. Since ear flattening was affected only by lesions of a smaller zone located in the middle of the pathway for vocalization, and pupil dilation and piloerection were unaffected by any of the lesions, the pathways for the different components of the threat pattern are differentiated to an appreciable extent at this level of the brainstem.

When unilaterally lesioned cats were blindfolded and tested for biting responses to touch on each lip, the impairment of hypothalamically induced biting was greatest for touch applied to the lip contralateral to the lesion, while the release of spontaneous biting was greatest for touch applied to the ipsilateral lip. These findings, together with similar laterality phenomena found by Flynn and his associates with hypothalamically elicited attack (Bandler & Flynn, 1971a, 1971b; MacDonnell & Flynn, 1966), constitute additional evidence that an innately organized neurological mechanism underlies the basic core of attack behavior.

It is unclear whether the hypothalamic output pathways that have been traced to specific portions of the midbrain reticular formation are only passing through or are more directly related to reticular function. The widespread connections and complex influences of the ascending and descending output of reticular structures could play a potentially important role in the motor integration, attention arousal, habit reinforcement, and memory retrieval that accompany the attack behavior. Further studies of the continuation of these paths into lower levels of the brainstem may yield evidence regarding this possibility.

THERMOREGULATION

While electrical stimulation offers significant advantages in precision of control, reversibility, and localization, it suffers from the disadvantage that it acts nonspecifically on all neurons within its effective field, and often excites two or more normally unrelated mechanisms (Roberts, 1969). Even when its effective field contains cells belonging to only one functional system, the current acts nonspecifically on the dendrites, soma, and axons of afferents, interneurons, and efferents, with consequent disorganization of local integrative processes, coupled with an undifferentiated increase in output resulting from direct excitation of efferent axons. While this yields information regarding the effects of increased output from the area, it tells nothing about normal input, local information processing, or the normal functional independence of mixed responses. Chemical stimulation is somewhat more specific, but the improvement is only relative, since the number of functional systems and the diversity of cell and synapse types within the diffusion field surrounding a cannula tip is often so much greater than the number of proposed transmitters and their subtypes that pure excitation of a single type of synapse is improbable. In addition, some synapses may involve the sequential release of more than one transmitter, such as acetylcholine and norepinephrine (Burn, 1971), which would make them sensitive to both substances.

An alternative method of improving the specificity of stimulation is to apply physical or chemical stimuli for which specific receptors exist in the brain, such as heat, cold, osmolality, glucose levels, hormones, etc. For several years, we have used localized diathermic warming to study central thermoregulatory mechanisms without simultaneous arousal of other behavior systems that adjoin or partially overlap them (Roberts, Bergquist, & Robinson, 1969; Roberts & Robinson, 1969). In our experience with over 100 opossums, cats, and rats, localized warming has never induced any of the nonthermoregulatory responses that can be readily elicited with electrical stimulation through the same electrodes.

The most consistent response to warming of the preoptic and hypothalamic region in opossums, cats, and rats was relaxation and lying down. In cats this usually culminated in sleep. A similar process in humans may explain the lethargy and sleepiness that are often induced by elevated environmental temperatures or large meals, which raise body temperature. Other responses to central warming were grooming or spreading saliva over the fur in rats and opossums, escape-like activity in rats, panting in cats and opossums, and vasodilation of the tail in rats. Figure 2 shows some preliminary data on the brain areas where localized warming induced relaxation,

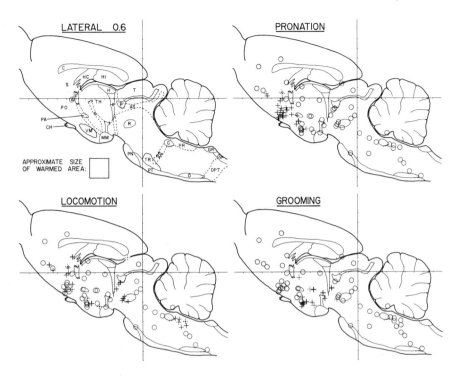

Figure 2. Locations where diathermic warming induced prone relaxation, locomotion, and grooming in rats. Crosses indicate centers of warming electrodes that induced each behavior, circles indicate ineffective electrodes. Heavy crosses represent lowest threshold cases, dashed crosses weak or high threshold cases. All electrodes located near midline.

grooming, and locomotion in the rat. Prone relaxation was obtained from the classical thermoregulatory area in the preoptic region and anterior hypothalamus, while grooming was induced from the posterior hypothalamus and ventral midbrain. Activity was obtained from more widely distributed areas, principally the septal region, ventral midbrain, and dorsal medulla, although a few warming electrodes in the preoptic and hypothalamic zones for relaxation and grooming were also effective. Because of this structural differentiation, most effective warming electrodes (77 percent) induced only one of the three behavioral responses, and only 3 percent elicited all three. It therefore appears that largely separate channels exist for the three responses from central receptor to final effector. A similar differentiation of the central actions of estradiol in female rats has been reported by Wade and Zucker (1970), who found that the increased locomotion and depressed appetite that normally occur together during estrus or following systemic estradiol injections can be separately induced by implants of estradiol in the preoptic area or ventromedial hypothalamus, respectively.

Thus, the correlated modulation of disparate elements of complex behavioral syndromes, such as thermoregulation and estrus, does not require unitary integrating centers, but can be accomplished by general physiological stimuli that produce correlated activity in different sets of receptors controlling different elements. A similar mode of organization may characterize other motivational systems that are modulated by general physiological states, such as hunger, thirst, maternal behavior, fear, etc.

QUESTIONS FOR FUTURE RESEARCH

Motivation is principally concerned with three types of usually reversible and often oscillatory changes in behavior that occur in the absence of learning experience or changes in the stimulus environment: (a) increases and decreases in the capacity of goal object stimuli to elicit unlearned bioadaptive behaviors, such as eating, drinking, mating, fighting, etc., (b) associated shifts in the effectiveness of specific rewards and punishments associated with the behaviors, and (c) correlated shifts in the probability and strength of learned responses that assist in procurement of goal objects or increase the efficiency of unlearned responses. It may be anticipated that further studies of centrally induced behaviors will contribute to understanding of the brain mechanisms underlying the first two and possibly all of these motivational phenomena.

During the last few years, it has become apparent that hypothalamic efferents do not exert a sufficiently dominant influence on the motor systems for many bioadaptive behaviors to produce the movements automatically, but instead act like motivational factors to potentiate the ability of certain specific environmental stimuli to elicit the responses (Roberts, 1970). Thus biting attack induced by brain stimulation requires both stimulation and an attack object, and ceases if either is removed. In the opossum, one component of attack, head tossing, is displayed only with objects that move, but not with anesthetized or dead objects, indicating that head tossing is critically dependent on stimuli (probably tactile) produced by the object's movement (Roberts et al., 1967). In the absence of movement, the opossum shifts his bites over the body of the object until he encounters the head, where he engages in repeated rhythmic biting, indicating that stimuli provided by this portion of the body are preferred cues for biting. The most elaborate and detailed analysis of specific stimulus-response elements of elicited attack has been made by John P. Flynn and his co-workers with cats (Bandler & Flynn, 1971, 1972; MacDonnell & Flynn, 1966). They have analyzed a number of reflex-like components of biting attack in cats that consist of relatively simple but specific stimulus inputs, such as touch of localized areas of the lip or paw and vision of an attackable animal through one eye, that elicit relatively simple but specific movements involved in attack, such as turning the head toward the stimulus, opening the mouth, striking with the paw, and lunging toward the stimulus. These specific sensorimotor elements resemble reflexes in that the receptive fields for application of the stimuli correspond to particular nerves or dermatomes, are graded in size to the intensity of hypothalamic stimulation, and are larger and more effective on the side of the body opposite the side of the hypothalamus stimulated. These findings suggest that a large part, if not all, of the innately organized core of the complex biting attack pattern may be composed of a number of specific reflex-like components that are simultaneously potentiated by hypothalamic output.

It is probable that efforts to determine the generality of the relatively mechanistic, multiple-reflex model of attack to other behavior patterns, such as mating, eating, drinking, etc., will constitute an important aspect of future research. The varied incompleteness of centrally induced mating and threat in opossums and cats suggests that such efforts are likely to meet with some success. Development of techniques for testing separate components of eating and drinking would also make it possible to determine whether these behavior patterns are always induced in complete form, as general observation suggests, or whether they sometimes consist of incomplete combinations of elements that appear to be complete because of the sequential organization of feeding and/or learned habits acquired during previous feeding experience. If such incompleteness does occur, it is possible that combinations lacking the initial components of the ingestive chain might explain why some cases of centrally induced eating and drinking appeared only after considerable delay in the experiments of Valenstein et al. (1968, 1969, 1970).

It may also be possible to make similarly specific analyses of the sensory stimuli that produce the reward effect associated with bioadaptive behaviors. Such analyses would involve identification of the adequate stimulus, the sensory field, critical peripheral nerves, and possible patterning effects involving specific combinations of stimuli. If the reward stimuli potentiated by hypothalamic stimulation could be identified and controlled, it might become feasible to trace their central pathways and effects, perhaps even as far as the unknown sites where the lasting changes that underlie learning occur. It is likely that more than one type of sensory feedback is rewarding for some behavior patterns, since it has been found that preintromission or preejaculation elements of natural or hypothalamically induced male mating behavior are rewarding in the absence of the reward associated with ejaculation (Roberts et al., 1967; Whalen, 1961). It would be interesting to know whether the reward stimuli are the same as those that elicit the responses, and whether the different reward stimuli are potentiated by the hypothalamus in varied incomplete combinations with response elements.

A related question concerns the relationship of the reward directly produced by the onset of stimulation (see the article by Olds) and the reward associated with performance of hypothalamically potentiated responses. Since both kinds of reward are often produced by the same electrode, it is tempting to speculate that they may result from the same neurons. The initial synaptic drive following the onset of stimulation might be strong enough to evoke an active discharge in reward neurons, followed by adaptation to a level too low to maintain the discharge, but sufficient to facilitate sensory input from performance of the response. If the reward stimuli normally associated with the responses could be identified and applied artificially without the responses, it might be possible to test whether the mechanisms underlying the two types of reward are the same by determining the effects of lesions in the output paths of the hypothalamus on response-related reward. The efferents producing stimulation-related reward are diffusely distributed, since destruction of any one pathway has relatively little or no effect, while the efferents producing motivational responses follow a more specific descending course into the midbrain, where they can be readily blocked by lesions (Bergquist, 1970; Berntson, 1971; Valenstein & Campbell, 1966).

A variety of experimental questions remain to be answered regarding the specific sensorimotor mechanisms of hypothalamically induced behaviors. For example, do all hypothalamic efferents that potentiate bioadaptive behaviors descend to lower midbrain levels, and where do they go from there? Do the cerebellum, basal ganglia, and sensorimotor cortex play essential roles? Do separate inhibitory components exist in the lower brainstem, as in the case of biting attack? Are the inhibitory and facilitatory influences of the amygdala and other forebrain structures (Flynn, 1967) exerted on the hypothalamus or on levels closer to the final motor paths? Most of these questions can be answered with various combinations of stimulation and lesion techniques. However, because of the likelihood that stimulation or destruction of some structures may induce interfering responses or other effects that would cause general impairment in free-moving tests, it will be necessary to supplement free-moving tests with restraint tests in which goal objects can be directly presented to the relevant receptors.

REFERENCES

Andersson, B., Larsson, S., & Persson, N. Some characteristics of the hypothalamic "drinking center" in the goat as shown by the use of permanent electrodes. *Acta physiol. Scand.,* 1960, **50,** 140–152.

Bandler, R. J., & Flynn, J. P. Visual patterned reflex present during hypothalamically elicited attack. *Science,* 1971, 817–818.

Bandler, R. J., & Flynn, J. P. Control of somatosensory fields for striking during hypothalamically elicited attack. *Brain Research,* 1972, **38,** 197–201.

Bergquist, E. H. Output pathways of hypothalamic mechanisms for sexual, aggressive, and other motivational behaviors in opossum. *J. comp. physiol. Psychol.,* 1970, **70,** 389–398.

Berntson, G. G. Blockade and release of hypothalamically and naturally elicited aggressive behaviors in cats following midbrain lesions. *J. Comp. physiol. Psychol.,* 1972.

Burn, J. H. Release of noradrenaline from sympathetic endings. *Nature,* 1971, **231,** 237–240.

Flynn, J. P. The neural basis of aggression in cats. In D. C. Glass (Ed.), *Neurophysiology and emotion.* New York: Rockefeller University Press, 1967. Pp. 40–60.

Flynn, J. P., Vanegas, H., Foote, W., & Edwards, S. Neural mechanisms involved in a cat's attack on a rat. In R. E. Whalen et al. (Eds.), *The neural control of behavior.* New York: Academic Press, 1970. Pp. 135–173.

Garcia, J., Ervin, F. R., Yorke, C. H., & Koelling, R. A. Conditioning with delayed vitamin injections. *Science,* 1967, **155,** 716–718.

Hess, W. R., & Brügger, M. Das subkortikale Zentrum der affektiven Abwehrreaktion. *Helv. physiol. pharmacol. Acta,* 1943, **1,** 33–52.

Hutchinson, R. R., & Renfrew, J. W. Stalking attack and eating behaviors elicited from the same sites in the hypothalamus. *J. comp. physiol. Psychol.,* 1966, **61,** 360–367.

Kagan, J., & Berkun, M. The reward value of running activity. *J. comp. physiol. Psychol.,* 1954, **47,** 108.

King, J. A., & Weisman, R. G. Sand digging contingent on bar pressing in deermice (*Peromyscus*). *Anim. Behav.,* 1964, **12,** 446–450.

MacDonnell, M. F., & Flynn, J. P. Control of sensory fields by stimulation of hypothalamus. *Science,* 1966, **152,** 1406–1408.

Montgomery, K. C. The role of the exploratory drive in learning. *J. comp. physiol. Psychol.,* 1954, **47**, 60–64.

Myer, J. S., & White, R. T. Aggressive motivation in the rat. *Anim. Behav.,* 1965, **13**, 430–433.

Richelle, M. L'amassement comme motivation dans le conditionnement du hamster: Etude preliminaire. *Psychologica Belgica,* 1967, **7**, 67–74.

Roberts, W. W. Rapid escape learning without avoidance learning motivated by hypothalamic stimulation in cats. *J. comp. physiol. Psychol.,* 1958, **51**, 391–399. (a)

Roberts, W. W. Both rewarding and punishing effects from stimulation of hypothalamus of cat with same electrode at same intensity. *J. comp. physiol. Psychol.,* 1958, **51**, 400–407. (b)

Roberts, W. W. Fear-like behavior elicited from dorsomedial thalamus of cat. *J. comp. physiol. Psychol.,* 1962, **55**, 191–197.

Roberts, W. W. Are hypothalamic motivational mechanisms functionally and anatomically specific? *Brain Behavior Evol.,* 1969, **2**, 317–342.

Roberts, W. W. Hypothalamic mechanisms for motivational and species-typical behavior. In R. E. Whalen, R. F. Thompson, M. Verzeano, & N. M. Weinberger (Eds.), *The neural control of behavior.* New York, Academic Press, 1970. Pp. 175–206.

Roberts, W. W., & Bergquist, E. H. Attack elicited by hypothalamic stimulation in cats raised in social isolation. *J. comp. physiol. Psychol.,* 1968, **66**, 590–595.

Roberts, W. W., Bergquist, E. H., & Robinson, T. C. L. Thermoregulatory grooming and sleep-like relaxation induced by local warming of preoptic area and anterior hypothalamus in opossum. *J. comp. physiol. Psychol.,* 1969, **67**, 182–188.

Roberts, W. W., & Carey, R. J. Rewarding effect of performance of gnawing aroused by hypothalamic stimulation in the rat. *J. comp. physiol. Psychol.,* 1965, **59**, 317–324.

Roberts, W. W., & Kiess, H. O. Motivational properties of hypothalamic aggression in cats. *J. comp. physiol. Psychol.,* 1964, **58**, 187–193.

Roberts, W. W., & Robinson, T. C. L. Relaxation and sleep induced by warming of preoptic region and anterior hypothalamus in cats. *Exp. Neurol.,* 1969, **25**, 282–294.

Roberts, W. W., Steinberg, M. L., & Means, L. W. Hypothalamic mechanisms for sexual, aggressive, and other motivational behaviors in the opossum, *Didelphis virginiana. J. comp. physiol. Psychol.,* 1967, **64**, 1–15.

Sarty, M. E. Species-relevant visual stimuli as reinforcement in the chick, Gallus domesticus. Doctoral dissertation, University of California at Los Angeles. Ann Arbor, Michigan: University Microfilms, 1968, No. 69-5347.

Simmons, R. The relative effectiveness of certain incentives in animal learning. *Comp. Psychol. Monog.,* 1924. **2**, No. 7.

Stevenson, J. G. Song as a reinforcer. In R. A. Hinde (Ed.), *Bird vocalizations.* London: Cambridge University Press, 1969. Pp. 49–60.

Thompson, T. I. Visual reinforcement in Siamese fighting fish. *Science,* 1963, **141**, 55–57.

Trapold, M. A. Are expectancies based upon different positive reinforcing events discriminably different? *Learning and Motivation,* 1970, **1**, 129–140.

Ulrich, R. E., & Azrin, N. H. Reflexive fighting in response to aversive stimulation. *J. exp. Anal. Behav.*, 1962, **5**, 511–520.

Valenstein, E. S., & Campbell, J. F. Medial forebrain bundle-lateral hypothalamic area and reinforcing brain stimulation. *Amer. J. Physiol.*, 1966, **210**, 270–274.

Valenstein, E. S., Cox, V. C., & Kakolewski, J. W. Modification of motivated behavior elicited by electrical stimulation of the hypothalamus. *Science*, 1968, **159**, 1119–1121.

Valenstein, E. S., Cox, V. C., & Kakolewski, J. W. The hypohtalamus and motivated behavior. In J. Tapp (Ed.), *Reinforcement and behavior.* New York: Academic Press, 1969. Pp. 242–285.

Valenstein, E. S., Cox, V. C., & Kakolewski, J. W. Reexamination of the role of the hypothalamus in motivation. *Psychol. Rev.*, 1970, **77**, 16–31.

Wade, G. N., & Zucker, I. Modulation of food intake and locomotor activity in female rats by diencephalic hormone implants. *J. comp. physiol. Psychol.*, 1970, **72**, 328–336.

Wasman, M., & Flynn, J. P. Directed attack elicited from hypothalamus. *Arch. Neurol.*, 1962, **6**, 220–227.

Whalen, R. E. Effects of mounting without intromission and intromission without ejaculation on sexual behavior and maze learning. *J. comp. physiol. Psychol.*, 1961, **54**, 409–415.

Wyrwicka, W., Dobrzecka, C., & Tarnecki, R. The effect of electrical stimulation of the hypothalamic feeding center in satiated goats on alimentary conditioned reflexes, Type II. *Acta Biol. Exper.*, 1960, **20**, 121–136.

Modification of Motivated Behavior Elicited by Electrical Stimulation of the Hypothalamus[1]

ELLIOT S. VALENSTEIN, VERNE C. COX, and JAN W. KAKOLEWSKI

The Fels Research Institute

Hypothalamic stimulation in the rat may elicit behaviors such as eating, drinking, and gnawing (Coons, 1964; Coons, Levak, & Miller, 1965; Fantl & Schuckman, 1967; Greer, 1955; Mendelson, 1967; Mendelson & Chorover, 1965; Miller, 1960; Mogenson & Stevenson, 1966, 1967, Morgane, 1961a, 1961b, 1961c; Roberts & Carey, 1965; Steinbaum & Miller, 1965; Tenen & Miller, 1964); previous reports have emphasized both specificity of the neural structures activated and similarity of the behavior to that occurring during natural-drive states. As satiated animals exhibit the behavior only during the period of stimulation, the term "stimulus-bound" behavior has been applied. From the fact that animals that exhibit such behavior will perform some learned task (instrumental behavior) to obtain a relevant goal, it has been concluded that the stimulation does not trigger a stereotyped motor act, but activates a motivational state such as hunger or thirst.

We studied the development of "stimulus-bound" behavior and the possibility of modifying the elicited behavior in the absence of any change in stimulation site or stimulation parameters. Our results indicate that there is a learning component involved in the association of hypothalamic stimulation with such behavior as eating, drinking, or gnawing. Hence, we question those theoretical positions based on the conclusion that electrical (and perhaps chemical) stimulation activates fixed neural circuits mediating natural-drive states.

Bipolar electrodes (Valenstein, Hodos, & Stein, 1961) were implanted in the lateral hypothalamus of mature Holtzman albino rats of both sexes. With the dorsal surface of the skull level between bregma and lambda, the electrodes were positioned 2.50 to 3.50 mm posterior to bregma, 1.25 to 1.50

1. Supported by NIH grants M–4529, career scientist award MH–4947, and research grant NsG–437 from NASA. We thank Laura Lande and Debra Singer for assistance.

TABLE 1. EATING (E), DRINKING (D), AND GNAWING (G) BEHAVIOR ELICITED DURING HY-
POTHALAMIC STIMULATION. EACH TEST HAD 20 STIMULATION PERIODS. MAX-
IMUM SCORE FOR ANY ONE BEHAVIOR IS 20, BUT THE ANIMAL COULD EXHIBIT
DIFFERENT BEHAVIORS DURING EACH PERIOD. THE DASH (—) IN THE SECOND
SERIES OF TESTS INDICATES WHICH GOAL OBJECT HAD BEEN REMOVED. RP,
RECTANGULAR PULSES; SW, SINE WAVE. ALL ANIMALS EXCEPT 80S WERE MALES.

Animal	Behav-ior	First Series			Second Series		Compe-tition	Stimulus Parameters (μa)
		1	2	3	1	2		
60S	E	0	0	0	15	17	11	RP,80
	D	20	20	20	—	—	14	RP,80
	G	0	0	0	0	0	0	RP,80
61S	E	0	0	0	20	20	15	RP,120
	D	20	20	20	—	—	12	RP,120
	G	0	0	0	0	0	0	RP,120
63S	E	0	0	0	0	0	0	RP,500
	D	0	0	0	20	20	12	RP,500
	G	20	20	20	—	—	8	RP,500
74S	E	0	0	0	20	20	12	SW,20
	D	20	20	20	—	—	13	SW,20
	G	0	0	0	0	0	0	SW,20
80S	E	19	16	12	—	—	10	RP,120
	D	1	5	8	19	16	10	RP,120
	G	0	0	0	2	2	6	RP,120
89S	E	0	0	0	18	20	16	SW,24
	D	19	19	20	—	—	4	SW,24
	G	0	0	0	0	0	0	SW,24

mm lateral, and 8.25 to 8.50 mm below the top of the skull.[2] Animals were
stimulated with either 30-second trains of 60-cycle sine waves or biphasic
rectangular pulses (frequency, 100 pulses per second; pulse duration, 0.2
msec). The stimulus parameters used with each animal are provided in Table
1. All stimulation was programmed by automatic equipment and was not
delivered under the experimenter's control.

After surgery but before any stimulation, the animals were placed in-
dividually in Plexiglas cages which served as living quarters and testing

2. The electrode tips were located in neural sites previously reported to yield "stimulus-bound" behavior. The electrode tips of animals 60S and 61S were located in the zona
incerta dorsal to the fornix, and the electrode tips of animals 74S, 80S, and 89S were
located in the dorsal part of the lateral hypothalamus. No histology is available for 63S
due to dislodgement of its electrode pedestal.

chambers. Light in the room was on from 7:00 A.M. to 7:00 P.M. each day. The cages contained three goal objects: pellets (Purina Lab Chow), a water bottle with a metal drinking tube, and a pine wedge mounted either on the wire-mesh floor or one of the walls. During preliminary screening to determine an appropriate stimulus intensity, animals were stimulated for a 30-second period followed by a 60-second interstimulus interval. The intensity was adjusted until the stimulus elicited a forward-moving "searching" behavior. If, after a period of time, the animal did not exhibit either eating, drinking, or gnawing in response to stimulation, the intensity was raised or lowered to what appeared to be a more promising level. If no specific behavior pattern emerged, the animal was stimulated throughout the night for 30 seconds every 5 minutes (night schedule). If no "stimulus-bound" behavior was evident, the sequence was repeated during at least one additional night before the animal was rejected. With this procedure, approximately 25 percent of the animals exhibited "stimulus-bound" eating, drinking, or gnawing on the pine wedges.

The animals that exhibited "stimulus-bound" behavior were then given a series of three standard tests (30 minutes in duration, with twenty 30-second stimulation periods, each separated by a 60-second interstimulus period). There was a minimum of 30 minutes between each test. During these tests, the three goal objects were present. After this first series of tests, the goal object to which the rat oriented was removed, and the animal was left overnight with the other two goal objects and stimulated on the night schedule. If, for example, the rat exhibited "stimulus-bound" drinking during the first series of tests, the water bottle was removed during the night, and only the wood and food pellets were left in the cage. *The stimulus parameters remained unchanged.* If the animal did not exhibit a new "stimulus-bound" behavior, it was stimulated additionally on consecutive nights. In most cases, however, one night was sufficient time for a new behavior to emerge, although for animals 60S and 89S several nights were necessary. In general, the earlier the onset of the first behavior during the preliminary stimulation sessions and the more consistently this behavior was displayed, the sooner the animal switched to a second behavior pattern when the first goal object was removed. Animals were then given two additional standard tests with the initial goal object still absent. Finally, the animals were given a competition test with all three goal objects present. Prior to all tests, animals were provided with an opportunity to satiate themselves on food and water.

Eating and drinking were scored only when there was clear evidence of consuming the food or water (Table 1). The food pellets were held with the front paws, and pieces were bitten off; the drinking tube was lapped, and the animal could be observed ingesting the water. Gnawing consisted of biting off pieces of wood from the wedge. In most cases, the animal began the "stimulus-bound" behavior within 1 to 2 seconds after the onset of the stimulus and stopped abruptly after its termination. The duration of the "stimulus-bound" behavior was variable. In a number of instances, the animal ate, drank, or gnawed for the entire 30-second stimulation period, and in a few cases the behavior was observed for only a 5-second period. Only in rare instances was any scoreable behavior observed during the interstimulus period. Table 1 illustrates that the "stimulus-bound" behavior during the first series of tests was exhibited consistently with almost every stimulus presentation. The second series was administered after the animal spent a variable amount of time receiving stimulation without the first goal object present. In most cases the second "stimulus-bound" behavior was exhibited as consistently as the first behavior (Table 1). During the competition test, when all three goal objects were present, approximately equal amounts of the two "stimulus-bound" behavior patterns were displayed in most instances, although the second behavior—eating—dominated the behavior of 89S during the competition test. In the case of 80S (an animal that exhibited two behaviors initially), a third behavior pattern—gnawing—was observed during the second series of tests and the competition test. This animal had been placed on the night schedule for two consecutive nights with only wood and water present. In addition to eating, drinking, and gnawing, other behavior was observed to be elicited by the stimulation in some animals; for example, 80S frequently positioned itself in one part of the cage, and with the onset of stimulation a specific path was traversed on the way to the drinking bottle.

There were no cases of "stimulus-bound" behavior which could not be switched to another behavior with the stimulus parameters held constant. We cannot be certain that such a case might not exist, but, in addition to the data in Table 1, there were a number of instances in which there were "spontaneous" switches from one "stimulus-bound" behavior to another. For example, an animal that might exhibit "stimulus-bound" gnawing approximately 50 percent of the time might switch to drinking with approximately the same consistency. We regard these cases of "spontaneous" switching as additional evidence of the lack of specificity of the behavior evoked by electrical stimulation. This conclusion is also supported by animal 80S, as well as others that did not complete the test series, which exhibited more than one behavior from the beginning of stimulation.

In stressing the lack of specificity between a given behavior pattern and lateral hypothalamic stimulation, we are not advancing a position of neural equipotentiality. We were not able to evoke either eating, drinking, or gnawing from a number of lateral hypothalamic sites. Furthermore, in several animals in which electrodes were placed in somewhat different lateral hypothalamic sites on the left and right side, the animal exhibited "stimulus-bound" behavior only when stimulated on one of the sides.

It might be argued that all the animals used in our experiment were special cases in which stimulation activated simultaneously the neural circuits mediating two motivational systems. We disagree for several reasons. We did not select the animals, and we studied all that exhibited any "stimulus-bound" behavior. Only one of the animals exhibited more than one behavior pattern before our effort to modify their responses. Of the animals exhibiting only one behavior initially, those that displayed the most vigorous pattern (judged by the brief latency, long duration during stimulation, and great consistency) required the least amount of training for a second pattern to emerge.

As far as we could determine, most investigators of "stimulus-bound" behavior focused on a specific behavior. As a result, the animals received either or both special training or limited opportunity to display different patterns. Those few instances in which an animal was given a brief "competitive" test with another goal object present usually followed an extensive amount of opportunity to display the initial behavior pattern. We found that the more opportunity an animal has to exhibit a specific "stimulus-bound" behavior, the longer it may take for a new pattern to emerge.

A number of experiments demonstrated that animals exhibiting "stimulus-bound" eating, drinking, or gnawing have much in common with animals under the influence of natural drives such as those induced by deprivation. Animals will work to obtain appropriate goal objects and appear willing to tolerate aversive stimulation, such as shock or quinine additives, in order to obtain the desired objects (Morgane, 1961b, 1961c; Tenen & Miller, 1964). However, the fact that in our experiment animals that were "stimulus-bound" drinkers appeared just as motivated to obtain food, for example, raises the question of whether thirst and hunger motives are involved at all.[3] Apparently, there is considerably more plasticity in establishing connections between hypothalamic circuits and motivated behavior than commonly advanced interpretations of "stimulus-bound" behavior suggest.

REFERENCES

Coons, E. E. Thesis, Yale University, 1964. University Microfilms, Inc. 64–13, 166.

Coons, E. E., M. Levak, & N. E. Miller, *Science,* **150,** 1320 (1965).

Fantl, L., & H. Schuckman. *Physiol. Behav.,* **2,** 355 (1967).

Greer, M. A. *Proc. Soc. Exp. Biol. Med.,* **89,** 59 (1955).

Mendelson, J. *Science,* **157,** 1077 (1967).

Mendelson, J., & S. L. Chorover. *Science,* **149,** 559 (1965).

Miller, N. E. *Fed. Proc.,* **19,** 846 (1960).

Mogenson, G. J., & J. A. F. Stevenson. *Physiol. Behav.,* **1,** 251 (1966).

Mogenson, G. J., & J. A. F. Stevenson. *Exp. Neurol.,* **17,** 119 (1967).

Morgane, P. J. *Nature,* **191,** 672 (1961). (a)

Morgane, P. J. *Science,* **133,** 887 (1961). (b)

Morgane, P. J. *Amer. J. Physiol.,* **201,** 838 (1961). (c)

Roberts, W. W., & R. J. Carey. *J. Comp. Physiol. Psychol.,* **59,** 317 (1965).

Steinbaum, E. A., & N. E. Miller. *Amer. J. Physiol.,* **208,** 1 (1965).

Tenen, S. S., & N. E. Miller. *J. Comp. Physiol. Psychol.,* **58,** 55 (1964).

Valenstein, E. S., W. Hodos, & L. Stein. *Amer. J. Psychol.,* **74,** 125 (1961).

---

3. Animals that were switched from "stimulus-bound" drinkers to "stimulus-bound" eaters have been observed to eat the dry pellets in the absence of water almost to the point where they appeared to be choking.

Commentary

ELLIOT S. VALENSTEIN

By 1967 there were numerous descriptions of the elicitation of such behaviors as eating, drinking, and gnawing, from what was reported to be specific neural sites located mostly in the hypothalamus (the reader may wish to refer to the historical overview in the front of this volume). These "stimulus-bound" behaviors were reported to share many properties with the same naturally occurring behaviors. For example, an animal displaying stimulus-bound eating would work to obtain food, even though it had just eaten, during periods of stimulation. The sites from which one could elicit these behaviors appeared to be located primarily within the neural structures that would support self-stimulation behavior, and therefore many investigators began to speculate about the possibility that specific areas within the reinforcement system were each concerned with strengthening responses relevant to particular biological need states.

My own background directed me to examine critically the anatomical evidence for the claim that specific behaviors were elicited from discrete areas. A review of the literature indicated that there was an impressive amount of overlap in the anatomical sites from which different behaviors could be elicited. It was difficult to justify the impression given by some investigators and most textbook writers that there were discrete areas associated with specific behaviors. Indeed, it seemed more than possible that the behavior observed in many studies was determined by the fact that experimenters frequently restricted their observations to one behavior. We therefore designed an experiment to determine to what extent the behavior elicited by electrical stimulation was influenced by the experimental conditions. The results we obtained, described in the preceding article, raised a number of additional questions which were then explored further.

When the results described in this brief note in the journal *Science* were first presented at a psychological convention, the reaction from many of my colleagues was strong and, in some instances, quite emotional. Some of the reactions I could dismiss as they seemed to be implying nothing more than an attitude of: "Sit down! You're rocking the boat." In short, our report seemed to be muddying up a seemingly clear story of the organization of the hypothalamus into specific motivationally relevant regions. Others, who had invested a great amount of effort directed toward an anatomical charting of the function of specific hypothalamic regions, saw implications that they interpreted as threatening to their program and in some cases seemed to be reacting defensively. Still others maintained, in spite of overwhelming published evidence to the contrary, that no one had ever believed that there were discrete anatomical regions associated with specific motivated behaviors. Many of the critical reactions, however, were carefully considered and asked questions that could only be answered by a great amount of additional experimentation.

ANATOMICAL SPECIFICITY

The original brief report described the results obtained from only 6 animals and presented no histological information. It was important to study a larger population in order to determine the generality of our finding that different behaviors could be elicited from a fixed electrode and stimulation parameters. It was equally important to determine if the results were characteristic of only a limited anatomical region where separate functional systems might be in close proximity.

Verne Cox and I compiled the results obtained in our laboratory from stimulating 269 animals at 375 diencephalic sites. Without going into great detail (cf. Cox & Valenstein, 1969a), it was found that, with the exception of a few structures (anterior hypothalamic nucleus and ventromedial nucleus), the sites eliciting eating and drinking (and also gnawing) overlapped with the sites that elicit only nonspecific exploratory behavior. Furthermore, a more detailed analysis revealed that it was not possible to distinguish the sites that elicited eating from those eliciting drinking or gnawing. In subsequent work, it has been shown that the elicitation of male sexual behavior and feeding can frequently be obtained from the same electrode (Caggiula, 1970; Stephan, Valenstein, & Zucker, 1971). Other elicited behavior such as carrying of objects, grooming, and digging (as well as eating, drinking, and gnawing) were also often obtained from the same electrode (Phillips et al., 1969; Valenstein et al., 1969; Valenstein et al., 1970).

Our results demonstrating that anatomical placement seemed to be a poor index of the behavior that could be elicited by electrical stimulation should not be interpreted as implying that any behavior can be obtained from stimulation at any site. Such a conclusion was never drawn, as it was clear to us that only a limited range of behavior patterns was being studied and even within the anatomical limits explored there were some regions that did not produce positive results. Although we had not studied aggressive behavior, for example, it was noted that some types of attack behavior (cf. p. 20) could be elicited from the ventromedial hypothalamus—an area from which we were not successful in eliciting eating or drinking. Subsequently, Woodworth (1971) reported that the majority of the electrodes from which she could elicit attack behavior were located in the ventrolateral area. She expressed the opinion that aggressive behavior was elicited by stimulation ventral and lateral to the fornix column, while eating and drinking could only be obtained from hypothalamic regions dorsal and lateral to the fornix. It is possible that this distinction could be justified on a statistical basis, but there are too many exceptions to permit it to be a very useful generalization. For example, we have obtained eating and drinking from sites both ventral and medial (dorsomedial nucleus) to the fornix column and at ventral-posterior hypothalamic locations where the fornix column has terminated in the mammillary bodies. Also, Olds, Allan, and Briese (1971) have reported enhanced food- and/or water-rewarded responding during stimulation of very ventral sites in the lateral hypothalamus. Panksepp (1971a) has distinguished between different types of elicited aggression in the rat and finds that a behavior that resembles predatory stalking ("quiet-biting attack") is obtained primarily from regions dorsolateral to the fornix.

There were several other considerations that began to appear and to place the anatomical problem in a somewhat different context. It had been noted by several investigators that the neural areas from which it was possible to elicit a certain behavior by stimulation did not appear to be essential to that behavior. Although Roberts (1962) had elicited a fear-like crouching from the dorsomedial thalamic nucleus, Roberts and Carey (1963) observed that destruction of this nucleus did not interfere with normal fear responses. Similarly, although Flynn (1967) has described the elicitation of aggressive responses from hypothalamic sites, Ellison and Flynn (1968) note that cats are capable of integrated attack responses following surgical isolation of the hypothalamus. Panksepp (1971b) has made similar observations in regard to aggressive tendencies of rats following hypothalamic lesions. These observations raise questions about how critical the neural tissue at the tip of the eliciting electrode is for the behavior under study. It could be argued that the neural substrate for the observed behavior is located at some distance from the electrode tip. If this is indeed the case, then it should not be surprising to learn that there is not a very precise localization within the hypothalamus. Many areas may have the capacity to activate relevant pathways and structures when stimulated.

In a recent report, Huston (1971) observed that the stimulus-bound behavior obtained from hypothalamic sites can be modified by cortical spreading depression (CSD). CSD is a technique of selectively suppressing the normal electrical activity of the cerebral cortex, for varying periods of time, by direct application of different concentrations of potassium solutions. Huston noted that unilateral CSD often produces changes in the behavior elicited by hypothalamic stimulation. Animals have been observed to switch from stimulus-bound eating to drinking (or vice versa) under the influence of CSD. Interpretation of these preliminary results must be very tentative, but in any case the results make it additionally clear that the behaviors elicited by hypothalamic stimulation are not to be understood as simple reflections of the functional significance of hypothalamic "centers."

INDIVIDUAL DIFFERENCES

Additional evidence from our laboratory and that of others also tended to deemphasize the precise anatomical localization within the hypothalamus. We had noted that there was a tendency for animals to display the same stimulus-bound behavior from each of several electrodes in spite of differences in placement. Figure 1 illustrates a number of cases in which electrodes located at different sites in the hypothalamus of the rat elicited the same behavior in the same animal. Although this is certainly not always the case, we observed too many incidences of animals exhibiting even very uncommon behavior from two very different sites for this to be explained by chance. Phillips and Valenstein (1969) demonstrated that this was also true for hypothalamic stimulation in the guinea pig, where the pattern of elicitation of eating, drinking, and gnawing from different electrode sites was apparently reflecting some characteristics of the individual animal. It was partly for this reason that we suggested that the responses elicited by stimulation often reflect the "prepotent" tendencies of individual animals (Valenstein, 1969). More recently, Panksepp (1971a) has observed that the tendency of rats to kill mice under nonstimulation conditions seems to be an important determinant of the

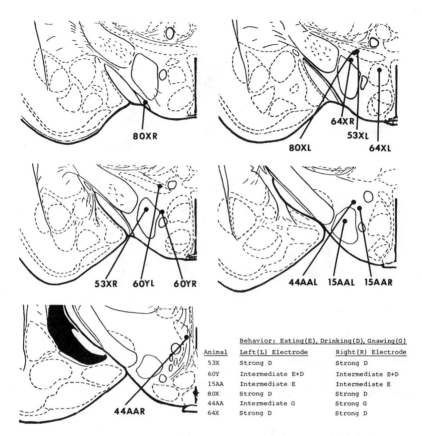

Figure 1. Examples of cases in which different electrode sites in the same animal elicited the same behavior. (After Valenstein, Cox, & Kakolewski, 1970.)

probability of eliciting aggression with stimulation. Panksepp concludes, "Thus, the electrically elicited response was probably not determined by specific functions of the tissue under the electrode but by the personality of the rat" (p. 327).

A striking example of the contribution of individual differences to the effects produced by hypothalamic stimulation has recently been presented by Wise (1971). This investigator used an electrode that could be gradually lowered through the hypothalamus in approximately 0.1 mm steps. In this way it was possible to explore a number of sites along a given plane in a single animal. It was found that 54 out of 243 sites explored induced eating and/or drinking (over 85 percent induced both), but the interesting finding was that the positive sites were all located in 6 animals. In the unresponsive animals, negative sites were found throughout the hypothalamus; however, in the responsive animals the negative sites were found only at the extremities of the approximately 2.0 mm area explored. Figure 2 illustrates the histological results with three of the responsive and unresponsive animals. It was noted that, within the limits of the positive area in responsive animals, movement of the electrode had little effect on current threshold and no effect on elicited

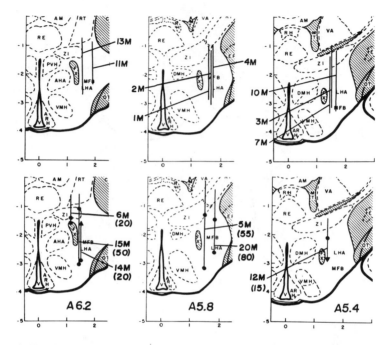

Figure 2. Hypothalamic sites explored with electrodes capable of being gradually lowered. Upper row depicts sites in animals not displaying stimulus-bound drinking and eating. The boundaries of positive sites in animals which did exhibit stimulus-bound behavior are marked by circles on the lower figures. Within the positive area, movement of the electrode had little effect on the current threshold (microamperes indicated in parentheses) or the behavior elicited in a given animal. (After Wise, 1971.)

behavior. As the electrodes were moved in a dorsal-ventral direction through the medial forebrain bundle, very different fibers must have been activated.

Wise made other interesting observations that should influence our interpretations of stimulus-bound behavior. He noted that for a given animal the threshold of the first electrode site explored gradually declined and during the same time the behavior tended to be elicited more and more reliably. In contrast, the thresholds and elicited behavior were stable from the outset of testing at subsequent sites within the same animal. Wise concluded, "The fact that threshold declines and response emergence are not observed at each site tested, and that stability of responding once established at the initial training site transfers to all other testing sites, indicates the neural changes underlying this learning are not local to the specific lateral hypothalamic site stimulated" (p. 572). Further support for this conclusion could be derived from the observation that the current threshold for eliciting stimulus-bound behavior differed between animals, but tended to be constant for all the positive points within one animal. Unresponsive animals were unresponsive at all sites, low-threshold animals had low thresholds at all sites, and high-threshold animals were similarly constant. The possibility that these results were due to some characteristic of the electrode was ruled out by interchanging electrodes between animals. (This could be done with Wise's electrode assembly.) Taken together, these results would appear to provide good support for the conclusion that the response given to hypothalamic stimulation is governed by neural systems located at a distance from the site of stimulation, and it also reflects some characteristic response tendency of the animal.

Species characteristics as well as individual factors contribute to the responses elicited by stimulation. We have observed that it was possible to elicit object carrying from a wide array of hypothalamic sites in the rat, but were not successful in eliciting this behavior in guinea pigs (Phillips et al., 1969). Rats normally carry objects in connection with nest building, maternal behavior, hoarding, and many other adaptive behaviors, whereas the guinea pig does not seem to possess a basic carrying pattern, probably because it uses natural burrows rather than building nests and does not carry its young, which are born very mature. Our analysis of the conditions necessary to elicit this biologically significant behavior in the rat have forced us to conclude that anatomical details cannot substitute for an examination of the environmental factors which tend to make particular species-specific behavior patterns prepotent. Under some circumstances very nonspecific factors may release the prepotent responses of a species. For example, Jacobs and Farel (1971) have reported that subanesthetic doses of sodium pentobarbital may trigger a great amount of eating by rats. Similarly, Huston and Bureš (1970) have observed that cortical spreading depression may induce "stereotyped eating, drinking, and exploratory behavior."

ELICITED BEHAVIOR AND MOTIVATION

The evidence that stimulation often induced a variety of behaviors forced us to question the frequent assertion that natural motivational states were being aroused. Commonly when stimulation elicited eating it was concluded that the eating was the result of the activation of hunger, elicitation of drinking was said to be produced by the activation of thirst, and so forth. In those many cases where we observed several different behaviors elicited by the same stimulation, what were we to conclude? Was the stimulation making the animal hungry in one instant, thirsty in another, arousing the animal sexually at still another time? While it was possible that the stimulation could elicit different motivational states from moment to moment, the interpretation was not quite so acceptable as it seemed when it was believed that only one behavior was normally observed from stimulation at a given site. Furthermore, there was a paradox that was bothersome. Stimulation at sites that elicited specific patterns had been observed to be positively rewarding as animals would self-stimulate. Did it make sense to think that animals would initiate stimulation that made them hungry, thirsty, etc., when the goal objects necessary to satisfy these motivational states were absent? These thoughts prompted us to investigate the nature of the motivation underlying the behavior elicited by stimulation.

We reasoned that if stimulation was inducing a state comparable to hunger, then rats displaying stimulus-bound eating of one food should readily switch to another food when the first food was removed. This should be particularly true if the second food was the familiar laboratory chow pellets that they ate in their home cages. Animals that primarily displayed stimulus-bound eating of a cat-dog food were tested with this food removed and only food pellets and water available. Not only did the animals fail to switch readily to eating the food pellets when stimulated, but when they eventually displayed a new stimulus-bound behavior it was often drinking that was elicited. Moreover, if the same food was simply changed in texture (as when the food pellets are pulverized), the animals do not readily switch to the modified food when stimulated (Valenstein, Cox, & Kakolewski, 1968). These animals certainly did not behave like hungry animals.

In a somewhat similar experiment it was shown that animals exhibiting stimulus-bound drinking from a water bottle did not readily switch to drinking water from a dish when stimulated (Valenstein, Kakolewski, & Cox, 1968). This was true in spite of the fact that the animals were thoroughly familiar with the water dish and demonstrated no hesitancy in drinking from it when known to be thirsty. It was also shown in this same study that animals had different preferences for solutions when drinking followed water deprivation than when it was in response to hypothalamic stimulation. Thirsty animals prefer water to a 30 percent glucose solution, but when the same animals are drinking in response to stimulation they prefer the glucose. These and other experiments suggested that the behavior elicited by stimulation was significantly different from the same behavior when it was evoked by natural motivational states.

SOME CONCLUSIONS

Where there are differences of opinion, there is a tendency on the one hand to overstate the position of a protagonist, while on the other hand to carefully refine and qualify one's own views. This frequently leads to an oversimplification of opposing positions and produces labels that caricature rather than characterize. On the present topic this trend has produced such polarizing phrases as "plastic *versus* specific" conceptions of neural actions. In fact, no one believes the nervous system is either "plastic" or "specific," as all would agree that organisms, at least above a certain level, are capable of modifying their responses to the same physical stimulus. Stimuli acquire significance and the responses to them are modified, and in this sense, therefore, the nervous system has plastic (modifiable) characteristics. Similarly, it is not necessary to have to document the fact that a number of connections in the nervous system are specified by the genetic code and are probably highly resistant to modification. Furthermore, there can be no denying that motivational states can be specific and that animals are capable of distinguishing between being thirsty, hungry, aggressive, and so forth. There obviously is a physiological counterpart of these motivational states that enables one to be distinguished from the other.

The main questions at issue are concerned with the extent to which electrical stimulation of discrete hypothalamic sites is capable of duplicating the physiological conditions of specific motivational states. Our own work has led us to conclude that: (a) The sites capable of eliciting stimulus-bound behavior are much more widespread than previously appreciated. (b) Most electrodes seem capable of eliciting several behaviors. Therefore, it may be necessary to reevaluate any conclusions based on the assumption that response to electrical stimulation (as, for example, in studies involving self-stimulation performance) is reflecting the excitability of the neural substrate of one particular motivational state. (c) The behavior elicited by electrical stimulation reflects some characteristic response prepotency of individual animals. (d) The fact that stimulation at many different sites in the hypothalamus often elicits the same behavior suggests that the neural substrate for that response is organized elsewhere (probably outside of the hypothalamus) than directly under the electrode tip. (e) Animals displaying eating or drinking in response to stimulation do not behave as if hungry or thirsty when the testing situation is modified.

A number of explanations for the anatomical diffuseness may have to be considered. Among these are the artificiality of electrical stimulation, the proximity of functionally discrete systems, the likelihood of stimulating the same fibers at different anterior-posterior positions in the hypothalamus, and individual differences in anatomical arrangements. Each of these possibilities could be commented on extensively as they all may be partially valid. Concerning electrical stimulation, however, I do not think the prospects are encouraging that we will be able to use stimulus-bound behavior to locate with any precision the neural substrate for specific regulatory behavior. Chemical stimulation has not been any more successful in locating specific sites for eliciting discrete behavior, but the picture may change with refinement of technique (cf. Miller's discussion of the alpha and beta adrenergic system, pp. 64–65).

One observation from our own work with electrical stimulation that has been of particular interest to me concerns the gradual development of an association between stimulation and a particular response. Our original paper on this topic, reprinted here, was entitled "Modification of Motivated Behavior Elicited by Electrical Stimulation of the Hypothalamus." Most of the debate seems to have focussed on the word "modification." It was not too difficult to accommodate to the finding that most electrodes elicited several behaviors, as the chemical stimulation data had accustomed people to think of separate systems in close proximity. The word "modification," however, implied that relationships were not fixed and opened up a "hornet's nest" of problems.

In retrospect, it seems to me that we had not included adequate controls to justify the implication that we were modifying anything by our environmental manipulations. Roberts (1969) has argued, correctly I believe, that testing animals with several goal objects simultaneously available may be misleading, as a weaker response to the same stimulation may not have had an opportunity to be expressed. He recommends that animals be tested with each object separately before concluding that the stimulation does not have the capacity to elicit other behaviors initially. This is probably good advice and there is now no doubt that one will find a number of cases where single goal-object tests will reveal behaviors that were not evident during the multiple goal-object tests. What may be most interesting, however, are those cases in which a second stimulus-bound behavior was not at all evident initially, by any testing method, but nevertheless *gradually* emerged. Not only did the additional behaviors appear gradually, but over time they were elicited more and more reliably and often became the dominant stimulus-bound behavior. We have described such cases (Cox & Valenstein, 1969b) and more recently Mogenson

(1971) has noted that, while some animals exhibit a second elicited behavior immediately after removing the preferred goal object, in other cases "the modification occurred only gradually after a large number of presentations of stimulation" (p. 257).

I have continued to study the gradual emergence of additional stimulus-bound behavior patterns because of the possibility, even if remote, that the phenomenon may be used as a model for a special type of learning. Figure 3 illustrates an example of a case in which the association between stimulation and behavior was strengthened. Only stimulus-bound eating was observed initially in spite of careful testing. This behavior was elicited more reliably over successive tests. Stimulus-bound drinking was not observed at all initially, but gradually this behavior appeared in response to stimulation and was "strengthened" until it became the more frequently elicited behavior. (The legend to Figure 3 provides some additional experimental details.)

It is difficult to prove conclusively that all the stimulus-bound patterns that eventually emerge are not reflecting preexisting connections between the hypothalamic area stimulated and the neural substrate underlying the elicitation of the responses. Our own experience with this phenomenon has led us to conclude that it is unnecessary to make such an assumption. The many instances we have observed in which a stimulus-bound behavior emerges only after a very long period of testing, and then gradually becomes elicited with greater frequency, suggests that in some ways an association is being developed. The assumption that there always exists a fixed association between the hypothalamic area stimulated (or the state induced by such stimulation) and a

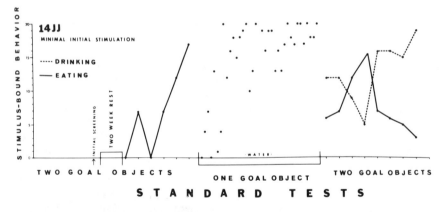

Figure 3. Illustration of the gradual strengthening and emergence of stimulus-bound behavior. After the animal received minimal screening (just long enough to demonstrate the presence of stimulus-bound eating), no additional testing was administered for two weeks. After this "rest period" stimulation induced only a low level of eating, but over a regular testing schedule this behavior was induced more and more reliably. Although the water bottle was present during this time, no stimulus-bound drinking was evident. When the food was removed the animal started to display stimulus-bound drinking only after a long interval and a great number of stimulations (not shown on chart). At this time, 30 stimulation tests with only water present (one goal-object tests) revealed a gradual increase in the elicitation of drinking. A final series of stimulation tests with both water and food present (two goal-object test) revealed that stimulus-bound drinking was evident at least as frequently as eating. All tests were conducted with identical stimulation parameters. Twenty stimulation trains were administered during each test; therefore a score of 20 represents 100 percent elicitation. During the final series of two goal-object tests the animal sometimes displayed both behaviors during a single stimulation period. (Adapted from Valenstein, 1971.)

specific response does not seem justified. The many examples, particularly at the human level, of eating, drinking, sexual behavior, aggression, etc., occurring under conditions unrelated to the regulation of biological needs suggest that connections are not completely fixed. The instances of one behavior, or symptom, substituting for another also supports the conclusion that there must be some plasticity in these relationships. It is unlikely that any arbitrarily selected response can be associated with stimulation at any hypothalamic site. Evidence is accumulating, however, which indicates that it is possible to establish and strengthen the association between the effects of at least some hypothalamic stimulation and a specific "mode of expression." The "mode of expression" has to be compatible with the state induced by stimulation, but it is not predetermined by it. If we could learn more about the rules governing the development of associations between affective states and behavior, or how some of the less specific motivational states can be "channeled" into one or another response, we might be in a better position to explain some of the strange and sometimes maladaptive behavior of our brethren.

REFERENCES

Caggiula, A. R. Analysis of the copulation-reward properties of posterior hypothalamic stimulation in male rats. *J. comp. physiol. Psychol.*, 1970, **70**, 399–412.

Cox, V. C., & Valenstein, E. S. Distribution of hypothalamic sites yielding stimulus-bound behavior. *Brain, Behavior, and Evolution*, 1969, **2**, 359–376. (a)

Cox, V. C., & Valenstein, E. S. Effects of stimulation intensity on behavior elicited by hypothalamic stimulation. *J. comp. physiol. Psychol.*, 1969, **69**, 730–733. (b)

Ellison, G. D., & Flynn, J. P. Organized aggressive behavior in cats after surgical isolation of the hypothalamus. *Archives Italiennes de Biologie*, 1968, **106**, 1–20.

Flynn, J. P. The neural basis of aggression in cats. In D. C. Glass (Ed.), *Neurophysiology and Emotion*. New York: Rockefeller University Press, 1967. Pp. 40–60.

Huston, J. P. Effect of cortical spreading depression on behavior elicited by electric hypothalamic stimulation. *Proceedings of the XXV International Congress of Physiological Sciences*, Munich, 1971.

Huston, J. P., & Bureš, J. Drinking and eating elicited by cortical spreading depression. *Science*, 1970, **169**, 702–704.

Jacobs, B. L., & Farel, P. B. Motivated behavior produced by increased arousal in the presence of goal objects. *Physiol. & Behav.*, 1971, **6**, 473–476.

Mogenson, G. L. Stability and modification of consummatory behaviors elicited by electrical stimulation of the hypothalamus. *Physiol. & Behav.*, 1971, **6**, 255–260.

Olds, J., Allan, W. S., & Briese, E. Differentiation of hypothalamic drive and reward centers. *Amer. J. Physiol.*, 1971, **221**, 368–375.

Panksepp, J. Aggression elicited by electrical stimulation of the hypothalamus in albino rats. *Physiol. & Behav.*, 1971, **6**, 321–329. (a)

Panksepp, J. Effects of hypothalamic lesions on mouse-killing and shock-induced fighting in rats. *Physiol. & Behav.,* 1971, **6**, 311–316. (b)

Phillips, A. G., Cox, V. C., Kakolewski, J. W., & Valenstein, E. S. Object-carrying by rats: An approach to the behavior produced by brain stimulation. *Science,* 1969, **166**, 903–905.

Phillips, A. G., & Valenstein, E. S. Elicitation of stimulus-bound behavior in guinea pigs. *Psychon. Sci.,* 1969, **17**, 131–132.

Roberts, W. W. Fear-like behavior elicited from dorsomedial thalamus of cat. *J. comp. physiol. Psychol.,* 1962, **55**, 191–197.

Roberts, W. W. Are hypothalamic motivational mechanisms functionally and anatomically specific? *Brain, Behavior, and Evolution,* 1969, **2**, 317–342.

Roberts, W. W., & Carey, R. J. Effect of dorsomedial thalamic lesions on fear in cats. *J. comp. physiol. Psychol.,* 1963, **56**, 950–958.

Stephan, F. K., Valenstein, E. S., & Zucker, I. Copulation and eating during electrical stimulation of the rat hypothalamus. *Physiol. & Behav.,* 1971, **7**, 587–593.

Valenstein, E. S. Behavior elicited by hypothalamic stimulation: A prepotency hypothesis. *Brain, Behavior, and Evolution,* 1969, **2**, 295–316.

Valenstein, E. S. Channeling of responses elicited by hypothalamic stimulation. *J. Psychiat. Res.,* 1971, **8**, 335–344.

Valenstein, E. S., Cox, V. C., & Kakolewski, J. W. The motivation underlying eating elicited by lateral hypothalamic stimulation. *Physiol. & Behav.,* 1968, **3**, 969–971.

Valenstein, E. S., Cox, V. C., & Kakolewski, J. W. The hypothalamus and motivated behavior. In J. Tapp (Ed.), *Reinforcement.* New York: Academic Press, 1969. Pp. 242–285.

Valenstein, E. S., Cox, V. C., & Kakolewski, J. W. Reexamination of the role of the hypothalamus in motivation. *Psychol. Rev.,* 1970, **77**, 16–31.

Valenstein, E. S., Kakolewski, J. W., & Cox, V. C. A comparison of stimulus-bound drinking and drinking induced by water deprivation. *Commun. in Behav. Biol.,* 1968, **2**, 227–233.

Wise, R. A. Individual differences in effects of hypothalamic stimulation: The role of stimulation locus. *Physiol. & Behav.,* 1971, **6**, 569–572.

Woodworth, C. Attack elicited in rats by electrical stimulation of the lateral hypothalamus. *Physiol. & Behav.,* 1971, **6**, 345–353.